HOW TO CLEAN ABSOLUTELY EVERYTHING

FROM CASHMERE TO CARPETS, AND SHOWER STALLS TO SLIPCOVERS, THE COMPLETE, UTTERLY COMPREHENSIVE GUIDE

YVONNE WORTH with AMANDA BLINKHORN

PROSPERO B·O·O·K·S

This edition produced in 2005 for
PROSPERO BOOKS
A Divison of Indigo Books & Music

ISBN: 1-55267-693-5

This book was conceived, designed, and produced by
THE IVY PRESS LIMITED
The Old Candlemakers
Lewes, East Sussex BN7 2NZ

Creative Director PETER BRIDGEWATER
Publisher SOPHIE COLLINS
Editorial Director JASON HOOK
Design Manager SIMON GOGGIN
Senior Project Editor CAROLINE EARLE
Designers WAYNE BLADES AND GINNY ZEAL
Illustrations PETERS & ZABRANSKY AGENCY
Graphic Artwork JOANNA CLINCH

Printed and bound in China

Every effort has been made to ensure that the instructions given in this book are accurate. However, they are
provided for general information only, and you should
always read and follow any manufacturer's instructions
and, where appropriate, seek professional advice.

CONTENTS

THE LOST ART OF CLEANING

"Begin somewhere. You cannot build a reputation on what you intend to do."

LIZ SMITH

Cleaning our homes has become a lost art. What was once as automatic as making coffee has turned into something we either farm out, ignore, or turn into a weekly drama, depending on our income and inclination. However, it doesn't have to be that way. For half the time and none of the money that so many of us devote to the gym, we can transform our homes into clean, comfortable havens that are a delight to live in. This is not about returning to a golden age of domesticity, nor is it about romanticizing what was for our grandmothers a never-ending treadmill of cooking, cleaning, and ironing. It is about taking pride in the things we work hard for. Why struggle all week to pay the mortgage if your heart sinks every time you catch sight of your kitchen floor? Why lust after a Philippe Starck sink if you can't get the toothpaste off your old one? And why invest in a pair of killer

Manolos if you don't dare go out in them in case you get them dirty? Housework has never been less hassle. We have the technology to get the best of both worlds. We can boil wash our Egyptian cotton sheets in the washing machine, air them on the line and a run a steam iron over them in the time it would have taken our grandmothers to strip the bed, stoke the boiler, and curse the rain. Why scrub a floor when you can laminate it, or sweat over an oven when it can clean itself? This is not a book for those who want to turn back the clock—it's for those who don't have time to mess around. We've taken the best tricks of the past and combined them with the quickest modern shortcuts we could find. Sometimes some old newspaper and a bottle of vinegar are all you need, other times a steam cleaner and some state-of-the-art carpet shampoo are essential. Just because your home gleams and smells of beeswax and lemons doesn't mean you've spent all day scrubbing away—it just looks as if you did. Remember, you have nothing to lose but your stains.

AROUND THE HOUSE

A ROUTINE MATTER

"Nothing is particularly hard if you divide it into small jobs."

HENRY FORD

Less than a century ago, most households followed the same, or similar, weekly cleaning routines. Baking was usually scheduled for the end of the week (after payday and in time for the weekend), which left the early part of the week as the traditional time for activities such as washing (Monday) and ironing (Tuesday, if the laundry was dry in time). Other household tasks, such as cleaning, dusting, sweeping, and scrubbing, were fitted around these and often carried out on a daily basis.

Nowadays, with the numerous appliances, sophisticated gadgets, and endless products that are available, coping with housework ought to be much easier and less time-consuming. We all know this isn't the case. With hectic lifestyles the norm, it can be extremely challenging to find enough time and energy to cope with the demands of keeping a house clean and tidy.

The most effective cleaning routine is the one that you actually do. Most people want to live in a clean house, but don't necessarily want to do any cleaning. It is essential to find a way of working that suits you and the way you live. Do you find it difficult to get started? Or, once you start, do you find that you become obsessive and can't stop? Whatever your approach to cleaning, the key is to come up with a system that fits as effortlessly as possible into your personal schedule.

For many people, a few minutes of daily maintenance seems to be the most effective method, while some prefer to do a major blitz, say once a week. Whatever way works best for you, the secret is to get into a routine and stick to it. This means that you will need to be honest about what you really can achieve on a daily, weekly, and monthly basis. It is essential to set yourself goals that are realistic and easy to fulfill, because this will give you the satisfaction, encouragement, and confidence to stick to your new cleaning routine.

5-MINUTE FLASH, 10-MINUTE FIX-IT

Whether you choose to clean in short, regular bursts or schedule longer, more intensive sessions, the trick is to stay on top of things. You don't want to let tasks build up and become overwhelming. Get into the habit of carrying out the small, simple jobs on a regular basis, and they will become automatic, leaving you extra time and energy to cope with your remaining chores. Even if you don't wash the mugs last thing at night, at least collect them and put them in the kitchen; recycle newspapers once you've done with them instead of letting them pile up; and always put items back where they belong once you're finished with them.

TIME YOUR VACUUM

SOUND THE ALARM

Got a few minutes to spare? Set a timer or alarm for the amount of time you have available and tackle the fingerprints on your doors and light switches, wipe the front of the refrigerator, or get out the vacuum cleaner.

IT'S ALL IN THE TIMING

☆ *Many people find it helpful to set themselves a time limit, rather than complete tasks. Decide on a length of time and stop whatever you're doing when time's up. (Choose the right kind of chore, like dusting.) You will be amazed at what you can achieve in just a few minutes if you do this regularly.*

☆ *Get into the habit of using your time efficiently. While you're waiting for the eggs to boil, your bath to run, or an important phone call, get busy instead of bored—clean a window, do some dishes, polish the table, or empty the trash can.*

⭐ *If you prefer to do an occasional blitz, or if extreme measures are called for, then make sure that you don't take on a task that you are unable to complete. The last thing you want to do is have to stop halfway and leave the house in more chaos than when you started.*

DUSTER BLITZ

CLEANING UP

Always be methodical in your approach to cleaning. Pick a task or two that you know you will be able to complete within the time available or can abandon easily if necessary. Even if you only do a few minutes here and there, you will start to notice the difference in no time.

The following tasks are best dealt with on a daily basis and should only take a short time to complete:

⭐ making beds
⭐ washing dishes
⭐ cleaning kitchen surfaces
⭐ taking out the trash
⭐ cleaning the bathroom sink
⭐ wiping down the shower or bath

Other tasks may only need addressing on a weekly basis:

⭐ laundry
⭐ vacuuming
⭐ floor cleaning
⭐ cleaning the kitchen and bathroom
⭐ changing the bedding
⭐ dusting

Certain tasks can be carried out every 4-6 weeks:

⭐ cleaning the refrigerator
⭐ sweeping out the garage, or any outside areas
⭐ polishing windows and mirrors
⭐ washing out the kitchen garbage can
⭐ cleaning the baseboards

CLEARING YOUR CLUTTER

Keeping your house clean is easier and much less time-consuming if you put things away when they're not in use. If everything has its place, then you always know where to find what you need when you need it. Chances are, if you don't have enough space for everything, then you've got too many belongings and it's time to get rid of some of them! Logically, of course, fewer belongings means that there is going to be less for you to clean, and if you clear your clutter, you'll reduce the buildup of dirt, dust, and grime, and the clear surfaces will be much easier to keep clean.

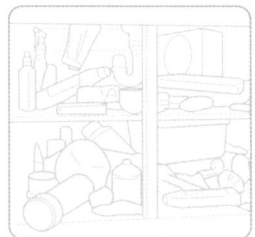

CUPBOARD NIGHTMARES

CUPBOARD LOVE

Cupboards and drawers that are kept neat and organized are much more efficient, as not only will it be easier for you to find and get to what you need, you will also be able to fit more into them in the first place.

RELEASE YOUR RUBBISH

Throw away items once you're done with them (e.g. jam jars, magazines, old lipsticks), and always resist any urge to hang on to things "just in case" they might come in handy at some point in the future. They probably won't, and they take up valuable space, acting as dirt and dust collectors. Some items simply need to be thrown away, while others can be recycled. If you haven't read the Sunday paper from last week by now, it's unlikely that you're ever going to get around to it. Get rid of it!

THINKING THINGS THROUGH

Need some time out to think things through, or do some problem solving? This may be the perfect opportunity to try some cleaning, tidying, or decluttering. Some light activity can actually help stimulate the thinking process.

FINISH WHAT YOU START

Always complete each task before you move onto the next one. Avoid beginning one task and then becoming distracted with another. If you continually find yourself unable to finish tasks, you are obviously setting yourself goals that are too high. Break down these chores into a series of smaller, more manageable jobs. Instead of attempting to clean all the windows, for example, restrict yourself to cleaning two or three. That way, you will never be left with unfinished business hanging over you.

HOOKED UP
To keep items neat and tidy, hang them up instead of storing them on the floor – invest in a few hooks to hold ironing boards, folding chairs, brooms and tools.

PROPER PLACES
Allocating specific places to everything makes cleaning a more straightforward process. It is much easier to put items away if you know exactly where they go and are not having to search for somewhere to store them, or having to stuff them into an already overcrowded drawer or cupboard.

TOOLS OF THE TRADE

Naturally, ideas of what represents an acceptable level of cleanliness and tidiness are bound to vary. Some people have to have everything immaculate, while others tolerate an astonishing level of messiness. Whatever your personal dirt threshold, having the right tool for the job makes any task much easier.

CLEANING KIT

CHOOSE CAREFULLY

There's a huge variety of cleaning appliances and products around today, all of which are designed to take the grind out of household chores. Always choose tools that are appropriate for your particular living space (in terms of both their cleaning ability and ease of storage) and are simple for you to handle. When choosing a new vacuum cleaner, for example, buy one that is light enough for you to lift and is easy to operate. Don't get talked into buying a model that is too powerful or complex for your needs.

CARING FOR YOUR EQUIPMENT

Appliances, tools, and equipment need maintenance. Care for them properly, and they will last longer and function more efficiently.

☆ *Regularly check plugs on all electrical equipment to make sure that no wires have worked loose.*

☆ Empty your vacuum or carpet sweeper frequently (or change the bag, if appropriate).

☆ Wipe down the outside of your vacuum every few weeks with a cloth that has been dunked in warm, soapy water and wrung out.

☆ Check the brushes and wheels of your vacuum cleaner and remove any threads, hairs, or dirt particles that may have collected there.

☆ Rinse brooms, brushes, and dustpans at least once a month in warm, soapy water, then leave them to dry thoroughly before putting them away.

☆ Don't stand brooms on their bristles. If possible, hang them up.

☆ Rinse mops after use and allow them to dry.

☆ Replace mopheads and spongeheads once they start to show signs of wear.

☆ Keep all cloths, sponges, and scourers as clean as possible, as they are a breeding ground for germs. Rinse them out after each use and spread or hang them out to dry.

BASIC CLEANING KIT

☆ vacuum cleaner

☆ broom

☆ dustpan and brush

☆ mop and bucket (with strainer)

☆ scrubbing brush(es)

☆ old toothbrush(es)

☆ dishwashing brushes

☆ sponges (including the nylon, non-stick variety)

☆ scourers

☆ dusting cloths and rags

☆ paper towels

☆ polishing cloths

☆ protective gloves

A CLEAN SWEEP

Good-quality brooms, brushes, and mops are great for dealing with dirty floors, but from time to time your floors will benefit from a good session with a bucket of warm, soapy water and a stiff scrubbing brush.

MULTI-PURPOSE MAGIC

GREEN AND CLEAN

Don't throw squeezed lemon halves away. Keep them in the refrigerator and use them to descale, clean and freshen faucets, sinks, and drainers.

CLEANING PRODUCTS

The number of modern cleaning appliances is matched by the array of chemical cleaning products on the market today. With their brightly colored packaging and promises of instant cleanliness, you will be tempted to keep adding to a large collection. You may fully intend to use the product when you buy it, but rarely (or never) actually do, so it ends up at the back of the cupboard gathering dust. Clear out your cleaning cupboard and use up what you already have, then focus on keeping a supply of useful, multi-purpose products (non-chemical, where possible).

EASY DOES IT

Even if you choose to resort to heavy-duty cleaners or strong chemicals, use them sparingly. Harsh cleaners can be harmful to the environment and their overuse can deplete our immune systems and give rise to conditions such as asthma and eczema. Frequently, mild cleaners or natural substances such as baking soda, vinegar, or lemon juice can clean just as effectively.

CUPBOARD LOVE

Organize your cupboard so that you can find what you need quickly and easily, and always put products back in their allocated place when you're done. If you do not have space to keep cleaning supplies in each area of your house, consider investing in a large plastic bucket filled with cleaning products, protective gloves, and a variety of cloths and sponges that you can carry around with you.

ANTI-ANTI?

Anti-bacterial products are not essential, whatever their labels say. Indeed, some people even argue that we overclean nowadays, and the blanket destruction of all bacteria may be counterproductive. Unless you suffer from specific health problems, you do not need to create an absolutely sterile environment and can go easy on the anti-bacterial products. A few bugs never hurt anyone. In fact, we are not designed to live in a sterile world, and a little exposure to some germs may help strengthen our immune systems and improve our ability to fight off illnesses.

BASIC CLEANING MATERIALS

☆ baking soda

☆ lemon (or lemon juice)

☆ salt

☆ white vinegar

☆ glass cleaner (optional)

☆ non-abrasive cream cleanser

☆ powdered or abrasive cleanser

☆ spray cleaner

☆ liquid or spray polish

☆ detergent

☆ disinfectant

PICK YOUR BASICS

KITCHENS

"A woman is like a tea bag. You never know how strong she is until she gets in hot water."

NANCY REAGAN

The kitchen and bathroom are the two rooms that usually require the most upkeep. The kitchen is where we prepare and often eat food, and it is essential, therefore, to keep it as clean and germ free as possible. It may also be the place we do laundry and deal with the garbage, and perhaps walk in from the garden, bringing in dirt from outdoors.

It can be tempting to rush out of the house in the morning, leaving the kitchen in a state of chaos to be dealt with later. In fact, the best way to keep your kitchen clean and tidy is regular maintenance. It can be difficult to know where to start, but try doing a little each day. Begin by clearing up after yourself: wipe up any spills immediately (whether on a counter, on the floor, or in the refrigerator); clean up whenever you prepare food; do dishes or load the dishwasher after each meal (or at least stack the dirty dishes neatly, leaving pans and dishes to soak if necessary); and wipe all surfaces. Make sure you sweep (or vacuum) the floor and take out the trash every day.

To supplement daily maintenance, make up a list of weekly and monthly tasks, such as scrubbing, cleaning the sink, mopping the floor, wiping down the cabinets and doors, and cleaning the refrigerator, the oven, and other appliances.

Wear protective gloves where possible, particularly when using harsh cleaners, and make sure you have a good supply of kitchen towels, so that you always have a clean, dry cloth on hand. Allocate different cloths or sponges to different tasks—don't use the same one for doing dishees that you use for wiping counters and surfaces, and never use either of these for wiping the floor, however tiny the spill.

Before you go to bed, spend a minute or two doing a final cleanup: clear away any mugs, wipe down the draining board and counters, and put out fresh kitchen towels ready for the next day.

REFRIGERATORS AND FREEZERS

A TIDY REFRIGERATOR

Keeping your refrigerator and freezer neat and clean is essential to a well-run kitchen. Since they provide storage for fresh foodstuffs, it is vital to keep them spotless and germ free. Check the contents regularly and get rid of any items that are starting to spoil, or are past their use-by date. Don't wait for food to go moldy before you dispose of it—be honest with yourself, if you're not going to use it, throw it out.

CLEANING YOUR REFRIGERATOR OR FREEZER

Clean your refrigerator every week—preferably when stocks are low, to avoid having fresh food lying around—and reorganize your freezer every 1–3 months.

⭐ *Always turn the power off before cleaning or defrosting your refrigerator or freezer.*

⭐ *Empty the contents into a cooler if you have one, or a sturdy cardboard box lined with newspaper or a blanket to prevent frozen goods thawing too quickly. Place food in a plastic bag first. In hot weather, you can buy a big bag of ice to pack around the food and keep it chilled.*

STEAM CLEAN

To speed up defrosting, stand a bowl of steaming water inside the freezer. Lay towels on the shelves to enhance the effect of the steam.

★ Avoid using sharp or metal objects to scrape away ice because they may damage the internal surface of your refrigerator or freezer—it's best to wait for any buildup of ice to melt naturally. If necessary, use a rubber or pliable plastic spatula or a wooden utensil.

★ Remove all shelves and drawers and wash them in warm, soapy water.

★ Use a cloth soaked in warm, soapy water to clean the interior: wipe the top, interior side walls, the bottom, then the inside of the door. To prevent mildew, pour a little vinegar onto your cloth and wipe the inside of the refrigerator.

★ Carefully clean the rubber door seals with a cloth or an old toothbrush.

★ Wipe the outside surfaces, then replace shelves and restock.

★ Every few months, pull the appliance out and clean behind it, using a soft brush attachment to vacuum the condenser coil and remove dust. Don't forget to clean the piece of floor that the appliance normally stands on, too.

GREEN IDEAS

For a green alternative to detergent, use a strong solution of baking soda to clean your refrigerator or freezer. To treat tough stains, sprinkle a little baking soda directly onto the cloth.

LOOK, NO ICE!

For your freezer or freezer section to run efficiently, the interior must be kept clear of ice and the door seal needs to close properly. Unless you have a frost-free model, you will need to defrost it regularly.

WHAT'S COOKING?

A few minutes of daily upkeep, and cleaning your stove and cooktop will never again be a daunting task. Clear up spills, stains, marks, and burns as they occur (being careful not to burn yourself, of course), and wipe appliances and surfaces after each use. Set aside time every 2–4 weeks for a more thorough cleaning of your stove, oven, grill, and microwave.

OVENS

☆ Clean glass doors with baking soda sprinkled onto steel wool.

☆ Cover spills in hot ovens with salt. Once the oven has cooled, the spill will lift away. Very dirty ovens may need a heavy-duty oven cleaner (usually caustic). Rinse well and finish off with a nylon scourer.

☆ Clean range-style ovens (when cool) with warm, soapy water or a little vinegar. Hot ovens do not generally need to be cleaned because deposits usually burn away.

OVEN HOODS

☆ Clean outside surfaces with hot, soapy water to prevent a buildup of dust and grease.

☆ Scrub metal filters with hot, soapy water and a nylon brush, or, if appropriate, wash in the dishwasher.

FOILED AGAIN
• For easy cleaning, line the grill pan with aluminum foil.
• Spread aluminum foil over the bottom of the oven to catch drips, spills, and crumbs.

STAINLESS STEEL
Stainless steel hoods can be wiped with a few drops of baby oil to make them shine.

ASK THE EXPERTS
If you have a specialist, self-cleaning or non-stick oven, check the instruction manual for cleaning tips.

MICROWAVES

☆ *Wash the glass turntable in hot, soapy water.*

☆ *Apply some baking-soda-and-water paste to stains and leave for a few minutes. Or put a slice of lemon in a bowl of water and "cook" on high for several minutes.*

CARING FOR YOUR COOKTOP

Glass, ceramic, and halogen cooktops are easy to keep clean and can be wiped with a cloth dipped in warm, soapy water or cleaned with a specialist cleaner. Avoid letting stains build up and bake onto the surface.

Dismantle gas rings and clean with hot, soapy water and a nylon scourer or small brush. Electric cooktops can be wiped or scrubbed. If very dirty, apply a heavy-duty cleaner, leave for 1–2 hours, then rinse.

Solid fuel cooktops are extremely robust, but should be wiped after each use (though allow them to cool down first). Scrub occasionally with a wire brush to remove crumbs and food particles.

WASHING AND DRYING

It's easy to take your washing machine and dryer for granted, forgetting that they too can benefit from the occasional cleanup. Start by consulting the instruction manual for the manufacturer's special recommendations on caring for your particular appliance.

WHITER THAN WHITE

✅ *For white appliances that have started to yellow, mix ½ cup bleach, ¼ cup baking soda and 4 cups warm water. Apply with a sponge or cloth and leave for 10–15 minutes. Rinse thoroughly. When it's dry, finish off with car wax to eliminate small scratches and make the surfaces shine.*

For general maintenance, wipe outside surfaces and check the drum for any stray particles of dirt or small items, such as buttons, that may have become lodged there. Wipe the drum with a damp cloth to clean away any residual fluff or dirt particles. Check filters and door seals, and empty and clean when necessary. Remove lint and fluff from the dryer filter after each use, and vacuum every few weeks using the crevice tool to give the filter a thorough cleaning.

RUNNING ON EMPTY

Depending on how much you use your washing machine, flush it through by running a short, hot program on empty, either with or without detergent. If you live in a hard-water area, run the cycle with a lime scale remover to clean the heating element.

CLEAN AND CLEAR

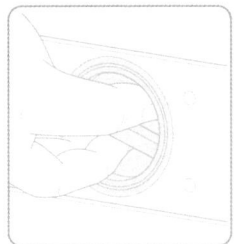

CLEAR THE FILTER

Clean the washing-machine filter regularly. It should be easy to remove. It is usually located on the front of the machine toward the base. As a precaution, place a small bowl in front of the opening to catch any water leakage. Get rid of fluff and small items that have collected there. Then rinse, scrubbing if necessary to dislodge any buildup of dirt and fluff. Finally, replace the filter, making sure that you fasten it securely.

CLEANING THE SEAL

The rubber door seal of your washing machine can become a trap for dust, dirt, detergent residue, and tiny pools of water. To prevent a buildup of grime and soap scum, and to prolong the life of door seals and keep them in good working order, clean them by washing with a cloth and some warm, soapy water. To reach awkward areas and remove caked-on dirt and stains, scrub with an old toothbrush. Wipe dry to finish.

RINSING THE DRAWER

Pull out the detergent drawer (it should slide out easily, although you may have to give it a gentle tug, or lift the front slightly to remove it) and rinse it under the faucet to get rid of any buildup of detergent and fabric conditioner. Leave the drawer to soak in warm water to loosen heavy deposits. Use a bottlebrush (or an old toothbrush) to scrub stubborn stains or patches of mildew.

SINKS, DRAINS, GARBAGE DISPOSALS

The kitchen sink is used when preparing food, washing dishes, generally cleaning, and, if you have a garbage disposal unit, disposing of leftover food and scraps.

☆ *Sinks and drains are traps for dirt and bacteria. To keep your sink as fresh, clean, and hygienic as possible, rinse thoroughly after each use, wipe down to prevent water marks and never leave bits of food lurking in the drain.*

☆ *To revive white ceramic sinks that are starting to discolor, fill the sink with cold water, add a cupful of bleach, then leave to soak for 30–60 minutes. Rinse thoroughly.*

☆ *Use a wooden skewer (or satay stick) to clean away dirt and grime from awkward corners of sinks that even bottle- and toothbrushes can't reach.*

☆ *Regular use of either a cream cleanser or baking soda is ideal for making most types of sink (stainless steel, ceramic, or acrylic) and drains sparkle, but check the manufacturer's instructions for advice on cleaning specialist surfaces. You may wish to use anti-bacterial cleaners and cloths to keep germs to a minimum.*

GREASE IS THE WORD
Avoid pouring grease or oil down the sink: wipe away any surplus from your pans and dishes with paper towels, or pour into an empty container or a cone made of newspaper and throw away.

CRYSTAL CLEAN
To keep your drains free from grease deposits, pour half a cup of washing soda crystals into the drain every few weeks, followed by a kettleful of boiling water.

☆ *To remove odors from garbage disposals and keep them fresh, "feed" them with some squeezed lemon or lime halves or orange peel before switching on. Alternatively, run warm tap water into the unit and trickle in some baking soda, or simply pour some vinegar into the unit or drain.*

GERM WARFARE

SINK FRESH

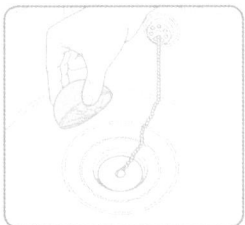

 Tea and coffee stains, watermarks, and lime scale can all be removed with a little lemon juice or by rubbing with half a squeezed lemon. Leave for a few moments and then rinse. Used regularly, this will help to prevent any lime scale buildup and also keep your sinks and drains deodorized.

 Never use steel wool pads to clean sinks because they will scratch and spoil most surfaces, making them more prone to stains in the future. Scrub drains and overflows with some non-abrasive cream cleanser or baking soda, using an old toothbrush or a small bottlebrush, to keep them clean and stain free.

THE SMALL STUFF

Kitchen countertops should be kept as clear as possible. The only small appliances, gadgets, and utensils that need to be kept nearby are ones that you use regularly. Get rid of any that you no longer need, and pack away ones that you use only occasionally, or, if you have sufficient space in your kitchen, store them in the back of a cupboard.

SPICK-AND-SPAN

Any items that are kept out on display, such as kettles, toasters, juicers, food processors, coffee machines, and even bread boxes need regular attention or they will become traps for dirt, dust, and splashes, and a consequent breeding ground for bacteria and germs. Every week, unplug or dismantle them and wash or wipe them with a cloth wrung out in warm, soapy water or a solution of baking soda. Then clean the counter behind, beneath, and surrounding them. If the surfaces are particularly dirty, you may need to use a stronger baking soda solution, or sprinkle some directly onto the cloth.

Clear your work space

✓ Apply the same principle to your cookbooks as to your appliances. Don't clutter up your countertop with books, gadgets, or utensils that you hardly ever use. Get rid of ones that are no longer useful, or pack them away and store them elsewhere. To keep surfaces clear, put up a shelf for any cookbooks you use regularly.

APPLIANCE SCIENCE

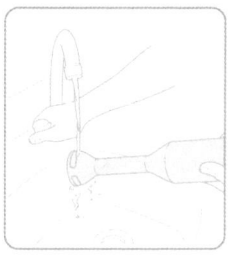

TOASTER TIPS

⏩ At least once a week, turn your toaster upside-down and shake out the crumbs into the sink or garbage. Make sure that the toaster is fully cooled first. To dislodge any burnt-on crumbs or trapped crusts, gently loosen them using the handle of a wooden or plastic utensil, not a knife or a sharp object that could damage the filaments. An easy way to control toaster crumbs is to place a small tray under your toaster. Any loose crumbs will collect on the tray and can be easily disposed of.

KETTLE DESCALING

⏩ To descale your kettle, use a proprietary descaler or simply fill the kettle with a solution of half water and half distilled white vinegar. Bring to a boil, then leave to soak for an hour or two to allow the lime scale to loosen. Rinse thoroughly, then fill the kettle, bring the water to a boil and discard to make sure that all traces of descaler or vinegar have been removed. A small shell or marble placed in the bottom of your kettle will help prevent lime scale from forming in the future.

CARING FOR UTENSILS

⏩ Some appliances, attachments and utensils that are out on display are used less frequently than others. However, these will still need to be washed or rinsed from time to time to keep them clean and free from a buildup of dust and grime. But remember, never immerse any electrical components in water. A regular rinse in clear water or a wipe with a damp cloth should be sufficient, but any item that is used for food preparation should be cleaned prior to use.

CUPBOARDS AND COUNTERTOPS

Work surfaces should be wiped down every time you use them. Put away any remaining foodstuffs first, because this will help to reduce the possibility of bacteria and keep your kitchen neat and tidy. Food cupboards should be checked every few weeks, and shelves and drawers emptied and cleaned. Glass, crockery, or pan cupboards only need thorough cleaning every few months, at which time you should wash any items that haven't been used for a while. Don't forget to clean the tops of wall cupboards occasionally, because they can get very greasy and attract dirt.

CHOPPING BOARDS

☑ Use two chopping boards: one for preparing meat and fish and one for vegetables.

☑ Rinse in hot water after each use and rub with half a lemon or lemon juice to remove stains and strong smells (such as garlic, onion, and fish).

COUNTERTOPS

☆ *Ceramic: wipe with a damp cloth or lemon juice.*

☆ *Laminate: wipe with a damp cloth dipped in warm, soapy water, or use a damp cloth sprinkled with baking soda.*

☆ *Marble: wipe with a little soapy water and a damp cloth, or use a little white vinegar or lemon juice and rinse it away immediately.*

☆ *Slate: pour a little milk onto a lint-free cloth and wipe over slate counters, to give them a slight shine.*

☆ *Wooden, unvarnished: rub with linseed or teak oil. For a more intensive treatment, work the oil into the surface with a piece of steel wool.*

CUPBOARD LOVE

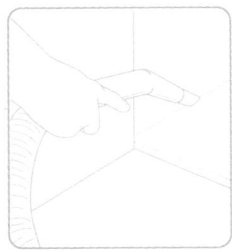

VACUUMING

Empty each of your cupboards, shelves, and drawers and throw away any items that are out of date. Vacuum thoroughly using the crevice tool or brush attachment to remove dust, dirt, or crumbs. If the idea of cleaning all your cupboards (or shelves or drawers) in one shot is too daunting, choose a different one to work on each week. That way they will all get cleaned in turn over a course of weeks.

WASHING

Wash down (or scrub, if necessary) your shelves, cupboards, and drawers with warm, soapy water. Then rinse and wipe them down with a clean cloth to dry them, or leave them to dry naturally. Wash (or scrub) the outsides of your cupboards and drawers, paying particular attention to hinges and door handles, where dirt and grime tend to collect. Then rinse and leave to dry.

CONTAINERS

Wipe jars, bottles, and tins with a cloth dipped in warm, soapy water and wrung out till damp, then dry them. Make sure that all containers are completely dry before refilling them. To keep your cupboards fresh, and also to discourage insects, hang sprigs of dried herbs such as mint, rosemary, or pennyroyal.

FOOD GLORIOUS FOOD

Any surface or container used to store or prepare food should always be as clean as possible to keep germs at bay and reduce the risk of cross-contamination. You can't be too careful when it comes to fighting bacteria and making sure that your kitchen is a safe, clean, and healthy environment.

BASIC RULES OF CLEANLINESS

☆ *Wash your hands before any food preparation—even if you wear protective gloves, because they can also carry and pass on germs.*

☆ *Don't sneeze or cough near food or countertops, and always wash your hands afterward if you do.*

☆ *Store raw meat, fish, and eggs away from vegetables and cooked foods.*

☆ *Place raw meats below fruit and vegetables or cooked foods, or store them in secure containers to avoid the risk of juices dripping and causing contamination.*

☆ *To prevent the spread of germs, use paper towels, rather than sponges or dishcloths, to clean up meat juices.*

☆ *Use separate boards or surfaces for preparing vegetables or cooked foods and raw meat or fish.*

Daily bread

✓ To prevent mildew from forming inside your bread box, wipe it with a little vinegar on a cloth. Leave it to air until the smell has disappeared.

✓ Line your bread box with foil or paper to catch any crumbs and make it easier to clean.

HEALTHY LIVING

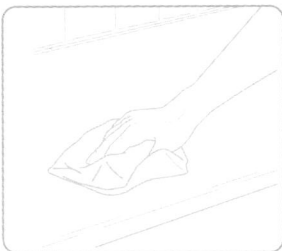

All items or areas that are involved in food storage or preparation should be washed before and after each use. Get rid of any crumbs and food remnants. Then clean with hot, soapy water.

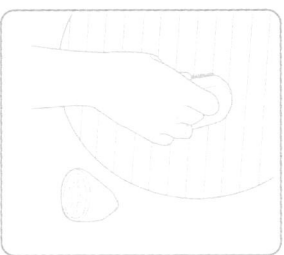

Wooden surfaces and chopping boards should be scrubbed clean with hot, soapy water. You can also use nailbrush and a lemon. Rub a little olive oil into the surface to seal it from time to time (see also pages 32–33).

Store dry goods (flour, rice, legumes, nuts, cookies, etc.) in tightly sealed glass or plastic containers to keep them fresh and prevent insects getting to them. If containers are out on display, make sure that they are placed in a cool spot, away from direct sunlight.

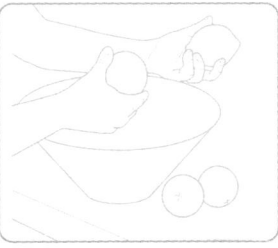

Regularly empty and clean fruit bowls, vegetable baskets, and refrigerator shelves and drawers—don't just keep topping them up. Get rid of any fruit or vegetables that have started to spoil, because they will spread rot, encourage mold, and attract insects.

DOING DISHES

Keeping dirty dishes under control is vital to a sparkling clean, well-run kitchen. The best method is to clean as you go, washing dishes after each meal, or loading and unloading your dishwasher immediately, so that you never have to tackle a mountain of food-encrusted, hard-to-clean pots, pans, and dishes. If you absolutely have to leave the dishes until later, rinse and stack your plates neatly, or leave them to soak in hot, soapy water. Rinse washed items in clean hot water. Preferably use two dishpans, rather than a running faucet, to save water.

YOU WILL NEED
- *A cloth, brush, or sponge*
- *Dishwashing liquid*
- *A plastic or rubber scraper or scourer*
- *Some scouring powder*
- *Rubber gloves*

GOLDEN RULES

DIRTY dishes piled into the sink are unsightly as well as unhygienic, encouraging the spread of germs and possibly even food poisoning.

STACK your items in the order in which you are going to wash them. Wash thoroughly and then rinse in clean, hot water.

WEARING rubber gloves will protect your hands and allow you to use hotter water, which will wash more effectively and kill germs.

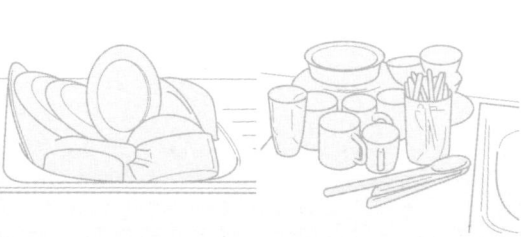

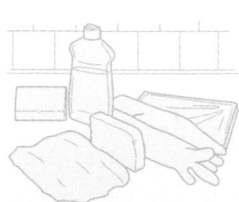

OPTIMUM ORDER FOR WASHING DISHES

1 Glasses (or change the water and wash them at the end)

2 Lightly soiled crockery: cups, mugs, tea and coffee pots, and side plates

3 Heavily soiled crockery

4 Cutlery and utensils

5 Pans and baking dishes

6 Small appliances

SPARKLE AND SAFETY

• Add a little vinegar to your rinse water to give your dishes an added sparkle.

• Invest in a good dish rack, to allow your dishes to drain efficiently and reduce risk of draining-board bangs and breakages.

CHANGE the water as often as necessary when washing or rinsing. As soon as your dish towel becomes damp, replace with a fresh one.

DRY dishes and put them away immediately. Finish off by wiping down the sink, faucets, and dish rack.

HALF a lemon placed on the top rack of your dishwasher will make your plates and glasses shine and will also cut down on lime scale.

CROCKERY AND GLASSWARE

Although there are some basic general rules that apply to washing most dishes, you should also be aware that utensils made of different materials call for slightly different cleaning techniques. Glasses, cups, plates, and dishes should be washed in hot water with a little dish soap, just enough to cut through the grease and dirt: extra bubbles will make your dishes difficult to rinse, and won't get them any cleaner. Use a plastic dishpan for washing dishes, or place a mat in the bottom of your sink, to prevent scratches to the sink or damage to your glassware and crockery. Avoid overstacking your drainer: dry and put away items as soon as the rack is full. Change kitchen towels and dishcloths regularly and wash them in hot water or soak them in a weak bleach solution.

SPECIAL BREW

DISHWASHING
Only put items in the dishwasher that you know are dishwasher-safe. Leave out handpainted items or plates and glasses with gilt decoration as they will fade.

TIME FOR TEA

⭐ *To remove coffee and tea stains from cups, mugs, and teapots, rub with a damp cloth dipped in baking soda. Alternatively, leave to soak for an hour or two in a solution of baking soda.*

⭐ *For stubborn stains, soak in hot water and enzyme detergent, but rinse thoroughly before using to remove all traces of soap.*

⭐ *To clean the spout of a teapot, pack it with salt and leave to stand overnight. Then rinse clean. Any stains should disappear.*

GLASS RULES

⭐ *Wash glass items individually (holding stemmed glasses gently by their stem).*

⭐ *Never leave glassware to soak in the sink where it can easily break and cause injury.*

WASTE NOT... Try not to run your dishwasher when it is only half full as it wastes water. Pre-rinse items, if necessary, and leave them in the dishwasher.

CLEAN AND CLEAR

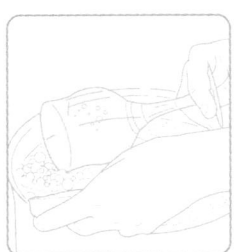

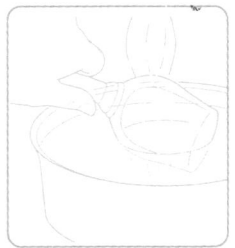

Glasses, which tend to only be lightly soiled, can be washed first. Or, if you prefer, save them until the end, but change the water. Glassware should always be washed in clean water to avoid smears and grease marks.

Before washing or scrubbing plates and dishes, scrape away any leftover bits of food, then rinse the plates briefly under the faucet to help loosen any remaining particles of food. Stack plates carefully.

Rinse glasses and china in hot water, not cold, because any sudden change in temperature can cause them to crack or break. Dry with a soft, lint-free cloth and put away immediately.

CUTLERY AND UTENSILS

A good time to wash cutlery is after the plates, cups, and bowls and before tackling heavy-duty pots, pans, and baked-on dishes (although heavily soiled utensils are probably best washed along with the dirty pans). Some people, however, prefer to wash cutlery second, after glassware. As with all dishes, cutlery should ideally be washed immediately after use. If this is not possible, rinse it under the faucet and put to one side. Never leave cutlery lurking at the bottom of the dishpan to be fished out at the end or dumped into the sink with the dirty water, and never leave any type of blade in the water as it could cause injury.

Given that cutlery is used to prepare food and to eat with, it should be treated with respect and thoroughly washed after each use, not simply given a token swill once the rest is finished. For safety, sharp knives used for food preparation are best washed and put away immediately after use.

OUT ON DISPLAY

Utensils that are stored out on display will gather dust and grease, particularly if you don't use them very often, so make sure you clean them from time to time and always wash before use.

KNIFE BLOCKS

✓ Knife blocks may seem to be a convenient method of storage, but they are difficult to clean and to keep free of crumbs and dirt. A better option is to store knives in a knife tray instead. It should be placed inside a kitchen drawer where items are less likely to gather dust.

CUTTING EDGE

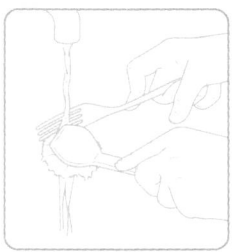

WASHING AND RINSING

Wash cutlery in hot water and a minimum amount of dish soap. Use a cloth or a soft brush: avoid using harsh scourers or brushes to remove dried-on food. Once it's clean, rinse thoroughly to wash away traces of soap and to avoid any "rainbow" staining, and then wipe dry immediately to prevent water marks forming.

CARING FOR CUTLERY

Cutlery and utensils can be left to soak in soapy water for a few minutes until you are ready to wash them, but don't leave them for any length of time as this can cause corrosion. Put cutlery and utensils to soak in a bowl or jug, making sure that wooden (or bone or ivory) handles are left out of the water, or put them to one side.

CUTLERY IN THE DISHWASHER

Only dishwasher-proof cutlery should be put in the dishwasher. To avoid tarnishing, separate silver cutlery from stainless steel and put them into different compartments in the cutlery basket so that they don't touch. For safety, put knives in the basket with the blades pointing downward, but make sure they are not poking through and likely to catch on something.

POTS AND PANS

When you're faced with dirty pots and pans and food-encrusted casseroles, it is very tempting to be slapdash, just swish a little greasy water around and ignore the burnt-on stains. Putting a little effort into keeping your pots, pans, and bakeware sparkling clean will prolong their lives and reduce the risk of festering germs and bacteria.

POT BLACK

☆ Pots and pans may come last in the cycle, but that is no excuse for sloppiness. Before you start, scrape away any leftover food and rinse pans quickly under the faucet. Next, fill pots and pans with hot, soapy water and put to one side.

☆ When you are ready to wash, change the water, making sure that it is as hot as possible, so that it is able to clean more easily and is more likely to kill germs.

☆ For difficult stains, use a scourer (remember to use the specially designed nylon variety for non-stick pans) along

Pan tips

✅ Make sure that pots and pans are completely dry before you put them away, to prevent mildew.

✅ Never reuse a pan without washing it first. It may seem like more work, but it is much easier to wash a pan twice than to have to scrub off twice-burnt stains.

with some scouring cream, or even a little scouring powder, if absolutely necessary. Don't forget to clean the underside of the pan, too.

☆ Wash lids thoroughly and check that there is no food stuck under the lip.

BANISHING BURNS AND STAINS

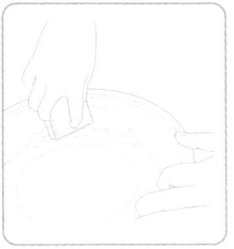

BLITZ WITH BAKING SODA

Rub a paste of water and baking soda into the burned area and leave for at least an hour. Rinse.

A GOOD OLD SOAK

Fill the pan, baking pan, or casserole with water, add a few drops of dish soap or some laundry detergent, and boil. For stubborn stains, leave to stand overnight.

SALT SCRUB

Sprinkle with salt, moisten with water, leave for 10 minutes and scrub.

CAST IRON CLEANING

To get rid of rust from cast-iron pans or woks, rub with the cut side of half a potato dipped in dish soap. Wipe the pan clean with a dry paper towel, the wipe again with a little cooking oil on a paper towel to prevent rusting in the future.

Never leave cast iron pots and pans to soak, or put them away while they are still damp, because this will cause them to rust.

TARNISHED COPPER

To remove tarnish from copper pans, rub with half a lemon dipped in salt, tomato ketchup, or Worcestershire sauce. Rinse thoroughly and then polish.

CLEANING COPPER

Put some fabric softener into the pan and leave to stand overnight. Wipe clean.

LIGHTNING LEMON

Clean non-stick pans with a combination of baking soda, lemon, and water.

ODOR BUSTING

An important part of having a clean kitchen is making sure that it smells nice and clean, too. Check regularly for potential offenders, such as drips under the sink, dampness, or mold under the flooring, or a buildup of dirt or grease behind cupboards, appliances or on top of cabinets. And make sure that there is nothing evil lurking at the back of shelves and cupboards. To keep your kitchen fresh, get rid of any foodstuffs if they start to spoil and wash curtains and blinds regularly. Clean cupboard tops and any hidden

DRASTIC PLASTIC

Plastic tends to absorb smells and can give off unpleasant odors. Go through your containers and throw away any that are past their best.

MAKING PERFECT SCENTS

AN OPENED box of baking soda in your refrigerator, freezer, or cupboard will absorb unwanted smells.

SCENTED candles are a quick and easy way to make any room smell lovely—even if you don't light them.

MIXING your own pot-pourri allows you to scent each room in whatever way you choose.

areas, sweep the floor, and take out the trash daily. Once you've made sure that you have gotten rid of any odor offenders, there are various ways to keep your kitchen, and your whole house, fresh and sweet-smelling.

JUICY FRUITS
- Grind up half a lemon and put it in the trash can to keep it smelling fresh.
- Place a cotton ball moistened with a few drops of vanilla essence in your cupboards and they'll smell heavenly.f

FRESH AIR AND AIR FRESHENERS

✔️ *There is no substitute for fresh, clean air—opening windows and doors and airing your rooms frequently will make a huge difference to your home's overall aroma. However, there are times when we need a little artificial help, too. There are numerous commercial air fresheners for you to choose from— plug-ins, aerosols, gels, liquids, crystals, oils, sprays, candles, and so on—and you can even buy sets of matching "smells" for different purposes. When selecting a product, check the fragrance and don't be taken in by pretty packaging. Never buy an item that you don't actually like the smell of. (The same applies to cleaning products.)*

SWEET SCENTS
For an irresistible fruity fragrance, simmer an apple and some cinnamon (or vanilla and orange or lemon peel) in a pan of water.

BATHROOMS

> ## *"Making movies is better than cleaning toilets."*
> ### KLAUS KINSKI

Your bathroom should be a retreat: a luxurious setting full of gleaming surfaces, fresh towels and delicious fragrances. It should be a place where you can prepare yourself for the day ahead, or escape from the world and relax in a soothing bath. With all that soap and hot water, it also ought to be the cleanest room in the house! Yet many people neglect their bathrooms, ignoring the buildup of lime scale around the faucets and the growing piles of dust and skin flakes in the corners. Are you one of those people whose bathroom only gets a thorough scouring when friends threaten to visit?

The best time to clean the bathroom is just after it has been used for a steamy bath or shower, when the dirt or scum in the bath or shower has not had time to set and when the warm steam has loosened any grunge on walls, fixtures, and fittings.

Buy yourself a good pair of rubber gloves for bathroom cleaning: heavy-duty ones are ideal. If you have enough space, keep a collection of cleaning products in each bathroom—all-purpose cleaner, glass cleaner, disinfectant, scouring powder, a small bowl or bucket, cloths, and paper towels. If you use a chemical cleaner, make sure that the bathroom is well ventilated to get rid of the harmful fumes. Old toothbrushes are invaluable for getting rid of dirt and grime from grout, drains, faucets, and awkward corners, but stick some tape around the handles so that they don't get used on teeth by mistake. Even the smallest bathroom should contain a cloth or sponge and an all-purpose cleaner for quick fixes and flash cleanups should an unexpected guest arrive.

If your bathroom hasn't been properly cleaned for a while, it will naturally take time to make it sparkle. But once it has been given a thorough overhaul, your task will be much easier. A few minutes every few days and a more thorough cleaning every month will be all it takes to keep it spotless and shining.

BATHTUBS

Cleaning the bath is easiest when it has just been used, while it is still warm. Keep a cloth nearby and encourage everyone to wipe the tub down after use to avoid buildup of dirt or rings around the bath. Avoid using scourers or abrasive cleaners that could scratch the surface of your bath.

WATERY WISDOM

☆ Wipe away bathtub rings with a cloth dampened with a little mineral spirits.

☆ Clean away bath oil immediately with a solution of dish soap.

☆ To get rid of mildew from awkward corners, dip some cotton balls in bleach and leave them to stand for a few minutes.

☆ Clear away lime scale from the bottom of your bath, or from whirlpool or jacuzzi nozzles, by rubbing with a little lemon juice or vinegar.

☆ Remove hard-water stains from porcelain or enamel baths by covering the area with a paste of baking soda and vinegar.

☆ Rub porcelain or enamel baths with coarse salt to make them shine.

☆ To revive yellowing enamel baths, rub with a mixture of salt and turpentine.

Bath time beauty regime

☑ Clear your bath of all bottles, brushes, soap, and washcloths.

☑ Wet the tub before using a cloth, nylon bath scourer, or a soft brush to cover the tub with a detergent. Leave for 10–15 minutes.

☑ Scrub gently, making sure that all the soap scum, dirt, and grime is removed. Rinse and wipe dry.

RUB A DUB DUB—WHAT TYPE OF TUB?

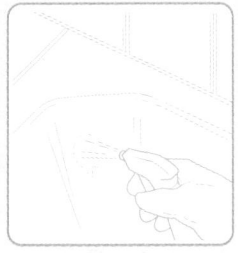
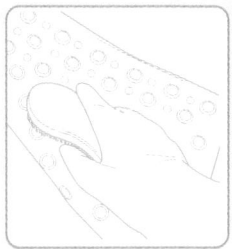

SURFACE CARE

To avoid damaging the surface of your tub, follow the manufacturer's instructions and only use products that are suitable for your type of bath.

PORCELAIN AND ENAMEL

Wash with a mild detergent and a cloth or sponge. Very dirty tubs can be cleaned with baking soda or cream cleanser, or soaked with a laundry-detergent solution. Wipe away stubborn stains with a little mineral spirits.

PLASTICS

For acrylic, fiberglass, or plastic, clean with a gentle spray cleaner or mild detergent and a cloth or sponge. If the tub is badly stained, rub with some diluted or undiluted dish soap, then pour a little white vinegar onto a cloth and rub.

A SHINY FINISH

Whatever type of bath you have, to finish, buff with a dry cloth or piece of towel to make the bath shine and prevent water marks from forming.

BATH MATS

Scrub plastic or rubber bath (and shower) mats with a stiff brush and hot, soapy water. To get rid of dirt or mildew, dip the brush in mineral spirits, or soak the mat in a washing-powder solution, then scrub clean. To store, always hang your mat up or roll it up and stand it on end—don't simply leave it sitting on the bottom of the bath to fester.

SINKS

Sinks are in constant use both in the bathroom and the kitchen, and they need regular maintenance to keep them looking good and free from soap scum, shaving cream, toothpaste, dirt, grime, and lime scale. A quick wipe after each use will make a huge difference to the overall state of your sink, but it's not only the sink that needs cleaning: the rim, the underside, and the pedestal need a weekly wipe or polish to keep them pristine, too. (*See also pages 54–55 and 62–63.*)

PEARLY WHITES
If you find any blobs of toothpaste in the sink, take a cloth and use the leftover paste to clean the sink and rim.

THAT SINKING FEELING

⭐ *Porcelain sinks: to make your white sink gleam, either leave to soak with laundry-detergent solution or line the sink with some paper towels and wet with a little bleach. Leave for 30 minutes, then rinse.*

⭐ *Vitreous enamel: this is best cleaned with detergent, but light stains and lime scale can be removed with a little lemon juice or baking soda. Never bleach an enamel sink: this will cause it to yellow.*

⭐ *Stainless steel sinks: for best results, clean with neat detergent and use a mild cream cleanser to get rid of stains and marks. Pour a little wood alcohol onto a cloth to wipe away water marks, but never use steel wool or heavy abrasives, because these will ruin the surface.*

SPARKLING SINKS

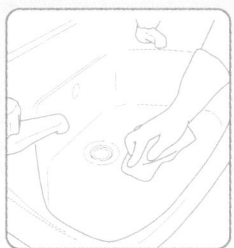

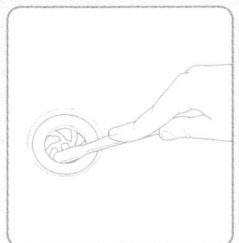

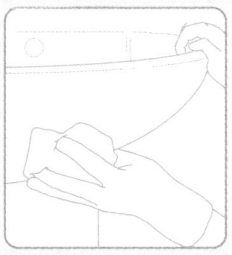

BASIC RULES

A simple wipe down after each use will keep your sink looking good, but for more persistent grime, or for a more thorough weekly clean, use a mild cream cleanser to rub away dirt. If your sink is very dirty, fill it with hot water and a little detergent and leave to soak. Clean colored sinks with mild detergent, vinegar, or baking soda, but never bleach, because this can cause fading.

AWKWARD CORNERS

Use an old toothbrush or a bottle brush and some liquid detergent, cream cleanser, or even some scouring powder to scrub away dirt and scum from the overflow, the drain, and even the plug itself. Regular rubbing with a squeeze of lemon juice will help reduce lime scale.

HIDDEN AREAS

Remember to include the less obvious surfaces of your sink in your weekly clean: the underside of the bowl can quickly become encrusted with soapy drips and dirt, while pedestals are favorite resting places for dust and grime, particularly if they have any slight detailing or recesses.

TOILETS AND BIDETS

Cleaning the toilet must be the most unpopular household chore of all, but it is essential nonetheless. Neglecting your toilet can quickly result in an unpleasant, smelly, and unhealthy bathroom. (*See also pages 62–63.*)

TOOLS OF THE TRADE

⭐ *Wear protective rubber gloves and use paper towels, which can be thrown away. If you prefer to use a cloth, make sure that it is kept purely for wiping the toilet and not for general bathroom cleaning.*

⭐ *Toilet brushes are very effective at keeping your toilet bowl clean but can act as a trap for bacteria. Flush the brush clean after each use and dip it in a disinfectant solution before storing.*

⭐ *There are numerous products on the market geared at keeping your toilet fresh and clean, but beware of mixing products because this can cause a chemical reaction, particularly if they are bleach or ammonia-based.*

FEELING FLUSHED

A continual cleansing block, gel, or liquid, which is activated with each flush, will keep your toilet sanitized and deodorized and make it easier to clean.

UNWANTED SMELLS

To eliminate unwanted smells in the bathroom, light a match and let it burn. For safety, don't leave the room while the match is still burning.

TOILET TRAINING

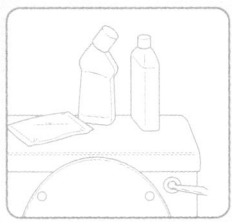

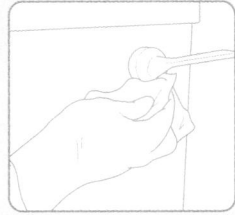

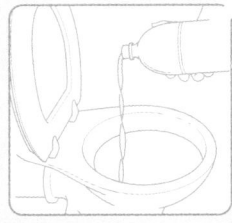

GOLDEN RULES

Every 2–3 days, clean your toilet bowl with a brush or cloth and some disinfectant or toilet cleaner. Use disposable wipes or paper towels and disinfectant or anti-bacterial cleaner to sanitize the toilet and seat.

FLUSH HANDLES

To keep the toilet as germ-free as possible, always wipe the flush handle. Take a few minutes each week to clean hidden areas such as the outside of the U-bend, which is a potential dust trap.

TIDE MARKS

To keep your toilet bowl ring-free, leave it to soak in some white vinegar, or drop two fizzy vitamin C or indigestion tablets into the bowl and leave for 30 minutes. Or pour in some cola, leave it for an hour or two, then scrub.

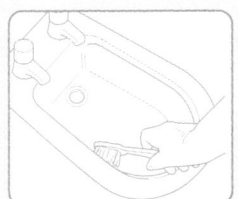

CARING FOR YOUR BIDET

If you have a bidet, this also needs to be kept clean and sanitized—again, don't neglect the underside of the bowl. To get rid of lime scale buildup on the spray cover, scrub with some lemon juice, baking soda, or vinegar solution.

FAUCETS AND SHOWERHEADS

Every item in a truly spotless bathroom must be clean and sparkling. Your tiles, mirrors, and bathroom suite may gleam, but if your faucets, shower system, and other fixtures are dirty and encrusted with lime scale, the overall effect will be ruined. It may take a great deal of effort to descale and destain everything, but once your bathroom is perfectly clean, it only takes a little regular maintenance to keep it shining.

BRUSHSTROKES
Old toothbrushes and bottlebrushes are ideal for scrubbing around the base of faucts and keeping your showerhead clean and in perfect working order.

⭕ KEEPING A CLEAR HEAD ⭕

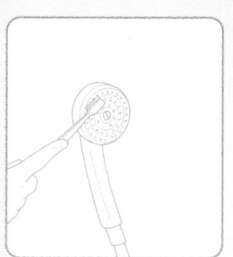

🔹 If your showerhead is spraying unevenly, it is almost certainly blocked with lime scale. You do not need to discard it and buy a new one— simply use a sharp needle to carefully poke away lime scale deposits and unblock the holes.

🔹 To keep your showerheads and faucets free of lime scale, scrub regularly with white vinegar or lemon juice and an old toothbrush or nailbrush. Or leave to soak in a hot vinegar solution for an hour and then scrub.

FABULOUS FAUCETS

 For heavy lime scale deposits, soak a rag or a piece of old towel in some white vinegar and wrap it tightly around the base of the faucet, then fill a small bag with white vinegar and tie it around the spout, making sure that it is fully immersed. Leave overnight, then scrub or wipe clean.

 To make your faucets really shine, finish by rubbing them with a little soap, liquid soap, dishwashing liquid, or a baby oil and then buffing with a soft, dry cloth or an old piece of towel. Never use abrasive cleaners or scourers on faucets, because they are likely to scratch the finish.

FINISHING TOUCHES

Chrome finishes can be cleaned with a specially formulated chrome cleaner (or a car chrome cleaner).

BRASS AND GOLD

Brass or gold-plated finishes should be wiped with a damp cloth and then buffed dry to make them shine and to prevent water marks.

TILES, MIRRORS, GROUT, AND SEALANTS

Humidity, dust, towel lint, and flakes of dead skin all help to make the bathroom a prime site for dampness, dirt, dust, and even mold. In no time at all, tiles and mirrors get covered with soap, shaving cream, and toothpaste splashes, while grout and sealants quickly become speckled with mildew. The result—a dull, dirty, musty-smelling bathroom. However, there are several quick and effective ways to revive your bathroom and keep it looking fresh and clean.

PAPER POLISH

☆ *An old favorite for making your mirrors glisten is to clean them with a few drops of vinegar and then polish with some old newspaper.*

FRESH VIEWS

Use spray air freshener to clean your mirrors; it cleans them beautifully and leaves the bathroom smelling wonderful.

WAX LYRICAL

Once you've cleaned your tiles, glass, grout, and seals, polish with a tiny amount of liquid car wax to keep surfaces moisture- and mildew-proof. Don't use the wax on the floor, because it will make it slippery. Reapply every six months.

TOP TIPS

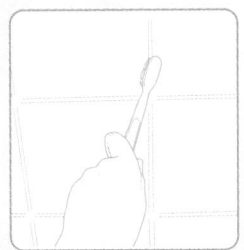

TILES

To dissolve dried-on stains, pour some concentrated cleaner onto a cloth or sponge and wipe onto tiles. Leave for a few minutes then wash clean.

Always wash tiles from the bottom up to avoid streaking.

Keep a squeegee handy to use after each bath or shower to wipe down tiles and prevent soap marks from forming.

MIND THE GAP

Caulking, or sealant, can be cleaned with cream cleanser, mineral spirits, or some weak bleach solution.

To revive discolored grout between tiles, scrub with an old toothbrush and a weak solution of bleach or vinegar. For larger areas, fill a squeeze bottle and apply the solution along the lines of the grout. Leave to soak for a few minutes, then scrub clean.

THROUGH THE LOOKING GLASS

Use a paper towel or a soft cloth and a little mild disinfectant or glass cleaner to clean toothpaste smears and splashes from mirrors. (For super efficiency, use the same paper towel to give the floor a quick swipe.)

Stubborn or dried-on marks can be wiped away with a few drops of wood alcohol or mineral spirits.

SHOWERS

Some showers are fitted over baths, while others stand in their own square- or rectangular-based units, fitted with shower curtains, glass doors, or partitions to prevent water splashing everywhere. In more European-style shower rooms, the shower is often part of a "wet room" with tiled walls and a sloping floor to ensure that waste water can drain away efficiently. Whatever shower system you have, your shower will benefit from a little dedicated maintenance to ensure that it stays fresh, clean, and scum free.

☆ *Rub or wipe glass shower doors with white vinegar to remove soap scum and lime scale and make them gleam.*

☆ *Clean and polish the metal frames of glass shower surrounds with furniture polish to remove marks and make them shine.*

☆ *Use a squeegee or sponge window cleaner to wipe away water from tiles and glass doors each time the shower is used. You will need to clean both the inside of the glass, where water drops collect, as well as the outside, where condensation forms.*

Shower stalls

☑ Shower surrounds and bases should be cared for in the same way as baths and sinks. Wipe bases after use to prevent patches of grime and a buildup of soap scum forming. Use neat dishwashing liquid, dishwasher liquid, or cream cleanser to remove stubborn marks, and make sure that the drain is kept free from hair.

CARING FOR YOUR CURTAINS

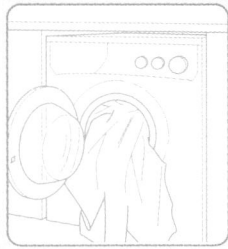

AIRING YOUR CURTAIN

 Open out the shower curtain after use to allow it to dry thoroughly and prevent mildew forming. If necessary, sponge or shower it down to get rid of soap splashes and then wipe with a cloth to stop water spots or lime scale from forming. Do not close until it has fully dried. Whether your curtain is fabric or vinyl, it should be cleaned regularly. But before you embark on a major cleaning spree, think carefully—maybe it's time to replace that aging curtain with a fresh one.

ELIMINATING MOLD

To clean, soak the curtain in warm water and baking soda and use lemon juice or a weak solution of bleach to wipe away patches of mold. Dab patches of mildew with cotton soaked in a little of your chosen solution and leave to stand for a few minutes, then wash and rinse clean. Finally, dip the curtain into a weak vinegar solution to discourage mold.

MACHINE WASHING

Alternatively, place the curtain in the washing machine along with some large towels. Add some soap powder, or half a cup of vinegar or a cup of baking soda. If the curtain is plastic or vinyl, remove before the spin cycle and hang to dry immediately. A little fabric softener added to the rinse cycle will help prevent soap buildup and make the bathroom fragrant.

BATHROOM ACCESSORIES

There is nothing worse than a messy bathroom, with a floor covered in soggy towels and a bath and sink teeming with grubby washcloths and slimy sponges. It's not only unattractive, it's also unhealthy, since it positively invites dirt and bacteria and encourages mildew. Such a mess can leave your bathroom smelling stale and fairly unpleasant, too. Towels, washcloths, and absorbent bath mats or rugs should be changed on a regular basis and always hung out to dry after each use.

HEAVEN SCENT
To give your bathroom a clean, fresh scent, place a fabric-softener sheet in the bottom of the bathroom wastebasket.

☆ *To clean and freshen sponges and loofahs, leave them to soak overnight in a solution of lemon juice or vinegar. If they are very dirty, boil them for a few minutes in the same solution.*

☆ *Place a small sponge in your soap dish, underneath the soap, to absorb wet soap. To clean, simply rinse out the sponge.*

☆ *Dirty soap dishes and toothbrush holders or mugs can be soaked in a solution of washing soda and very hot water for a few minutes and scrubbed. Alternatively, if they are dishwasher-safe, pop them in the dishwasher.*

☆ *To prevent a buildup of soap in holders and dishes, and to make them easier to clean in the future, rub their surfaces with a few drops of baby oil.*

TOWELS AND WASHCLOTHS

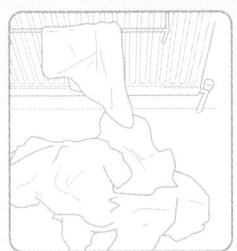

FRESH TOWELS

Leaving towels strewn in a heap on the bathroom floor means that they are unable to dry out and are almost certain to pick up dirt and germs.

Never fold or put towels away wet or damp. Even if your towel is being resigned to the laundry basket, allow it to dry out properly first.

CARING FOR TOWELS

Always hang towels (and washcloths) neatly to dry after use, and change them regularly to make sure that they are clean and fresh.

Launder your towels on as hot a wash as you can to ensure that they are as clean as possible and to discourage bacteria forming. Hang out to dry in the sunshine whenever possible.

WASHCLOTHS

Washcloths should be rinsed in hot water after use, then wrung out and hung up to dry. Change them daily, if possible, to avoid collecting and passing on germs, and wash them on a hot wash, or boil for a few minutes. You can even keep a pile of clean washcloths in the bathroom to be used as individual hand towels for visitors.

DRAINS AND PIPES

Keeping your drains clean and clear is vital if you want to maintain a clean, fresh-smelling bathroom. Give them some regular attention, and you will never have to deal with a clogged drain or blocked pipe again. Here are some simple tips for keeping your drains clear and problem free.

PREVENTIVE MEASURES

☆ *To help keep blockages from forming, pour a kettleful of boiling water down each of your drains once a week.*

☆ *To freshen drains, pour half a box of baking soda or drop two or three effervescent indigestion tablets down the drain, followed by half a cup of white vinegar. Leave for 30–60 minutes, then flush through with clean water.*

☆ *Half a box of baking soda poured into your toilet bowl each week will help to prevent U-bend blockages and deodorize your toilet. Leave for 20–30 minutes before flushing. Old boxes of baking soda that have been used to deodorize refrigerators and cupboards are perfect for this.*

Soda stream

To keep drains flushed and clear, pour a cup of washing soda crystals into the drain . . .

. . .followed by a kettleful of boiling water. This will dissolve grease, break down buildup, and prevent blockages from forming.

KEEPING DRAINS CLEAR

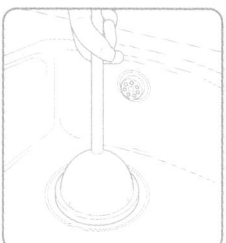

HAIR TODAY, GONE TOMORROW

 To clear drains of hair that can't be lifted out with your fingers, use a Q-tip, a pair of tweezers, a bobby pin, or piece of bent wire. Alternatively, squirt a little hair remover down the drain, leave for 10–15 minutes, and then rinse away.

 Prevention is the best and easiest course of action, so don't wait until your water starts to slow down or a drain becomes blocked. Get into the habit of cleaning your drains on a regular basis.

DOWN THE DRAIN

 To keep your drains unclogged and free of hair, either invest in some sink and bath strainers or fix a piece of netting over the drain. Strainers are easy to maintain, because trapped hair simply lifts away and the strainer can then be rinsed clean and repositioned. This simple device is an extremely effective way of preventing stray hair from getting trapped. Without one, hair can eventually result in a blocked drain.

EXTREME CASES

 If a drain becomes stubbornly blocked, position a sink plunger over the drain and pump it sharply several times to dislodge the blockage.

 If all else fails, you may have to resort to a chemical drain cleaner. Make sure the room is well ventilated, put on some protective gloves, and carefully follow the manufacturer's instructions. Never be tempted to mix chemicals or cleaning products.

HOT AND STEAMY

A steamy bathroom is inevitable, but you can do a great deal to counteract the excess moisture and humidity. Leaving your bathroom in a damp, unventilated state encourages mold and mildew and makes it impossible for towels and shower curtains to dry out effectively, while condensation leaves you with dripping surfaces that, over time, can result in peeling paint or wallpaper, eroding plaster and mold. Making the effort to keep your bathroom aired will give it a chance to dry out properly between uses and reduce the possibility of moisture and humidity-related problems.

MIRROR, MIRROR

✓ To stop mirrors from misting over, rub the surface with a little soap, liquid soap, dishwashing liquid, or even a squirt of shaving cream. Then polish with a clean, lint-free cloth.

DAMP DEALINGS

☆ *When preparing a bath, run the cold water first, then add the hot water to raise it to the required temperature. This will reduce condensation and prevent your bathroom from steaming up.*

☆ *Mildew does not grow in areas of strong lighting, so turn bathroom lights on while you take a hot shower or bath and leave them on for several minutes after you finish.*

☆ *Always wipe down the shower and bath area after bathing to help get rid of excess moisture. Wipe the shower curtain with a cloth or sponge and use a squeegee to clear the walls and tiles.*

✪ Always allow your bathroom to dry out as fully as possible between uses—including the bathroom floor. Don't just leave puddles on the floor to dry out eventually; wipe them up right away.

✪ In winter, turn on the heating in the bathroom to help burn off excess moisture.

✪ If condensation on the outside of your toilet tank is dripping and causing problems, empty out the tank, dry the inside with some rags or paper towels and apply a generous coating of floor or car wax. Leave to dry thoroughly before refilling the tank with water.

✪ If a damp bathroom is a consistent problem and nothing you do seems to help, you might need to consider investing in a dehumidifier. It's probably best to rent one first, though, to make sure that it has the desired effect.

NUMBER ONE FAN

☑ If you have an extractor fan in your bathroom, use it. If you don't, then at least open doors and windows after using the bath or shower to help the air circulate and reduce humidity.

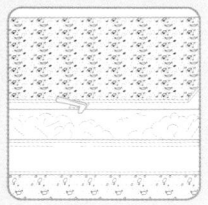

CHARCOAL

Placing pieces of charcoal or charcoal bricks in your bathroom or bathroom cupboards will absorb moisture and will also help to eliminate musty, damp, or unpleasant smells.

BEDROOMS

"O bed, o bed, delicious bed!
That heaven upon earth for the weary head!"

THOMAS HOOD

O f all the rooms in our home, the bedroom is the one that should radiate calm, comfort, and a sense of luxury and rejuvenation. This is where we go to shut off the chaos of the outside world—to escape, to relax, to rest, and of course to do our most intimate entertaining. The world of work and effort has no place here, so anything that reminds you of tasks left undone—heaps of clothes on the floor, coffee stains on the bedside table—undermines your sense of peace and comfort.

Think about your favorite hotel room—what is it that gives it that unmistakable air of luxury? The fact that it is CLEAN—the bed lined with crisp, fresh sheets; the sparkling surfaces; the twinkling lights; the scent of flowers wafting from an open window. You can re-create this scene in your own home: your first step is to banish anything that harbors, encourages, or attracts dirt.

You can't clean surfaces you can't see, and nowhere attracts clutter like a bedroom. Beds and chairs become dumping grounds for clean laundry and the floor for dirty clothes, while the dressing tables and chests of drawers seem to invite bits and pieces.

Don't be tempted to drape mirrors with shawls and necklaces, as they just attract dust and grime. If you can, move your beauty regime to the bathroom—cleaning a pool of foundation from a deep pile carpet is no picnic.

Children's bedrooms are a different story, and, as with everything, prevention is better than cure. Steer clear of flounces and frills, especially if the children are very young. Canopies look great—until the kids have a bout of food poisoning. Ditto with bunk beds and padded crib bumpers. They look cute but they are fiendish to change and keep clean, and they are a magnet for dust and mites. In any case, children find too much stuff overwhelming. Rotate toys and invest in some toy boxes you can stash away. Remember, the more you have the more you have to clean.

PILLOW TALK

We spend an average of eight hours a night between the sheets, shedding skin and sweat. Ideally we'd change our sheets daily, but a weekly laundering is the absolute minimum. Babies' bedding is another matter, and the number of times you change it will depend on circumstances beyond your control! As a general rule, change the bottom sheet daily, sponge down the mattress and air the crib covers.

Pillow protectors are a boon for those with allergies, but unless you have particular health problems it is simpler just to avoid irritants, such as feathers. Pillow protectors are not safe for young children so shake their pillows outside, air daily, and vacuum once a week.

BASIC BEDDING RULES

ALLOW your bed to air every day. Never simply throw the covers back over a bed that's still warm.

CHANGE your bedding at least once a week, including pillow protectors if you use them.

WASH or clean pillows, comforters, and blankets regularly, according to the manufacturer's instructions.

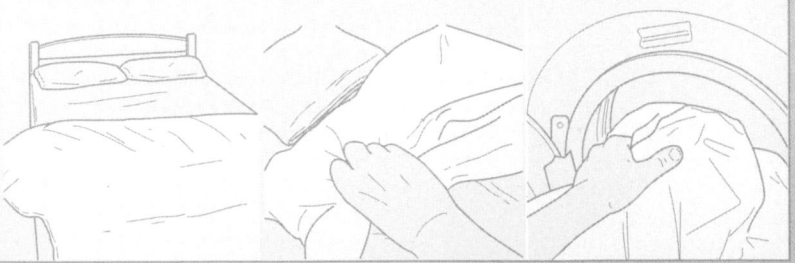

WASHING SHEETS AND PILLOWCASES

✯ Cotton and cotton/polycotton blends: *wash sheets and pillowcases at the highest temperature the label allows. Don't cram them into the washing machine, overloading the drum, because they need space to rinse and spin to be properly clean.*

✯ Linen: *linen requires special attention, but as long as you take care of it, it will get softer with each wash. Don't allow it to dry to a crisp, because it will become impossible to iron. Bring linens in off the line while they are still slightly damp and iron them immediately if possible. Then hang the folded sheets in a place where the air can circulate around them.*

✯ Drying: *hanging your sheets out is good for them. Sunlight acts as a bleach, helps kill mites, cuts down on ironing and means you avoid the scorching that is inflicted by some dryers.*

✯ Ironing: *invest in a good-quality ironing board and cover, a decent steam iron and some lavender or rose water with which to spritz. Never let sheets dry to a crackle—always iron them while they are still slightly damp.*

COMFORTERS

✔ *Synthetic comforters should be washed at the laundry, since the weight of a wet comforter can damage the mechanism of a domestic machine.*

✔ *Feather comforters need to be professionally cleaned, but deal with any one-off spills by sponging immediately, then shaking the stuffing away from the spill area and washing that part of the cover by hand with a mild detergent.*

MAINTAINING YOUR MATTRESS

If you don't want your mattress to dip in the middle or develop lumps and bumps, you need to take control from day one and turn it over regularly. For the first two months, rotate the mattress horizontally and flip it over vertically (head to toe) once a week. For the next three months, flip and rotate every other week. From then on, flip and rotate monthly.

A GOOD TURN

MATTRESS MINI CHECKLIST

✅ **Daily:** *throw back the bedding and allow to air for several hours to keep moisture levels down.*

✅ **Weekly:** *launder the bedding and mattress cover and give the mattress a good vacuum.*

✅ **Monthly:** *rotate horizontally and flip vertically to ensure it doesn't start sagging.*

PROTECTION

☆ *A washable, slip-on mattress cover will protect your mattress from stains. It will also help prevent moisture seeping through and mites taking residence. Wash it as often as you wash your sheets.*

☆ *A weekly vacuum will cut down on mites and dander (the scales of human skin, which collect in beds and carpets).*

FUTONS

☆ *A traditional Japanese futon should be aired daily, but even if you can't manage that, get it out into the fresh air at least once a week and ensure that it rests on a slatted base (not just flat on the floor) to allow some air flow.*

⭐ *If your futon doubles as a couch, a washable cover is essential. Folding it back into a couch every morning may seem like a drag, but it will help keep the futon ventilated and fresh.*

⭐ *Use a foaming upholstery cleaner to give your futon a "spring" clean every few months, and otherwise vacuum weekly as you would a normal mattress.*

MATTRESS MAKEOVER

Mix a few drops of tea tree oil into 2 pints (1 liter) of water. Sponge on gently and leave to dry. Use an upholstery cleaner to get rid of individual stains.

Sprinkle baking soda all over the mattress and leave for up to 24 hours. This will help absorb moisture and stale smells.

Vacuum the mattress completely the next day, using the upholstery attachment. Invest in a mattress cover to protect your newly cleaned mattress.

BEDKNOBS AND BLANKETS

Beds can be busy places, and if you use yours to eat, read, watch TV, or even just enjoy an early morning coffee, the bedstead can get as grimy as the kitchen table. It's not a pretty thought. Dust from nightly tossing and turning will also gather in the various nooks and crannies, so treat visible parts of your bed as if they were any other surface in the house. Covers and blankets may have little, if any, contact with your skin. That is still no excuse for neglecting to take proper care of them, as they can still harbor dust, dirt, and dampness.

POLISHED WOOD

✔ Wood that has a polished finish will stand the occasional wipe with a damp cloth but will fare better if you use a dusting cloth and wood polish.

WEEKLY AIRING

BLANKETS

Cashmere comforters and pashmina-style throws have brought blankets back out of the closet. Blankets can still absorb far more water than a sheet, and dust mites need damp to survive, although they don't like wool. A weekly airing on the line when you change your sheets will help keep dampness and bugs to a minimum, and a monthly trip to the washing machine (or dry cleaner for cashmere and the more delicate fibers) will do more. Dry outside if you possibly can. Sunlight kills mites, and they hate fresh air.

BEDSTEADS AND HEADBOARDS

IRON

Iron attracts dust like flames attract moths, but a weekly vacuum and sponge with a mild detergent should keep iron bedsteads looking good.

BRASS

Most modern brass has been lacquered to preserve the shine, but if yours is old, weekly attention with brass polish and a soft dusting cloth will work miracles.

WOOD

A simple, untreated pine bedstead looks good to start with, but it will absorb dirt and stains like a sponge. It really is worth getting it varnished or stained so that you have a washable surface to deal with.

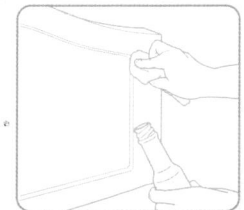

QUILTED OR UPHOLSTERED

It pays to have a few strategically placed pillows to minimize direct contact. Vacuum as you would the mattress and use a dab-on upholstery cleaner if and when things get grimy. Keep an eye on matching quilts and bedspreads. Even if they are washable, it may be better to treat them to a dry-clean to prevent them fading and spoiling the match.

CLOSETS AND CUPBOARDS

Y ou can close a closet door, but you can't hide from what's behind it. If you have a cluttered and chaotic bedroom, chances are you don't dare look inside your closet too closely. Now is the time to take courage. Organize your closet and the rest of the bedroom will soon fall into place.

REORGANIZING YOUR CLOSET

⭐ *Face it—you have more clothes than your closet can possibly accommodate. Devote three hours (no more, or you will probably abandon the job halfway through) to reorganizing. Equip yourself with a mirror and three garbage bags.*

CUPBOARDS & DRAWERS

GO THROUGH the same routine as you did for the closet with your drawers, chucking anything worn out or embarrassing.	**VACUUM** and sponge down each drawer or shelf individually. Move the chest of drawers and vacuum behind and underneath it.	**PACK** away any out-of-season items and transfer some of the bulkier, wrinklier items to your new reorganized and roomy closet.

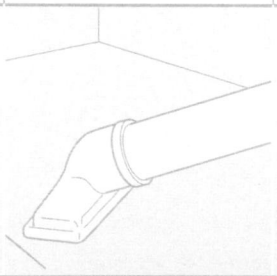 

⭐ **Empty everything out onto the bed**, *and that means everything—even those mysterious plastic bags you just don't want to deal with.*

⭐ **Sort everything into three piles**—*Keepers (because it fits, it suits you, and you like it), Fixers (because it suits you, you like it, but it needs cleaning, repairing, or altering), or Tossers (because life is just too short to await the return of the gilt-buttoned box jacket).*

⭐ **Sort your Keepers into seasons.** *Out-of-season clothes can be washed, dry-cleaned, pressed, and stored, preferably in a vacuum-packed bag. Don't store anything that hasn't been cleaned—dirty linen can attract permanent mildew stains in storage, and moths will ruin your wool and cashmere.*

⭐ **Clean that closet.** *Dust and sponge down shelves, vacuum the floor and lift the carpet if possible to get underneath. Moth larvae love dark, undisturbed corners and are more likely to settle in natural than synthetic fibers. If you discover any visitors, ask your pharmacist about insecticide strips that you can hang in your closet, then inspect and vacuum again in a week's time.*

CLOSET SENSE

✓ *Dig out those potpourri-scented clothes hangers and lavender bags that have been stuffed away since Christmas. Cedarwood helps keep moths at bay, but don't hang silk or linen on cedar because the natural wood resin may stain them. Rehang your clothes (seasonal Keepers only) in order of color and type—i.e. all seven pairs of black trousers together.*

SHELVES AND MIRRORS

SHELVING IT

✓ *If your bedroom has become a dumping ground, your shelves will be functioning as the final resting place for everything that doesn't have a home—including dust. It's time to get tough. Clear everything off the shelves, vacuum them, sponge them, dust, and polish them.*

We all need some sparkle in our lives, and cluttered shelves and grimy mirrors just reflect badly on you. Be ruthless—go through your ornaments and nick-nacks and ask yourself: "Is this a) useful b) beautiful c) loved?" If the answer is no to all three, then wave goodbye. Do not be clouded by misplaced sentiment. "But it was a present" does not count. "But it was the last present my mother gave me" only counts if you really like it. It was not the only thing your mother gave you, nor was it necessarily something she expected you to treasure. If she had a say, she might prefer you to make space for that graduation photograph showing you both together rather than cling onto that china dog she bought in a rare lapse of judgment.

BOOKS AND PAPERS

Paperwork has no place in the bedroom—all it does is gather dust and make you feel guilty for not dealing with it. Get rid of it. Sort through, edit, and tidy your books, magazines, and old bits of mail. Think restful lines rather than messy heaps.

COSMETICS AND ACCESSORIES

Again, apply the use/beauty/love rule and then find a discreet home for all those cosmetics or trinkets that aren't beautiful but don't deserve to be tossed. Think quality, not quantity. If you love Victorian dressing-table boxes, don't be tempted to buy every battered one you find—sell the imperfect ones and use the money to buy one gorgeous piece instead.

SHELVES

Unless we are one of the lucky few with more than enough storage space, we usually find we never have as many shelves as we need. However, this is no excuse to cram them to overflowing, particularly in the bedroom. Anything that you do not use regularly or is not deliciously decorative should either be disposed of or found a new home. Overpacked shelves are difficult and time-consuming to keep clean and neat and are much more likely to add an air of stress and frustration than contribute to a feeling of restful calm in your bedroom.

MIRRORS

✓ *Mirrors are not jewelry racks, hat stands, or notice boards. Left to their own devices, they reflect light and increase your feeling of space. Keep them clutter and dust free with a weekly polish. Either go retro with newspaper and vinegar, or a quick blast of glass cleaner on a soft cloth will do the job.*

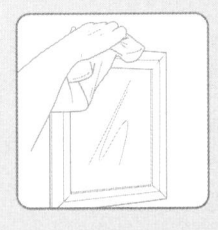

LAMP SHADES AND LIGHT FITTINGS

GLASS SHADES AND CHANDELIERS

✅ *First put on some strong protective gloves, then take down your glass lamp shade or chandelier very carefully. Line the sink with a folded towel to prevent chips occurring and wash the shade gently in hot water with a squirt of mild soap. Fill another bowl with clean water to rinse. You can add a few drops of ammonia to the final rinse to help it sparkle. Either leave it to dry naturally and polish with a soft cloth later, or dry gently. If you have an antique or very heavy glass shade, it may be safer to wash it in situ.*

Subdued lighting in a bedroom is one thing. Viewing everything through a veil of dust is something quite different. Get the stepladder out and carefully take down all your lamp shades. Shake first (this is an outside job), then vacuum or dust with a soft cloth. This will work for most, including cloth, plastic, and paper shades.

⭐ *You may prefer to clean all of your lamp shades at once, but if you find the thought of this too daunting, then work room by room instead, attending to each lamp shade at the same time as you give a thorough clean to a particular room.*

⭐ *Before you replace each shade, clean the fixture, check for signs of wear that may need dealing with and, if your shade has one, check the label to make sure that you are using the correct voltage bulb(s).*

⭐ *If you are washing your shade, make sure it is completely dry before replacing it. Collapsible shades (e.g., fabric) that cannot stand up on their own can be placed over the neck of a bottle and left to dry.*

DUST BUSTING

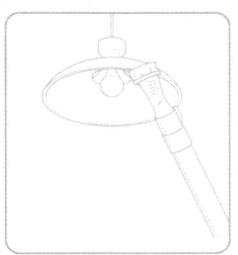

DUST AND VAC

Although it is preferable to take down lamp shades to clean them, for regular maintenance, particularly if you are in a hurry, you can use the soft brush attachment and vacuum shades gently in situ to remove dust and cobwebs.

FABRIC LAMP SHADES

If they are stitched, you can happily dunk them into a bath of warm, soapy water and then rinse using a shower attachment or a cup of fresh water. Don't panic if the fabric sags when wet—it will shrink back when dry. Dry the shade by hanging it over the bath using some string, but wrap it up first in an old towel to absorb most of the water.

HOMEMADE CLEANER

Make your own upholstery shampoo by whipping together ¾ cup mild detergent with ¼ cup water. Use an electric whisk for added entertainment, then use a sponge to wipe this mix over the shade while gently working it in. Wipe off the excess, then use a clean wrung-out cloth to rinse away the detergent. Dry and admire.

DEALING WITH DUST

The skin and hair we slough off in our sleep combined with the sheer amount of cozy cloth furnishings can make the bedroom possibly the dustiest room in the house. Everything in the room, from the face powder we put on first thing in the morning, to the fluffy slippers we kick off last thing at night, conspires to exacerbate the problem. Prevention, again, is your first step, and a clutter-free, well-organized room in which heaps of clothes and nicknacks are kept to a minimum will cut down on the work drastically.

SCARY FACTS
- A typical mattress is home to up to a million dust mites, each of which produces 20 droppings a day.
- Ten per cent of the weight of a two-year-old pillow is made up of dead dust mites and their droppings.

☆ *Invest in a vacuum cleaner which has a HEPA (High Efficiency Particulate Arrester) filtration system, which means that its filtration system is strong enough to absorb dust mites. Ordinary vacuum cleaners may just recirculate them, although they do pick up the dander (human skin and hair flakes) that the mites need to survive.*

☆ *To drastically reduce the amount of dust in your house, you will need to be disciplined about dusting and vacuuming thoroughly on a regular basis. And vacuuming does not simply mean the carpet, but drapes, beds, and any other upholstered furniture, too. Anywhere that dust can collect and settle should be vacuumed at least once a week.*

GETTING INTO THE DUSTBUSTING HABIT

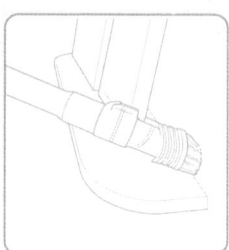

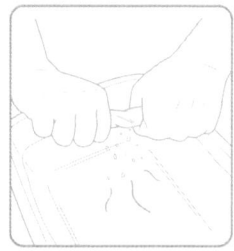

DAILY

Open the window first thing and shake out your pillows and, if you have them, throws.

Keep a small hand-held vacuum cleaner under the bed or in the closet and use it to give shelves the once-over after you've done your makeup.

DAILY

Put dirty clothes straight into the laundry basket and put clean laundry away immediately.

If you can't ban smoking in the house completely, at least banish cigarettes and ashtrays to downstairs areas. Empty used ashtrays immediately. This will prevent the ash from dispersing and help get rid of the ashtray stench.

WEEKLY

Use a feather duster to get at lamp shades, valances, and light fittings. Wipe shelves and flat surfaces clean with a damp cloth wrung out in mild detergent.

Vacuum from top to bottom, beginning with drapes, cushions, the mattress, and finally the floor. Empty the vacuum cleaner immediately into an outside garbage can to disperse any moth larvae.

LETTING THE ROOM BREATHE

Because we tend to be up and out of the bedroom quickly in the morning, it's easy to overlook how stale and musty the atmosphere can become. Not convinced? Try leaving the room sealed up one morning and then come back an hour later. Stale air in the bedroom is depressing and can make you ill. Dampness, mildew, and creepy crawlies thrive in a warm, damp fug, so do everything you can to make sure that your bedroom stays as fresh and airy as possible.

FRESH FRAGRANCES

☆ *If you have wide enough windowsills, fill a window box (or two) with some lavender plants: the flowers will intoxicate you throughout the summer and the leaves will remain fragrant all winter. Hyacinths, lilacs, and narcissi will see you through the springtime, and at Christmas you can invest in a few winter-flowering potted jasmines to create a delicious scent inside the bedroom. Remember, this is the room in which you spend most of your time, so it's worth making the effort to turn it into a sweet-smelling, restful haven.*

☆ *If you don't have a windowsill, either invest in some scented potted plants to keep in the bedroom, or set out a dish or two of dried lavender, rose petals, or potpourri to keep the air smelling sweet and fresh.*

Getting rid of odors

✅ If your bedroom has a tendency to smell musty, try to eliminate the cause. Maybe there is some dampness in your cupboards that needs treating, or maybe it's that old pair of sneakers at the bottom of your closet. They need to be thrown out, or at least taken out of the bedroom.

IMPROVING THE ATMOSPHERE

NO SMOKING
Smoke clings to drapes, carpets, and bedding, polluting the atmosphere and creating a deeply unpleasant smell that is difficult to eradicate. If you can't ban smoking completely in your home, at least ban it in the bedrooms.

FRESH AIR
Open the windows and doors first thing every morning, or, if it's warm, quiet, and safe enough outside, keep the windows partially open all night. Throw back the drapes and the bedspreads every morning to allow the room and the bedding to air and the bedclothes to dry out properly.

CUT FLOWERS
Freshly cut flowers are a delightful addition to any room and will contribute to a feeling of freshness. When choosing flowers, if you are buying scented ones, make sure that they have a perfume that you appreciate. You will be much more sensitive to scents in your bedroom, the place where you relax, than you would be anywhere else in the house. At night, if possible, it is best to remove plants and flowers from bedrooms and sleeping areas.

FLOORING

*"My idea of superwoman is someone
who scrubs her own floors."*

BETTE MIDLER

K eeping floors looking gorgeous is one of the toughest jobs in
the house. Aside from kitchen countertops they are probably
the most hardworking surfaces in your home, and therefore the
most difficult to keep clean. If yours are dirty, you can bet it's
the first thing people notice.

Your first job is to make life easy for yourself—try to make the
surface fit the workload. Avoid carpet in rooms where dirt is a daily
inevitability, such as those that lead directly outdoors (those
immediately inside the front or back door, or leading onto a garden,
balcony, or patio), or kitchens and bathrooms. (Think about it—
carpeting in these rooms can be more trouble than it's worth.)

Hard surfaces, wood, laminate, and tiles are easier to clean than
carpet, but can be harsh in winter and less than cozy in living rooms
and bedrooms. Introduce some comfort with a handwoven rug. It

will look fabulous and lend an air of elegance, and even the most beautiful can work out to be cheaper, and more lasting, than a fitted carpet. Rugs also have the advantage of being portable—simply roll them out of the way when not required.

Kitchens and bathrooms need to be hygienic, so it's tempting to go for light colors for that pristine look, but try not to saddle yourself with something that shows every paw print or drop of coffee. Some of the new glittery resins are brilliant for bathrooms—they literally sparkle, but you don't need to scrub them on the hour to keep them clean.

A stone floor can look wonderful in a kitchen, but is unforgiving when it comes to china and toddlers. The uneven shades and surfaces have the advantage of not showing the dirt, but a perfectionist might say they never look quite clean, either.

Before you start, take a look at every room in your home and decide whether the flooring you have is working for you. If not, think about changing it for something that earns its keep.

EQUIPMENT

Half the hassle of cleaning floors is finding the right tool for the job when you need it. Devote half an hour or so to some strategic thinking. Drag everything out of your broom cupboard (or cupboard under the sink, or heap of buckets and brooms lurking behind the front door). If your broom has more bald patches than bristles and the mop is moldering away like something out of Monsters, Inc., retire them. You can replace them for the cost of a pizza.

BROOMS AND MOPS

☆ *If you have the space, keep a collection of brooms of varying stiffness. If you can't face a forest of brooms, buy three sets of dustpans and brushes. Keep one in the kitchen, one in the bathroom cupboard and a third in whichever room is messiest and furthest away from the kitchen.*

☆ *A mop—choose whichever works for you, but make sure it has a detachable head and that you know where to get replacements. Avoid the traditional poodle-style mop unless you are prepared to wash and wring it out after each use and can leave it to dry.*

MOP MAGIC

MAGIC MOPS

High-tech "magic mops," the kind that come with a box of baby wipes and a detachable bottle of cleaner, are fun but expensive to refill. If you have the space and money, they can be useful for quick on-the-spot cleanups, but don't rely on them for regular cleaning of large expanses of floor.

CARING FOR YOUR FLOORS

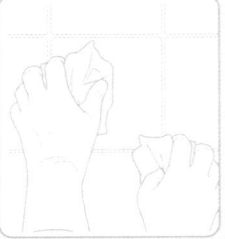

PRODUCTS

A basic, multipurpose floor detergent will work on most hard surfaces, including plastic, linoleum, laminates, and stone, terra cotta, and vinyl tiles, as well as painted or varnished wood. Oiled or untreated wood requires a specialist detergent. Polishing solutions that promise to leave vinyl, plastic, and tiled surfaces gleaming only work well on scrupulously clean floors and can leave an annoying residue. Wax polishes for wooden floors are a once or twice a year commitment.

CLEANING MACHINES

Steam cleaners are the bread machine of the flooring world—so tempting, so efficient, so difficult to store. The steam cleaner is a wonderful invention that could change your life, but weigh up how much you're likely to use it with the cost of hiring a professional carpet cleaner once or twice a year. For most people, particularly those with carpets, a good vacuum cleaner, preferably one with a useful set of tools, is the only essential electrical item.

TWO HANDS ARE BETTER THAN ONE

When cleaning or polishing, try using both hands instead of just one. That way you can do twice the amount of work in half the time and give your upper body a short workout as you go. Don't overdo it, though; it can be strenuous work. Alternatively, you can try strapping cloths to one or both feet and using them to polish. This stretches your legs and prevents you from getting a backache from being hunched up on the floor.

CARPETS

Clearing the decks before vacuuming any carpet is a drag, but it's extremely worthwhile. It is amazing how quickly you can shrink a room by simply lining the walls with piles of books, magazines, and other bits and pieces. Cleaning right up to the edge of a room at least once a week is vital if you want to keep mites and vermin at bay. Mice, in particular, will hug the edges of rooms and find ways in and out through corners and gaps in the floorboards, so don't neglect that undisturbed run behind the couch.

MAX VAC

Always start with an empty machine (for bag-free type vacuums), or check that the bag is not overfilled (for machines with bags), to ensure maximum oomph.

☆ *A daily run over your carpet with the vacuum cleaner will keep dust and mites at a minimum and help protect a short-pile carpet from scuffs and marks. Empty your vacuum regularly and change any filters according to the manufacturer's recommendations to keep it working efficiently.*

☆ *Regular, gentle vacuuming is vital to keeping long-pile carpeting looking its best, because even light spills can turn a dusty, shaggy carpet into a muddy swamp.*

☆ *The lighter your carpet, the more it will show scuff marks from rubber heels or damage from stilettos (if it is short-pile), or trapped dirt and mud (if it is long-pile), so encourage everyone to leave their shoes at the front or back door, where possible.*

THE LONG AND SHORT OF IT

SHORT-PILE CARPETS

Short-pile carpets look sleek, and although stains and marks will show, they are easy to clean. They're ideal if you want the comfort of a carpet in a busy room such as a living room. Light-colored carpets can show stains easily, but, on the upside, absorbent powder cleaners, which are sprinkled on and then vacuumed up, will cope with on-the-spot stains, and home shampoos are easy and effective.

LONG-PILE CARPETS

Long-pile carpets absorb stains well but should be limited to rooms where activity is at a minimum (adult bedrooms and quiet living rooms). Long pile is not a good idea in kitchens, bathrooms, or children's rooms. Powder shampoos will not penetrate long pile and are difficult to vacuum out. Home shampooing is possible, but is heavy going and takes a long time to dry.

VACUUMING WISDOM

Whatever the type of carpet, move all the furniture to the middle of the room each week, then use the brush attachment to vacuum the outside edge. Switch to the main brush head once you have a clean border. That way you avoid sweeping dirt into the corners. Move furniture back into place as you go, trying not to replace it in exactly the same spot, to avoid making permanent dents in the carpet.

SHAMPOOING YOUR CARPET

However scrupulous you are with daily vacuuming and dealing with spills, carpets need deep cleaning at regular intervals. If you have pets, children, or throw a lot of parties, your carpet will need shampooing or steaming every few months. If you are careful with your carpets, an annual cleansing should be enough.

YOU WILL NEED

⚙ When shampooing, choose a cleaning product that is suitable for both the machine and your type of carpet.

BUY?
Before buying equipment that you may only use occasionally, make sure it's going to earn its keep. Rent and try first.

STEAM OR SHAMPOO?

Combined vacuum cleaners (steam or shampoo) can be hard to assemble and heavy to operate. Steam cleaners sound magical, but cheaper models are not always

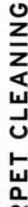

CARPET CLEANING

MOVE as much furniture as possible out of the room, and stack the rest in the center.	**VACUUM** the entire carpet, lifting drapes, chairs and couch covers, and cables out of the way as you go.	**PLACE** plastic saucers or aluminum foil under the legs of furniture you cannot move out of the room, to minimize staining and dents.

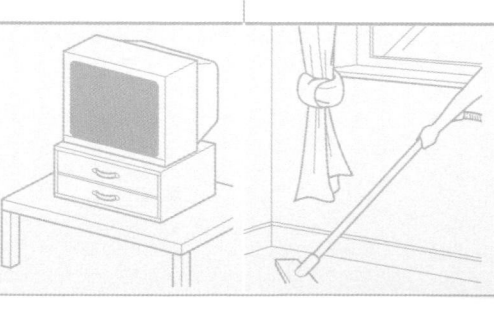

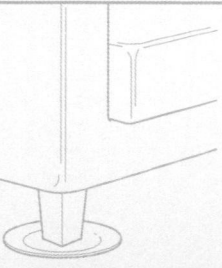

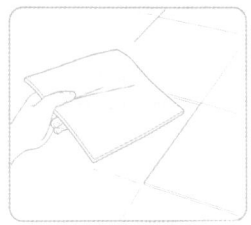

LIFT UP CARPET TILES

efficient. Cleaners that spray on a detergent solution and then suck it up immediately can leave your carpet dirt free and virtually dry.

COPING WITH SPILLS

If you spill red wine or coffee all over your newly cleaned carpet, don't panic. Blot up what you can with a rag or old towel. (Lift up individual carpet tiles to make them easier to clean.) Saturate what's left of the stain with club soda. Blot the area again with a clean cloth and repeat until the stain disappears.

SATURATE WITH SODA WATER

OPEN the windows and work your way from the farthest corner to the door, to avoid trampling over a newly cleaned patch.

PILE PREENING

✔ For carpet that looks flat once it's dry, a quick vacuum, especially one with a rotating brush, will lift the pile to its former fluffy level and remove any shampoo residue, which also tends to flatten or crush the pile.

✔ To get rid of furniture dents, brush with a soft handheld brush. If this doesn't do the trick, use a warm iron over a sheet of parchment or waxed paper (test on a hidden spot first to avoid scorching or melting the fibers).

WOODEN FLOORING

Wooden floors are like horses: the better you treat them, the better they look and the more gasps of admiration they draw. It is true, you can get away with a quick sweep and a cursory once-over with a mop and a gentle detergent, but you know they deserve better.

YOU WILL NEED

- A broom
- Mops
- Dusting cloths
- A vacuum cleaner: there is no need to drag the vacuum cleaner out every time, but it is useful if it's upstairs and the broom isn't. And it is better than a brush at keeping dust to a minimum in bedrooms

VACUUM TOOLS
As a general rule, anything that rotates is designed for carpets, so that it can lift dirt from the bottom of the pile.

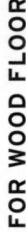

CARING FOR WOOD FLOORS

A DAILY sweep (or even three times daily if children and food are involved) with a soft broom is the bare minimum.	**KNOW** your vacuum cleaner. Work out which attachment is for carpets and which works on bare floors.	**THE LONGER-HAIRED** attachment is designed for bare floors. If you try it on carpet it will just drag you down.

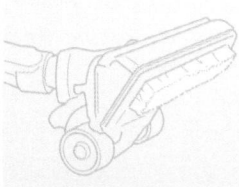

☆ Regularly sweeping your wooden floor will keep dust, grit, and dirt particles and other gunk to a minimum and help to prevent scratches from occurring. It will also reduce the amount of dirt being tracked through the rest of the house.

☆ Bring out the shine of your wooden floor by mixing a mug of cider or cider vinegar into approximately 1 gallon (4 liters) of warm water. Using a new or scrupulously clean mop, give the floor (make sure it's freshly swept) a careful once over with the solution. Allow to dry thoroughly, then buff well.

CARING FOR WOOD

✓ With all wooden floors, ban your friends from stamping over them in steel-capped boots or stilettos. But don't be frightened of parquet; it may look fragile, but if it's been properly sealed and varnished, it needs no special treatment and can be maintained like any other wooden floor.

DUST MOPS may seem old-fashioned, but they are fabulous for removing fluff from under beds and for reducing risk of scratching polished floors.

PARQUET FLOORING that has been properly treated simply needs sweeping, then cleaning with a wood detergent.

ONCE your wooden floor is clean and thoroughly dry, use a soft, dry cloth and some elbow grease to buff it to a shine.

FLOOR TILES

The advantage of tiled flooring over wood or carpet is that it's more durable and you have so much to choose from. A tiled floor, whether made from stone, quarry, or some of the latest plastics, can come in a wide range of colors and textures we could only dream of a few years ago.

⭐ *Over time, if not properly cared for, carpets and wooden flooring will at best spoil and at worst totally disintegrate, whereas tiles are infinitely more robust. If laid and finished correctly, most tiled floors will survive almost anything you can throw at or on them, needing nothing more than a scrub with warm, soapy water every few days to keep them looking sharp.*

Dust to dust

☑ The grout and mortar in newly tiled ceramic or quarry floors often leave behind a dusty buildup that can drive you to distraction. However hard you try, nothing seems to get rid of it. However, this simple technique can be extremely effective: try wiping the floor with a mixture of diluted vinegar, leave until completely dry, then sweep as normal.

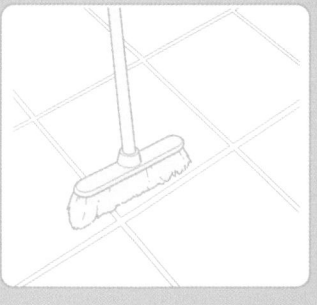

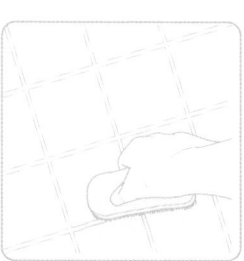

TILE STYLE

TILE WISDOM

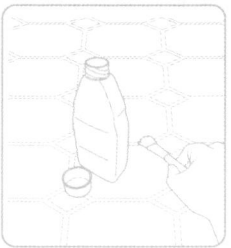

BE PREPARED

 Preparation is the key to a long-lasting, beautiful tiled floor. Quarry tiles will look wonderful for years, but they should be sealed once they have been laid or restored. If new, use a paintbrush to brush on a solution of linseed oil and mineral spirits mixed in a ratio of 5 to 1. When dry, buff with a light wax polish.

SHINING CERAMICS

Once sealed and waxed, your tiles can be washed simply and quickly using warm water and any normal detergent designed for floors. Ceramic tiles can become dull over time, especially in bathrooms, but adding two tablespoons of washing soda to the detergent-and-water mix will bring out the shine.

GROOVY GROUT

Your tiles may be indestructible, but the grout in between is vulnerable. If old or left unsealed, it can attract dirt or wash away with too much enthusiastic scrubbing. A specialist sealant, applied with a small paintbrush, will protect it, but make sure the floor is clean first, or you'll seal in dirt, too.

TYPES OF FLOOR TILES

Tiles come in a range of hard-wearing, low-maintenance materials. Some, such as cork, can be very inexpensive, whereas marble or even terra cotta tiles can be extremely costly. Whatever material you choose, to get the best out of your flooring you need to treat it with respect. Soft tiles such as cork and vinyl can become pitted with heel marks, and even tough stone flooring will show scratch marks and may even crack if you drop something heavy enough onto it.

APPLY EMULSION POLISH

GREASY FLOORS

If you spill any grease on your floor, simply rub an ice cube over the spill. This will harden it and enable you to scrape it off with a broad-bladed knife. If the blade is very sharp, be extra careful not to scratch the floor or to cut yourself.

SLATE, STONE, AND TERRA COTTA

☆ *Stone and slate floors are tough, but they benefit from the protection of a water-based emulsion polish, which provides a "sacrificial" layer against dirt, grease, and scratches. Unlike wax finishes, emulsion polish will protect the slate or stone without actually sealing it—natural stone is porous and needs to breathe. Applying a layer of sealant to stone or slate finishes will cause moisture to build up under the seal.*

☆ *Stone floors can look extremely elegant and are very durable, but they are very cold to walk on. Ceramic tiles are elegant and easy to clean, but they're also cold. Terra cotta tiles (and brick floors) are more forgiving underfoot because they tend to retain heat. However, their surfaces are prone to scratches.*

VARNISH VERSUS OIL

⭐ When it comes to deciding whether to use varnish or oil on flooring, there is really no contest—high-maintenance oil versus 5-10 years of trouble-free varnish. As long as you are not painting over layers of dirty or chipped varnish, you are creating a tough, durable, waterproofed surface that will need nothing more than a gentle wipe with a mop wrung out in a detergent solution. Oil-treated floors look lovely, but they require regular reapplication of oil.

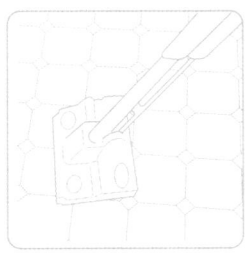

MOP VARNISHED TILES

CORK

✅ Cork flooring is hugely vulnerable to damage and staining until it has been sealed, and even then it must be treated with a certain amount of caution. Think of it as the soft wood it is, and don't let it be subjected to spiky heels, work boots, or anything sharp or heavy. Once sealed, sweep daily with a soft broom—anything harsher may cause damage.

THE HARD STUFF

Don't be fooled into believing that hard flooring will look after itself. It may look indestructible, but all natural materials need to be treated with care in order to stay looking their best.

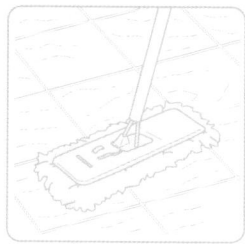

SWEEP STONE FLOORS

STONE

⭐ *Harsh detergents can cause stone to become ultra absorbent and leave it vulnerable to water penetration. To clean your stone flooring, choose a natural soap that is specially designed for stone surfaces, which usually has the added advantage of providing a protective seal, too. A daily sweep with a dust mop will pick up any debris and give your floor a gentle buff.*

BUFF PAINTED CONCRETE

SLATE

⭐ *Slate is slightly porous, so it tends to absorb any floor-cleaning products that are used on it. Some cleaners can actually make marks look worse, so read the instructions carefully beforehand. If you use the wrong stuff, scrub it off with dish soap and seal with a little olive oil. Some people use milk instead—it sounds sticky, but if you rub it down, it will shine nicely*

MARBLE

Marble is porous and susceptible to acid, so be particularly vigilant with things like red wine. Mop up any spills immediately. For everyday cleaning, mix a solution of soap flakes or dishwashing liquid with warm water and scrub thoroughly. Rinse with clean water and a cloth until the water runs clear, allow to dry, then buff with a soft, dry cloth.

MOP MARBLE FLOORS

CERAMIC TILES

Glazed ceramic tiled floors should be swept regularly to get rid of dirt and grit that might scratch the surface. Apart from sweeping, a once- or twice-weekly wash with soapy water is all that is required.

FLOOR WASHING

Half a cup of washing soda added to a bucket of warm water will bring a shine to floors with a painted finish. Allow to dry, then buff to a shine with a soft cloth.

STICKING THE KNIFE IN

✓ *There are some things you can't clean off with soap and water. Chewing gum, grease, wax, and obstinate bits of cheese cling like glue, especially to stone or mock-stone floors. A blunt knife will pry off stubborn blobs of dirt, and the rest can be scrubbed away.*

MAN-MADE FLOORS

Man-made floors are probably the most economical, longest-lasting, and versatile of all the types of flooring there are to choose from. We've certainly come a long way from marble-effect black-and-white floor tiles. Nowadays you can choose to cover your bathroom floor with plastic beach pebbles, or tile your child's bedroom with wall-to-wall candy patterns. There is sand effect for your bathroom or you can even have vinyl daisies sprouting up all over your living-room floor. Reward your creativity by making small, regular efforts at keeping your lovely floor looking its best.

YOU WILL NEED
- A bucket
- All-purpose or floor-cleaning detergent
- Non-scratch cream cleanser
- A mop and strainer bucket
- Polishing cloths
- Finishing polish

A DAMP mop and some mild detergent dissolved in a bucket of hot water are all you need for day-to-day cleaning.

A CAPFUL of baby or mineral oil added to your final rinse water will help preserve a linoleum floor and give it a light shine.

CREAM scourers can remove stubborn marks, but go easy. You can still scratch and dull the surface, so choose a variety that is mild and non-abrasive.

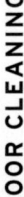

FLOOR CLEANING

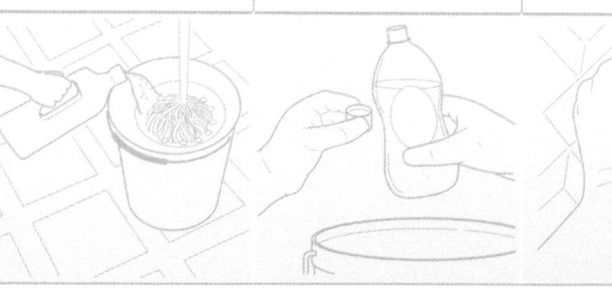

CARING FOR YOUR FLOORING

Whenever possible, try to clean up as you go. Wiping up spills and splashes as soon as they happen and giving your vinyl floors a quick daily spruce with a broom will prevent dirt and grime from building up and prevent sticky residues and stains from forming.

KEEPING YOUR FLOOR CLEAN

The state of your floor determines the overall look of any room, so it's worth making the effort to keep your floors clean and uncluttered.

VENTILATION
When using any kind of chemical or cleaning product that gives off even mild fumes, open the windows to allow the air to circulate, and always wear protective gloves.

A PASTE of baking soda mixed with water rubbed on with a damp cloth will remove black heel marks on most types of flooring.

REMOVE layers of old wax polish with a solution of three parts water to one part rubbing alcohol. Scrub in well and rinse thoroughly.

DAMPEN the mop with a mild detergent to make sure it is clean. Rinse, wring out well and allow to dry. Then apply a fresh layer of finishing polish.

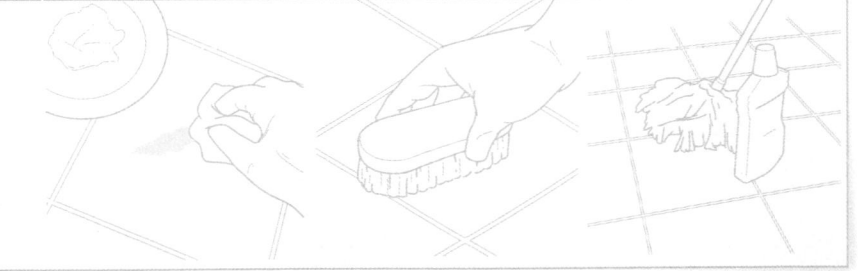

MATTING AND WOVEN FLOORING

Natural floor coverings such as seagrass and sisal are an exotic and unusual alternative to wood or carpets, and can be a wonderful choice in a garden room where you want to celebrate and soften the boundaries between garden and home. They may be durable, but that doesn't make them indestructible or particularly easy to clean, so avoid natural fibers in rooms where either pets or children are free to roam.

BLOT SPILLS IMMEDIATELY

SPILLS

Blot up any spills on natural flooring as soon as they happen. If slops and spills occur frequently in your house, it may be worth investing in a stain-protecting solution, or even arranging to have your floors professionally treated.

SEAGRASS FLOORING

Seagrass is created from salt-marsh grass, which can be woven into a variety of different patterns and textures. It is naturally anti-static and resists dust and dirt, but if it is laid in a room that leads to the great outdoors, it makes sense to put a coconut mat or some other type of barrier mat inside each of the doorways to minimize outside dirt being tracked into the house. A quick session with a non-beater vacuum will prevent dirt becoming embedded. If your seagrass flooring gets muddy, allow it to dry fully, then brush along the grain with a broom or handheld brush and vacuum clean. If it gets really dirty, it is possible to wash it, but choose a specialist cleaning solution designed for the purpose.

SISAL MATTING

Sisal, the hardest wearing of all natural flooring, is woven from the fine leaves of the subtropical *Agave sisalana* plant. Unlike seagrass, it can be dyed in a range of colors, but like seagrass it is anti-static, vacuums well and is extremely durable. However, as with all natural floors, sisal does not take kindly to shampooing, steam cleaning, or any kind of saturation cleaning. Spills should be wiped away as soon as possible with a clean cloth in order to prevent water marks from forming. Clean the surface, if necessary with a cloth wrung out in soda water, working from the edge of the spill in toward the center, to prevent a water mark.

BRUSH SISAL MATTING

GOING BAMBOO

These days, bamboo is often used as an appealing and practical alternative to wooden flooring, but narrow strips of bamboo can also be woven into attractive and durable floor matting.

COIR

Coir is excellent for high-traffic areas because its strong coconut-husk fibers are able to withstand a great deal of wear and tear. Sweeping or vacuuming should be sufficient to keep coir floors clean. As with sisal, wipe away spills and marks immediately, and if you do need to wash a patch, allow it to dry thoroughly.

MATS AND RUGS

However delicate or valuable the rug, it is liable to get the Cinderella treatment of the flooring world. We kick it around, flop down on it, and then just roll it out of the way when we hold a party. Consequently, rugs tend to pick up more than their fair share of dust and muck.

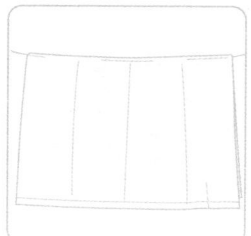

HANG OUT YOUR COTTON

DEALING WITH DELICATES

Handmade or antique rugs cannot cope with carpet shampoos, so don't attempt it— even on spot stains—as you could end up with a bright "clean" patch in the middle of your rug.

COTTON PICKING

Many rugs and mats, such as the cotton ones we use in bedrooms or bathrooms, or novelty children's rugs, can simply be thrown into the washing machine. Cotton ones will actually improve after a few washes, becoming softer in texture and more user-friendly. If your mat is a particularly hairy or lint-prone variety, try washing it inside a pillowcase or comforter cover to save yourself a tiresome session de-linting the washing machine filter. Cotton rugs absorb water like a sponge, so hang them outside to dry, if possible.

FURS AND FAKES

Sheepskin rugs are surprisingly hardy. You can keep most dirt at bay by combing the rug with a wide-toothed comb and then beating it on a clothesline. If you do need to wash it, put it in the washing machine (on the wool setting) but use a detergent designed for that purpose and a softener afterward to protect the skin. Fake fur is not quite so tough, so choose a mild liquid detergent solution for specific stains, using a soft brush or sponge to work the foam into the stain with a gentle circular motion. Pat as dry as you can with a clean, dry cloth. Leave the rug to dry completely and then brush it in the direction of the fur.

SPONGE FAKE FUR

RAGS TO RICHES

Rag rugs may be made from scraps, but they shouldn't be treated as such. Use cold water and a mild detergent to prevent colors from running and then dry outside, but not in direct sunlight (to prevent colors from fading). Delicate handmade or antique rugs also need to be treated gently. Gentle vacuuming is fine, but don't use a rotary brush because it may pull the threads. If it is particularly fragile, vacuum through muslin to prevent pulls and snags. Silk, Turkish, or any particularly valuable or antique rugs should be cleaned by a specialist.

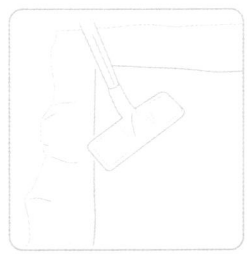

VACUUM THROUGH MUSLIN

PROTECTIVE MEASURES

A staggering 98 percent of the dust in our homes gets trampled in from outside, so it's no wonder that doormats harbor twice as much dust as any other surface in the home. You don't have to start laying plastic matting everywhere, but you should make sure that everyone who comes into the house actually uses the doormat in the way it's intended. You should also insist that everyone removes their shoes and leaves them at the front door. Both of these measures will reduce the dust carried into your home by half.

A good way to keep your home looking clean and tidy is to avoid unnecessary dirt and damage in the first place. Floors take a lot of wear and tear, so make the effort to keep them looking their best.

CAST-IRON CASTERS

Caster saucers can also be placed underneath those fiendish metal bolts that go under cast-iron baths to even out the height of the feet.

Be prepared

✔ Any simple measures you take for looking after your flooring and preventing unnecessary damage or wear and tear will reap huge and long-term rewards. Scratches, marks, dents, and stains all contribute to making floors look shabby and old, even if they are relatively new, so make sure that any areas that are at risk from dirt or damage are protected. This applies in the long term as well as the short term. Never carry out any messy activity (such as painting or cleaning) without putting down an old piece of sheeting or newspaper. Accidents do happen, so be prepared.

PROTECTING YOUR FLOORS

PLASTIC PROTECTION

Plastic runners or mats near outside doors are a good temporary measure and ideal for moving days, letting the builders in, or the sudden arrival of a home mechanic or bicyclist. But if you find plastic runners turning into a permanent fixture in your hallway, then carpet obviously isn't the right flooring for this space. Think about getting rid of it and putting down a floor that is more suitable.

ABSORBENT MATS

Wooden flooring is beautiful, tough, and versatile, but too much water will stain, warp, and ultimately ruin it. An absorbent bath mat is essential on a wooden bathroom floor, but be careful not to leave wet ones lying around. A simple, washable mat or a plastic mat is a good idea in front of the kitchen sink, but again, make sure it provides a barrier between water and wood, and doesn't just keep the wood permanently damp.

PREVENTING DENTS

Furniture legs can cause dents and marks on carpets, especially if the furniture is particularly spindly or oiled. Felt disks that you can stick beneath table and chair legs will protect wooden floors from scratching when furniture is banged around, and you can buy caster "saucers" to slip underneath chair legs to spread the weight on carpets. They also allow your furniture to slide, making it easier for you to clean underneath.

FURNITURE

"Well then, I'll buy some furniture and give the cat a name."

HOLLY GOLIGHTLY, *BREAKFAST AT TIFFANY'S*

F ar too many of us have far too much furniture. Yet furniture can feel almost impossible to get rid of. The reason may be part sentiment, part the memory of how much it cost us (either in terms of the actual expense, or how much time and effort it took to get it up the stairs), and part the pack rat's mantra: "But one day, it might come in handy."

It may come in handy at some future date, but chances are that it won't. So before you commit to beeswaxing that battered old bureau yet again, take a few minutes to do a thorough inventory. Visit each of your rooms in turn, and, in much the same way as you blitzed your closet, take a long, cool look at the bits of wood, plastic, and upholstery that stand between you and your walls. Exactly when was the last time someone expressed surprise and delight on learning that you found that office chair in a dumpster?

If the answer is "never," then perhaps it's time it found its way back there. And that pine bookshelf perched on top of your mahogany one—is it really such a good use of space, or has it become a dumping ground for yet more paperbacks that you will never get around to rereading?

Of course, no one is suggesting that you ditch any family heirlooms (unless you want to that is), but you need more than elbow grease to make your furniture shine—you need light, and for that you need plenty of space. So be brutal with the junk, and make sure that the treasures have room to be seen. If you don't have sufficient space for them, lend them to a friend who does, or beg, borrow, or rent a space in a self-storage place until you do.

Remember, no house is ever really big enough to store spare mattresses, broken desk lamps, or "spare" VCRs, and life is certainly much too short to have to spend time vacuuming and dusting them all on a regular basis.

LEATHER AND SUEDE

Leather couches are no longer the preserve of the wealthy, but they need as much tender loving care as they ever did. Treated well, leather and suede will last four or five times as long as fabric upholstery. Placing a couch is dictated by many factors, but try to keep leather away from sunlight (which can dry and fade it) and direct heat (which will cause it to dry and crack)— aim for at least 3 feet (1 meter) away from heating vents, fires, or radiators. Finally, keep it out of the main thoroughfare of the house, so that it doesn't become a dumping ground for scratchy school bags, or have

YOU WILL NEED
- *Dusting cloths*
- *Warm, soapy water and a sponge or cloth*
- *Soft polishing cloths*
- *Specialist leather cleaner*
- *Leather conditioner*
- *Waterproof protector*
- *Suede brush*

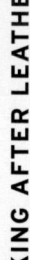

LOOKING AFTER LEATHER

CRUMBS, grit, and coins can all spoil leather, so a weekly vacuum, followed by a gentle dusting with a soft cloth, is essential.

REMOVE all the cushions and vacuum, making sure that you get right into the crevices to remove all traces of dust and dirt particles.

EVERYDAY spills can usually be cleaned up by using a damp cloth that has been squeezed out in warm water and mild detergent.

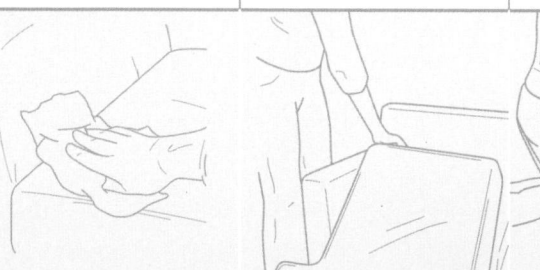

to suffer muddy-sneakered feet or cats' claws. As part of your cleaning regime, vacuum leather and suede furniture regularly. This will keep the pores of the leather and suede clear and reduce the chance of scratches and discoloration that can be caused by grit, debris, and dirt if it is allowed to build up.

When cleaning spills and splashes, go easy on the amount of water you use—avoid wetting the leather, because this may result in ugly stains.

SOAP

Don't be tempted to use normal upholstery shampoo or saddle soap to clean up spills and spot stains; the resulting marks could be worse than the original stain.

POTENTIALLY serious spills, such as red wine on pale leather or anything greasy or sticky, need to be treated with a specialist leather cleaner.

A SUEDE brush or sponge will clean away dry dirt. For soiled suede, use a specialist suede cleaner and rub in gently with a sponge.

ONCE cleaned, or every six months, both leather and suede need their waterproof/stain-resistant layer to be reapplied.

UPHOLSTERY

Loose covers have transformed the way we treat our furniture. We no longer use antimacassars or, as a rule, keep the plastic covers on our couches to protect the upholstery. These days we have washable throws and spare covers, so the only thing standing between us and clean upholstery is the time and energy to change the damn things.

☆ Frequently the hassle of struggling to remove and then fighting to replace loose furniture covers is far more effort than actually washing or cleaning them. It is consequently a task that we tend to put off until it is practically forced on us. The key is to use as many preventative measures as you can to keep your upholstery looking clean and neat. As always, deal with any spots and spills as quickly as possible, working from the outside of the mark in toward the center to prevent the stain from spreading further.

☆ Regularly vacuum your furniture, using the small upholstery attachment and the crevice tool to get rid of dust and dirt. You might even consider acquiring some washable fabric guards for the arms and backs of your couch and chairs.

☆ Remember, covers are not meant to last forever. If yours are starting to look shabby, then maybe it's time to buy some nice new ones.

That shrinking feeling

☑ If you are concerned that your removable upholstery covers may shrink, wash them in cold water. Then stretch them back into shape and hang them out to dry naturally. Put them back on the furniture while they are still slightly damp.

CLEANING WASHABLE LOOSE COVERS

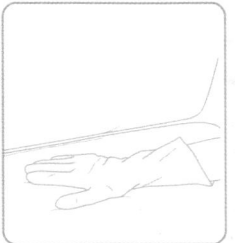

SURFACE SWIPING

Hurry things along by donning some rubber gloves and swiping the surfaces of chairs and couch. This is the speed queen's answer to removing dust and pet hairs. If going for a full cleaning operation, doing this first will save time.

CORNER LABELING

You'd think the cushions on your couch were the same size, but they often vary in subtle ways. Use an indelible marker to mark the inside or label of the cover and the underneath of the cushion so you can match them again later.

MACHINE WASHING

Don't overload the machine—if there's anything more time-consuming than doing your covers, it's doing them twice. Spray obvious stains with stain remover and leave for a couple of minutes, then wash on the hottest cycle the labels allow.

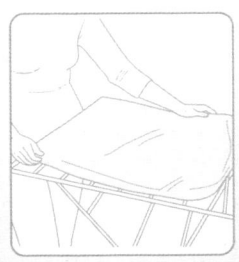

DRYING AND REFITTING CUSHION COVERS

Stretching your covers out flat will reduce the chances of them getting misshapen when wet and will cut down on ironing. The bottom cushions usually fit snugly, but loose cushions will look better with a quick iron. Replace the covers while they are still slightly damp so that they can shrink to fit.

MAINTENANCE AND SPOT CLEANING

You can cut down on the hassle of regularly removing and washing every loose cover in the house by devoting a few minutes every day (or at least every two to three days) to dealing with any dust, spills, and stains on your chairs and couches.

PLUMP CUSHIONS DAILY

PLUMP YOUR PILLOWS

Some people can't get to sleep at night if they haven't plumped the couch cushions before they go to bed. It's not as ridiculous as it sounds, because it is possibly the quickest way to make your living room look complete. Vacuuming your cushions weekly, not forgetting the crevices underneath, will keep mites and dust at bay, while plumping cushions daily will keep them dust free and in good shape.

WHIP OUT THE SHAMPOO

COVER UP

Why wash a cushion cover when you can simply turn it over and use the other side? Because you can only do it once, that's why. If you really can't face getting out a bucket of water and a bottle of shampoo and foaming it up yourself—and who can every time they get careless with a plate of spaghetti?—then invest in an aerosol can of upholstery shampoo that you can whip out in emergencies.

HOT AIR

Once you've shampooed the stain and revived your upholstery, there is no need to decamp to the floor for the night—a gentle blitz with a blow-dryer and you're back in business. Go easy though, depending on the power of your blow-dryer, and avoid using the hottest or most powerful setting—you don't want to replace a spill stain with an even-more-difficult-to-remove scorch mark. Do not use furniture until it is thoroughly dry.

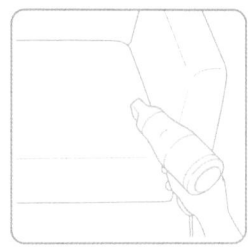

WIND POWER

A HAPPY ENVIRONMENT

Your furniture will fare better in a drier environment, because damp atmospheres can wreak havoc with fabrics and ruin colors. Also, slightly damp surfaces tend to encourage dirt and dust to stick to them.

TOP TIP
Before applying foam cleaner to couch or chair cushions, fold an old piece of terry cloth and slide it in between the fabric and the actual cushion to absorb any excess fluid.

PATCH TEST
Always test upholstery cleaners on an out-of-sight patch of fabric first. That way, if it does cause the color to fade a little, you won't have ruined your couch finding out.

WOODEN FURNITURE

To keep your wooden furniture looking its best, follow this simple tip: don't use a dry cloth on polished wood. Always apply a little polish, either wax or a spray, which will pick up any dust or dirt. However, make sure you refold the dusting cloth after every couple of sweeps, otherwise you are simply moving the dust around.

Aim to clean your wood furniture in this way every two months to get rid of dirt and avoid actually polishing in grime, which may possibly scratch your furniture. Many people make the mistake of adding polish on top of polish without ever cleaning the wood.

SOAP AND WATER

Soap and water should not be used to clean wood—unless you want to develop a "limed" look on scrubbed pine—as it will stain your furniture.

RING DAMAGE

To remove a heat stain from polished wood, mix up a solution of one part turpentine to one part linseed oil. Dip a cloth into the mixture and wipe gently over the white mark. Polish as usual when dry.

Tea time

A little-known tip for caring for wooden furniture:

☑ Use cold tea to clean varnished woodwork and polish with a soft, lint-free duster. The tannin in the tea helps to counteract grease and enhances the color of the wood.

GENERAL CARE AND CLEANING

SPILLS AND MARKS

Immediately wipe away sticky marks or messy spills that have occurred. Quickly remove any residue with a cloth that has been well wrung out in a mild detergent solution, or sprayed with a little polish that is suitable for your particular wood surface.

DUSTING

Carefully dust down the entire surface with a clean, soft cloth that has been lubricated with a tiny amount of polish to get rid of any dust and dirt. Never skip this step: it is essential that you get rid of any particles before giving the surface a final, nourishing polish.

WHICH POLISH?

Pick the right polish for the job and stick to it. Alternating between wax and oil-based polishes may cause streaking. To enhance the shine, rub over with a cloth dampened with vinegar before you give the surface a final polish.

ELIMINATING SCRATCHES

Light scratches can be magically removed by rubbing them with a Brazil nut or walnut. Break, or cut, the nut and rub the scratch with the freshly exposed, oily surface. Use a soft cloth to work the nut oil into the surface and polish. To get rid of heat marks, coat the area of the heat mark with a layer of mayonnaise. Leave to stand for an hour, then wipe clean and polish.

CANE, WICKER, AND BASKETWARE

Woven cane furniture is tougher than it looks, but it can be easily ruined simply by leaving it outside for a few days. Rain, or even dew, can warp, dry out, or lead to enough mildew to ensure it is permanently banished to the shed.

PAINT WORK
Treat painted wicker and cane as you would painted wood. Try not to soak it—a damp cloth or sponge is usually sufficient.

MILDEW
To get rid of mildew, clean the affected area with salty water or a weak vinegar solution.

WASH DAY

Cane and wicker furniture may be hosed down once a year as long as it can be left to dry outside fairly quickly—choose a windy day. Saggy cane chairs will benefit enormously from a scrub with hot, soapy water. Rinse with salt water, and the shape will tighten and improve as the chairs dry. If you can't wash your furniture down outside, put it in the bath or shower, but remember it won't stand being kept wet for too long. Use a fan heater, fan, or blow-dryer to dry it as quickly as you can.

HINTS AND TIPS

☆ *Take the headache out of dusting cane furniture by using a clean paintbrush sprayed with furniture polish.*

☆ *Use a soft brush dipped in cold salty water to clean bamboo furniture. Dry with a soft cloth. Leave to dry fully, outdoors if possible.*

CARING FOR WICKER

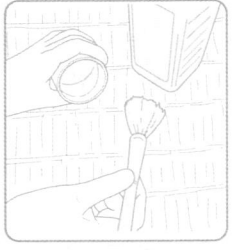

VACUUM AND DUST

Woven textured furniture can be a trap for dust and dirt. Regularly dust and vacuum using the brush attachment or the crevice tool, as appropriate, to keep your furniture dust and dirt free and to prevent any buildup of grime and grit.

WIPE CLEAN

Clean everyday dirt from cane and wicker furniture with a damp cloth and the judicious use of a paintbrush, toothbrush, or even steel wool dipped in a solution of baking soda and water, if something really nasty has been dropped onto it.

PROTECTIVE COATING

Furniture can be prevented from drying out by applying a minimal amount of vegetable oil on a soft cloth, or, preferably, on a small paintbrush.

PLASTIC PIECES

With most plastics, a regular dust and a wipe with a clean, damp cloth are all you need to keep them looking good. Don't be tempted to use any detergent or a cleaning product, as you will simply strip the shine from the surface.

CHILDREN'S FURNITURE

☑ A quick vacuum and a scrub down with warm water and dish soap will be enough for most plastics. Don't be tempted to use strong scouring creams or powders or anything alkali, because they will take away the surface shine and may cause permanent scratches. Wipe dry—if you leave it to dry naturally, water spots may form.

HARD PLASTIC CHAIRS AND TABLES

☆ White plastic can be kept clean by washing with a mixture of 7 pints (3.5 liters) warm water and three teaspoons of dishwashing detergent. The dishwasher powder contains a mild bleach that will revive the white. Wipe the solution on with a sponge and use a brush to scrub away at stubborn marks. Leave the solution for 10 minutes, then rinse and dry with a clean, dry cloth.

SHINY DESIGNER PIECES

☆ A regular dusting and a wipe with warm water and mild detergent will keep most plastics looking good and help them keep their sparkle.

☆ If white appliances begin to yellow, you can revive them with a mix of 3 fl oz (100 ml) bleach, 2¼ oz (60 g) baking soda, and 1¾ pint (1 liter) of warm water. Using protective gloves, apply with a sponge, leave for 10 minutes, rinse well and dry with a clean cloth.

CARING FOR SOFT PLASTICS

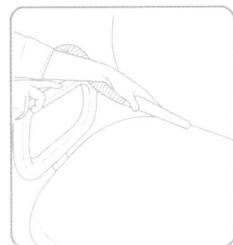  

 Dust with a soft cloth or, if necessary, vacuum to get rid of dust, dirt, and crumbs that may be trapped in ridges and corners.

 Wipe the surface clean with a damp cloth or sponge. Sticky marks and stubborn stains can be removed with a little mild soap and water or a weak solution of baking soda.

 When dry, buff with a soft cloth. If the surface has become dulled, use a small amount of a vinyl car-seat polish to restore its shine.

☆ *Most plastics are washable, but avoid using harsh detergents or abrasive cleaners because these can scratch or dull surfaces. Stick to mild detergents, baking soda, or vinegar solutions, or even a weak solution of ammonia. If you are at all uncertain, test on a hidden section first.*

GO GENTLY
If you use the crevice tool to reach those awkward places, be careful not to scratch the surface of the plastic with any hard edges.

GLEAMING GADGETS

Electronic equipment is getting smaller, but that doesn't make it any easier to clean. In fact, it probably makes it even trickier. Gadgets are certainly more sensitive to dust and grease than they used to be.

STICKY PATCHES

☆ A clean damp cloth wrung out in warm water and dishwashing liquid will get rid of surface stickiness from electronic equipment, but remember to wring it out until it's virtually dry before you get to work. If things still seem sticky it's time for a trip to a technician.

ICONS

☆ To avoid disconnecting the computer instead of the table lamp when you want to plug in the vacuum cleaner, buy a pack of transfer stickers printed with symbols of lamps, televisions, stereos and so on, and label your plugs accordingly.

☆ Electronic equipment may be sensitive to dust, but it seems like a magnet for it and consequently needs regular dusting. If you wish to use polish on the plastic casing of any of your electrical equipment, choose a non-abrasive type that repels dust, cleans, reduces static and will give a shine to all types of plastics.

Twinkling TV

✓ When you clean your television screen, add a little fabric conditioner to the final water to discourage dust from sticking to it. The fabric conditioner will make your room smell nice, too. Alternatively, polish with a dryer sheet and buff.

COMPUTER CLEANLINESS

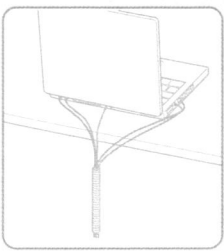

SCREEN CLEANING

Plexiglass and plastic are particularly easy to scratch, so clean your screens using a clean, damp, soft cloth, sprayed with a small amount of glass cleaner (or anti-static spray cleaner) before you dust. Remember to fold the dirt away and use a fresh surface of the cloth after each sweep. That way you avoid grinding dirt and grit into the surface.

KEYBOARDS

Day-to-day dust and fluff on keyboards or electronic control panels can be puffed away using a special compressed-air aerosol. If you snack at your screen and your keyboard is starting to rattle with crumbs, you need to take drastic action. Place some thin muslin over the keyboard and gently vacuum through it.

WIRE JUNGLE

Messy wires and cables are unsightly, a dirt trap, and potentially dangerous. Coils of wire can heat up and catch fire if left untended. With the possible exception of the VCR, most machines can be unplugged when not in use. Switch everything off, then trace each cable from the plug to its destination and ensure that it has as clear a route as possible. Use cable organizers to fix cables to the backs of cabinets (rather than each other), but be careful not to stretch them.

CUSHION COVERS AND THROWS

BANG OUT THE DUST

WIPE IT DOWN AFTERWARD

MATCHING SETS
Washable covers can be thrown in the machine and cushions hung up to air in the sunshine, but avoid washing separately if they are part of a set because fading may occur.

TAPESTRY OR EMBROIDERED CUSHIONS

☆ *Gently shake cushions and bang them with the flat of your hand to get rid of dust.*

☆ *Wipe the surface clean with a barely damp cloth, wrung out in warm, soapy water.*

☆ *Apart from the arms, cushions are in the first line of attack when it comes to gathering dirt and dust, so it pays to keep them vacuumed and fluffed up.*

THROWS AND QUILTS

☆ ***Wool and cashmere:*** *these can be freshened up by hanging out on the line to air and bashing with a carpet beater. Most wool can cope with the delicates cycle on the washing machine, but stick to hand-washing for cashmere. Roll it in towels to squeeze out the excess moisture and dry flat so it won't stretch.*

☆ ***Patchwork quilts:*** *test for colorfastness by wiping a patch with a piece of white cloth. If the color runs, take the quilt to the dry cleaner. If all the patches are colorfast, you can probably risk a hand-wash, but not if the quilt is antique, because water may damage the fibers.*

☆ *Intricate embroidery or a mixture of fabrics:* steer clear of water. Using a handheld vacuum cleaner, remove the brush, fasten a layer of muslin over the suction pipe with a rubber band, and gently clean the fabric surface. You may need to do it from a short distance if the fabric is fragile.

☆ *Silks and satins: if colorfast, hand-wash in cool* water. Never use bleach on silk or satin. If the color runs, dry-clean, but if the piece is antique or involves particularly fragile-looking embroidery or stitching, check first with a specialist.

☆ *Fleece: this is practical, cozy, and possibly the* easiest type of throw to keep clean as it can be vacuumed or thrown into the washing machine. The slightly fluffy texture can mean that fleece collects dirt and debris, so it will benefit from regular washing.

VELVET TOUCH

☆ *Brush velvet throws and cushions with a soft* brush to get rid of dust and to raise the pile. Cotton-based velvet can be steam cleaned, but rayon and acetate velvet must be dry-cleaned.

MATCHING SETS
Take care with on-the-spot upholstery cleaners—they remove spills, but may leave you with a glaringly "clean" patch.

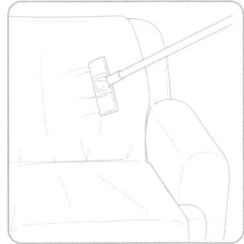

FLEECE CAN BE VACUUMED

CARING FOR ANTIQUES

Antiques require regular maintenance to make sure that they remain in tip-top condition, but treat them gently—put your modern technology and harsh cleaners away and give them a little old-fashioned tender loving care.

MUSTY SMELLS

☑ Cupboards, closets, and drawers can harbor all sorts of dank smells. Once you have gotten rid of the source (see Mildew opposite), use beeswax to polish and help dispel any smells on the outside, and sprinkle the insides with cat litter to absorb anything lingering. Sweep the cat litter away and vacuum after 24 hours, then invest in some lavender bags or drawer liners.

PROTECTING YOUR INHERITANCE

☆ *Clocks:* it's very often dust that causes grandfather clocks to stop, never to start again. Solve the problem without risking any damage to the mechanism by soaking some cotton wool in turpentine and putting it inside the door at the base of the clock. The resultant fumes may be enough to lubricate the mechanism and shift the dust. This works for any clocks with enclosed internal works, where you can slip in a cotton ball without dislodging anything.

☆ *Piano keys:* to improve the color of yellowing keys, squirt a blob of toothpaste onto a damp cloth and rub it into the keys. Wipe dry and buff with a clean, dry cloth. You can use the same method on bone cutlery handles—if necessary, soak in a 50/50 solution of bleach and cold water first. Once dry, polish with talcum powder.

SIMPLE CLEANING TIPS

Use a soft cloth or a clean feather duster to keep fragile, awkward-to-clean items free from dirt, dust, and grit.

Wipe away dust from tapestry or embroidery seating with a cloth or a soft brush such as a baby's hairbrush.

Use a cotton swab to clean awkward corners in antique wood carving.

Kids love to help out—a simple job such as dusting the twisted legs of a gateleg table is fun and set at just the right height for a child.

⭐ *Mildew on furniture: try washing down with a solution of 1 tablespoon bleach, 1 tablespoon dishwashing powder, and 18 fl oz (½ liter) of warm water. Dry with a soft cloth, leave overnight, then polish.*

DUSTING AND WOOD-POLISHING TIPS

Before you start, open the doors and windows and let the air circulate and the sunshine in. Use a clean feather duster on ceilings and moldings, and always work from the top down. For almost everything else, use a damp cloth, or if feeling flush, a disposable "baby wipe"-style duster. Otherwise, unless you are particularly scrupulous, if you use a traditional dry duster you may find that you are simply redistributing the dust around the room.

HELPFUL HINTS

☆ *To remove a water mark from polished wood, smear some olive oil around and over the stain. Then, using a soft cloth, mix it into a paste with a good sprinkle of cigarette ash. If it's an old stain, leave it as it is overnight. Otherwise, rub the paste off and polish.*

☆ *Store glasses upside-down. It helps prevent them from getting dusty.*

☆ *Get rid of candle grease from a wooden table by softening it with a blow-dryer, then wiping as much as you can away with a paper towel. Wash the table with a solution of vinegar and warm water, then dry and polish.*

☆ *A wipe with a cloth wrung out in cold tea will erase fingerprints from polished wood.*

☆ *A shoe brush dipped in black polish will quickly brighten up dusty "coals" in an artificial fire.*

DUST TO DUST
A great opportunity for multi-tasking and getting in a few minutes of dusting is when you are chatting on the (cordless) phone.

DUSTING TIPS

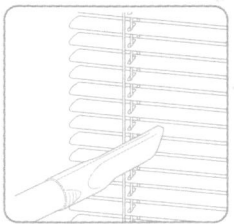

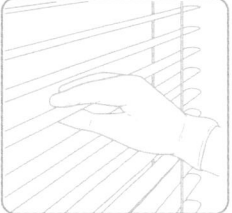

Venetian blinds are a magnet for dust. Depending on the type of blind you have, use either the brush attachment or the crevice tool to vacuum them clean. You can also invest in a specially designed duster with several fingers that slip in between the slats for easy cleaning.

Cotton gloves are extremely useful if you need to get into tiny, awkward areas, and they are the perfect accessory for cleaning tricky blinds. Put on a pair of cotton or fabric gloves and simply run the slats of the blind between your fingers. You can use the gloves for washing the slats, too.

Don't throw away old socks: keep them to wear over your hands when you polish. They make buffing surfaces much quicker and easier than trying to polish with a regular cloth.

Don't forget those hidden areas—turn chairs and tables upside-down and dust, vacuum and polish underneath. Make sure the chair is stable and well supported underneath to avoid putting any unnecessary strain on the back or overall structure of the chair.

SPECIFIC SURFACES

"Nature abhors a vacuum And so do I."

ANNE GIBBONS

It's easy enough to keep on top of the basics—such as a whiz around the living room with the vacuum, a quick spruce of the bathroom with some all-purpose cleaner and a sweep of the kitchen, but how often do we actually delve into the recesses and see what's hiding in the corners? This is what we tend to think of as "Spring Cleaning" territory, meaning that for most of the year, we avoid it. After all, it can be scary back there: there might not be any dragons lurking, but spiders and cobwebs you will almost certainly find, and, quite possibly, all sorts of other creepy crawlies, too. The trick with spaces we never really think we have time for is to whittle away at them gradually. Spending just three seconds wiping down the light switch and doorknob can transform a space from a student hovel into a room we actually enjoy sitting down in.

This is equally true for staircases. If you take that opportunity to vacuum them thoroughly on the way down, rather than simply thudding the vacuum cleaner down the stairs, trying to ignore the dirt and dust that has taken up residence, you're only a short step away from giving the banister the once over and winning the battle against grime. The same applies to walls and ceilings. No one wants to spend any more time on housework than they have to, but nor do we want to spend two hours blitzing a carpet, then look up, and instead of seeing a gleaming chandelier reflecting glory on our efforts, all you are aware of is the resident spider busy spinning herself a new penthouse.

Cleaning radiators is arguably the most soul-destroying way to spend a morning, aside from tackling the Venetian blinds, of course, but there are ways to reduce the tedium. Cleaning pictures and photographs can, by contrast, be almost satisfying, as can polishing jewelry and silverware—you just need to settle yourself down in front of a good movie.

WALLS AND CEILINGS

Admit it—you can't remember the last time you touched that ceiling, and the sight of those yellowing strips of masking tape with bits of crepe paper clinging to them is still driving you crazy. Steaming may be the best way to get rid of the tape residue, but it isn't an ideal technique to try up on a ladder, unless you already happen to be up there steaming the wallpaper off. Instead, use a cotton pad soaked in acetone to ease it away, but test first on an inconspicuous part of the wall or ceiling, in case it damages the surface.

FEATHERS FLYING

A feather duster is your best bet for getting rid of cobwebs and dusting ceiling molds, cornicing, and corners. Start with the ceiling and work your way down the walls, not forgetting to clean the moldings and chair rails. Use an extension handle, if possible, so you don't have to balance on a chair or stepladder.

QUITE WHITE

If your ceiling is painted white, but has any small, but obvious, marks, try disguising them by dabbing on a little white shoe or sneaker polish. Or color over the area with some white chalk.

HALLWAYS

Scuff marks from bicycle or stroller wheels can wreck the look of your hall wall, but you can get rid of them using a squirt of toothpaste on a damp cloth and rubbing the marks gently with a circular motion.

Soot marks

☑ Never get soot damp: use a bicycle pump to suck away any deposits from walls and ceilings. Brush away the rest with a clean, soft paintbrush, then rub away any remaining smudge marks with a pencil eraser.

WASH AND BRUSH

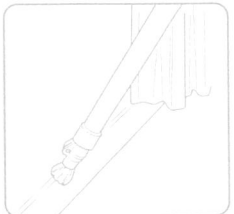

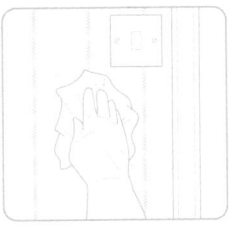

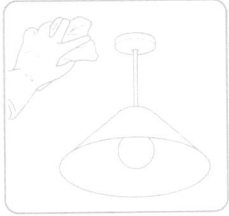

WALLS, RAILS, AND BASEBOARDS

 Painted walls, chair rails, and baseboards can be washed with a solution of 4 fl oz (125 ml) white vinegar, 2¼ oz (60 g) washing soda in 8 pints (4.5 liters) of warm water. Before you start, brush each area using the round brush attachment on your vacuum cleaner to remove dust and cobwebs. Then wash each wall in turn, starting at the top and working downward, wiping each area as you go with a dry cloth to stop drips, streaks, and water marks.

COATED WALLPAPER

 Varnished and vinyl wallpaper can be cleaned by wiping with a cloth wrung out in cold tea. As an alternative solution, mix a tablespoon of distilled white vinegar into 18 fl oz (½ liter) of water. To avoid drips and streaks, make sure that your cloth is wrung out well before you wipe.

CEILING MARKS AND STAINS

 Lighter stains can sometimes be removed with neat bleach. Place protective coverings over your carpet, drapes, and furnishings and, wearing rubber gloves, use a rag to dab the area until the stain disappears.

WINDOWS AND DOORS

To clean your doors, begin by dusting from the top of the door frame using a feather duster or soft rag, then work your way down the panels. Use a specific detergent designed for wood on untreated or oiled doors, and again wash from the top down, drying as you go with a clean, dry cloth. Use all-purpose detergent in warm water for painted or varnished doors.

FAIR WEATHER
Ideally, windows and external doors should be cleaned on a fine but dull day. Do not clean windows when the sun is shining directly on them, nor in frosty weather when the glass is more likely to break.

☆ Wipe the door handles and doorplates clean with a soft cloth wrung out in warm water and some all-purpose cleaner. Finally, using a soft cloth and a small amount of brass cleaner, polish door handles, knockers and lock plates, buffing to a shine with a clean soft cloth as you go. Use masking tape or a coil of children's modeling clay to protect the paintwork from polish, if necessary.

☆ Cleaning windows can be an annoying chore to carry out and is one that we often put off as long as possible, but being able to look through sparkling windows is well worth the effort. Clean glass will brighten and improve the look of the entire room.

☆ Regular window-cleaning sessions will prevent the buildup of dirt and grime that makes infrequent window cleaning a difficult and disheartening task.

CLEANING WINDOWS

We all know the old wives' tale about cleaning windows with vinegar—so how come it leaves streaks the first time we try it? The problem is that commercial window cleaners leave a residue behind that vinegar alone can't shift, so here's the secret.

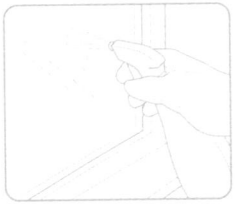

CLEANING SOLUTION

Mix up 18 fl oz (½ liter) of water with one squirt of dish soap and half a cup of distilled vinegar. Use a small bowl, or, if you have one, fill an empty, clean spray bottle (but label it clearly and keep out of reach of children).

SPRAY AND WIPE

Wring out a chamois leather in a bucket of clean warm water. Spray, or wipe, the window with your vinegar solution and use the chamois leather to rub away at the dirt, paying close attention to the corners where dirt collects.

RINSE AND DRY

Once all the dirt is removed, or at least loosened, rinse your cloth and change the water if necessary, wringing out the chamois so that it is barely damp. Wipe the glass clean, working from the top to the bottom, making long, single strokes and using a clean surface of the cloth with each sweep. Finally, polish with crumpled newspaper.

RADIATORS AND FIREPLACES

The days of cleaning the cinders out of the fireplace and grate are, thankfully, long gone, but we shouldn't completely neglect the fireplaces, radiators, heaters, and other appliances that help keep your home warm in winter and cool in summer. Dust and dirt are not only unsightly, but over time they will affect efficiency. Vacuum away dust and residual dirt from fireplaces and appliances, making sure that you clean behind and beneath the object from time to time.

YOU WILL NEED

❁ A good vacuum with a crevice tool and a brush attachment

❁ Cloths

❁ A wire brush (if you have a cast-iron fireplace).

❁ Mild detergent

❁ Specialist cleaning products

YEARLY CHECK
Even if they are rarely used, chimneys should be given an annual check and cleaning. Spring or summer is the best time—don't put it off or you'll regret it when winter comes around.

CLEANING A RADIATOR

HANG an old towel down the back of the radiator, leaving a little at the top so it doesn't fall off. Make sure it is long enough to reach the bottom.

USE A blow-dryer, or the reverse setting on your vacuum, if you have one, to blast the dust off the radiator and onto the towel.

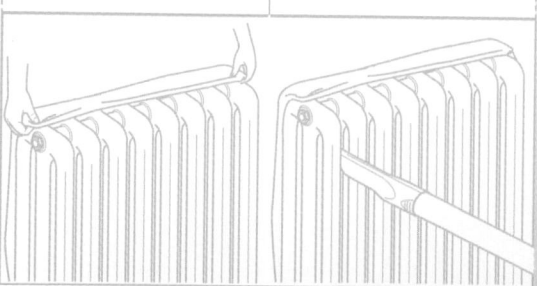

FIREPLACES

MARBLE

 Marble is porous, meaning it will soak up any spills and stains if you don't act quickly. It is also vulnerable to attack from acid, so be especially careful with red wine. To clean, dissolve some soap flakes in warm water and scrub away dirt, wiping as you go. Rinse using a clean, damp cloth and, to finish, buff with a dry cloth. Polish with an oil-based polish if it needs it.

SLATE

 Smooth slate can be washed down with a cloth wrung out in warm water and a squirt of dishwashing liquid. Rinse thoroughly with a clean, damp cloth, then dry and buff. To finish, polish with boiled linseed oil but avoid areas that are likely to get hot.

 Rough slate can be scrubbed clean with a scrubbing brush dipped in warm water and dish soap, and then rinsed. Do not use oil on rough slate.

CAST IRON

 Scrub with a wire brush followed by a rub with a squeeze of black metal polish will remove and halt the spread of rust. Buff with a soft cloth for a pleasing sheen.

DRAPES AND BLINDS

Drapes and blinds need shaking, dusting, or wiping down regularly to keep them free from dust and dirt. Allowing dirt to build up can cause fabric to deteriorate and make it much more difficult to clean properly.

CLEAN TRACKS AND POLES

MARK INSIDE CORNERS

CLEANING YOUR DRAPES

☆ *Don't neglect your drape rails, tracks, and valances. Run the vacuum over the top of and around them every couple of weeks, as well as over the drapes themselves. To keep them dust free, follow with a wipe with a damp cloth wrung out in warm, soapy water.*

☆ *When you next take the drapes down to wash or dry-clean them, use an indelible marker to label the inside corners so that you know which is left and which is right when you put them back up. You might find it useful to mark where the curtain rings go as well.*

COMPLETELY FLOORED

The hems of floor-length drapes pick up dirt quickly and may need extra attention. If the nature of the room means they are likely to become heavily soiled, spray on some fabric protector to discourage dirt and dust.

BLINDS

VENETIAN BLINDS

For a speedy way to dust Venetian and wooden-slatted blinds, invest in one of those fluffy blind cleaners that looks like five small feather dusters stuck together. Greasy Venetian blinds in the kitchen can be taken down and washed in the bath as follows:

Run a shallow bath of warm water and mild detergent.

Dunk the the opened-out blind into the water, and use gloved hands to wash each individual slat.

Rinse with the shower attachment and then hang over the bath to dry. Never wet wooden blinds, because water may cause them to warp or split.

ROLLER BLINDS

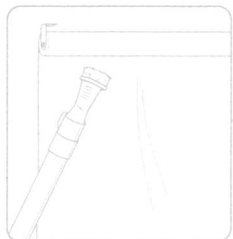

Vacuum fabric blinds to get rid of any dust, dirt, or dead insects that are caught in the fabric.

Sponge washable blinds clean with warm water and mild detergent.

If you have enough space, remove your blind and lay it flat to clean, then wipe it dry.

STAIRS AND BANISTERS

In many households, the stairs function as main thoroughfares. As each member of the household goes up and down, dust goes flying and dirt gets ground in. Staircases can be tricky to tackle, and the prospect of cleaning them thoroughly may feel overwhelming. In fact, they will benefit enormously from just a little attention on a regular basis.

⭐ *Carpeted stairways should be vacuumed every few days to raise the pile and prevent a buildup of dirt from damaging the surface. Vacuum from the bottom to the top to reduce the chance of the vacuum cleaner tumbling and falling on top of you. Use the crevice tool to vacuum in the corners and around stair rods or carpet risers, and the brush attachment to eliminate dust from any painted areas.*

STAIR RODS AND STRUTS

⭐ *Stair rods can be wiped down with a clean, damp cloth, then buffed to a shine with a dry one. Never use metal cleaner on them because most stair rods have been lacquered, and metal polish will probably damage the finish as well as stain the carpet.*

KEEPING IT CLEAN

Keeping your stairways clean is a good way to contribute to the overall level of cleanliness in the house, as it will get rid of dirt that would otherwise be distributed throughout the house every time anyone passes through.

CARING FOR YOUR STAIRS

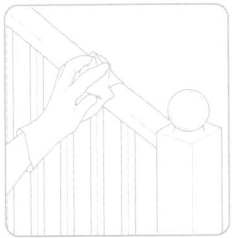

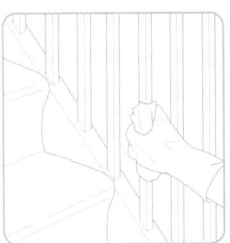

VACUUMING

Wooden, tiled, painted, or vinyl-covered stairs are the one uncarpeted area in the house for which it really is worth getting the vacuum cleaner and that soft brush attachment out. A broom is much too awkward to use on stairs, and if you use a dustpan and brush you can simply redistribute the dirt, spreading it down each step and sprinkling a generous amount into the base of the spindles along the way.

BANISTER CLEANING

Clean the banisters and handrails as you would any other painted or wooden surface, with a soft cloth wrung out in warm water and detergent. Use a separate cloth to dry as you go to avoid water marks and drips. Polished wooden banisters can be wiped down with a suitable wood detergent, then polished to a shine.

AWKWARD AREAS

Even after careful vacuuming and dusting, you may find that there are still remnants of dirt and dust lurking in the various corners, nooks, and crannies of stairways and banisters. Use a soft brush, such as a shaving brush or paintbrush, to get into those awkward areas and remove those final specks.

ALL THAT GLITTERS

Cleaning the silver used to be a weekly ritual as sacrosanct and essential as going to church. Now, unless it's Christmas, this particular chore seems to have fallen off the calendar completely. Dig out an old movie favorite, lay down some newspaper and bring some shine back into the house. But remember, silverware should never be left coated with polish or standing in dip for longer than two minutes, so only work on a few pieces at a time.

PIPE DREAM
Use a pipe cleaner to clean between the tines (prongs) of forks.

SILVER TIPS

☆ *As an alternative to silver polish, mix baking soda and water into a paste and apply with a soft cloth. Rinse, then polish to a shine with a fresh cloth.*

☆ *Bring the shine back to tarnished silver by soaking it for several minutes in a pan of water that has just been used for boiling potatoes.*

☆ *A very simple, but extremely effective way to clean silver is to spread a piece of foil (shiny side up) on the bottom of a heatproof glass dish. Add your silverware, sprinkle on a tablespoon of baking soda, and pour on enough boiling water to cover. The foil will draw away the tarnish from the silver. Leave to stand for 15–20 minutes, then remove the silverware, rinse, and polish.*

GOLDEN TOUCH

⭐ *Gold plate (or gold) items are easy to care for. Simply wipe them down, or wash them with hot, soapy water. Dry and polish with a soft cloth to prevent streaking and make them shine.*

⭐ *Revive dull and marked gold-colored items by polishing with a small squirt of toothpaste on a cloth.*

HI HO SILVER

Silver and lacquered silver can be washed in warm, soapy water, then rinsed. If the item is lacquered, make sure the water is not too hot, or it may remove the lacquer.

Once washed, dry with a soft, lint-free cloth. Don't wear rubber gloves when cleaning silver, because they may tarnish the silver—use plastic or cotton gloves instead.

Use a soft paintbrush to apply polish to ornate or particularly grimy or tarnished silverware. Rub until the tarnish is gone, rinse, dry, and polish with a cloth.

BOLD AS BRASS

Brass, copper, bronze, pewter, and chrome may be durable, but most items still need to be treated with care to avoid surface damage or scratching. As with silver, any objects that have been lacquered should be washed with mild detergent, because polish will ruin the finish.

BRASS AND COPPER

☆ Brass and copper can be wiped clean or polished with a specially formulated cleaner. Old and badly stained copper can be revived if immersed, briefly, in a solution of toilet cleaner and water. Keep an eye on it, though, and remove and rinse the moment it begins to change color. Polish with a soft, clean cloth as usual.

BRONZE

☆ Bronze does not tarnish easily and can be dusted and wiped clean with a damp cloth, or brought to a shine using a little vegetable oil or some colorless shoe polish. Avoid washing bronze items because it may cause corrosion.

PEWTER

☆ To keep pewter clean, wash it in hot, soapy water, rinse, dry, and polish with a soft cloth or brush to bring out the shine. Never put pewter pieces in the dishwasher. Pewter that has become highly discolored should be taken to a specialist.

CHROME

Chrome fixtures can be cleaned with a cloth wrung out in soapy water. To make them really shine, use a little baking soda on a damp cloth or some chrome polish. Alternatively, once your chrome items are clean, pour a few drops of baby oil onto a soft cloth and polish.

BRASSED OFF

RADICAL MEASURES

If you have neglected your brass (or copper) for a while and don't think that regular polish will be strong enough for the job, fear not. Once you have dusted the items— or, if they are very dirty, washed them in warm soapy water and then dried them—mix up a paste of vinegar and salt or lemon and salt, and arm yourself with some elbow grease and a few clean cloths

APPLYING THE PASTE

Liberally apply the paste with a sponge or soft cloth, or, if you are cleaning tricky door handles or intricate candlesticks, work in well with an old toothbrush or paintbrush. Leave to stand for a few minutes. This mixture is suitable for cleaning copper, too.

FINISHING TOUCHES

Wipe away the paste and then wash the item in hot, soapy water. Dry thoroughly, then apply your usual polish and buff to a glorious shine. Extremely dirty items, such as fire tongs, can be rubbed clean with some very fine sandpaper or steel wool, but use an up-and-down motion, not a circular motion, to avoid damaging the surface. Lacquered brass should never be polished; this will ruin the surface. Simply wash in warm soapy water and dry thoroughly.

JEWELRY

Most jewelry, with the exception of delicate stringed necklaces, can be safely washed in warm water with a squirt of mild detergent. Pieces that are set with glue, however, should be brushed or wiped clean, because water may loosen the setting. Intricate jewelry can be cleaned with a brief dip in jewelry cleaning solution, or by putting a few drops of ammonia into a bowl of warm water and brushing the solution over the jewelry with a small makeup brush or paintbrush. Rinse off using a clean brush in warm water, and leave to dry.

PASTE

Paste jewelry should be kept free of dust with a soft brush. Do not wash it because you may dissolve the paste. Wipe away any dirty marks with a clean cloth that has been dipped in a weak ammonia solution.

BAKING SODA CLEANS BEADS

PRECIOUS METALS

☆ *Gold, silver, and platinum can be washed in mild detergent, or polished with a soft cloth. You can use silver polish, or a silver cleaning cloth or dip, to revive your silver items, but in most cases, scrubbing them with a soft brush and some warm, soapy water will be sufficient.*

BEADS

☆ *Baking soda is an extremely effective substance for strings of beads. It's best to avoid any contact with water, which may not damage the beads themselves but can rot the thread. Brush the baking soda all over the beads with a soft brush, dust off, and polish with a soft cloth.*

DIAMOND BRIGHT

To avoid your diamonds disappearing down the drain, clean jewelry in a bowl, rather than directly in the sink. Line the bowl with an old towel or cloth to prevent scratches and bangs.

Diamonds have a natural sparkle, so they don't need any special polishes—just use a soft brush to get rid of dust or any dirt ingrained in the setting and wash in warm, soapy water.

Dry with a soft cloth, buff to a shine, and admire. This method works for most precious metals and stones, but remember to treat elaborate and antique settings gently.

STRING OF PEARLS

Soft stones, such as pearls, opals, turquoise, and coral should be treated gently—polish with a soft cloth or chamois leather. As with beads, the stones may be immersed in water, but not if they are strung.

CHINA AND CRYSTAL

Fine china and crystal are not usually suitable for dishwashing and should be hand-washed. Ideally, wash them immediately after use, to prevent any food deposits from damaging the surface. If this is not possible, rinse and put them to one side. Fine china should never be scrubbed or left to soak, because this can damage the glaze and any patterning or gilt work.

WHITE FILM

Get rid of the white film around vases or from glasses that have been clouded by the dishwasher by washing first in diluted lime scale remover, then washing and rinsing as usual.

WASHING

★ Use a plastic dishpan filled with warm, soapy water, lining it first with an old towel to minimize chips and cracks—the combination of precious fragile objects and warm, soapy water can often spell disaster. Wash items one at a time to prevent them from knocking against each other. Use an old shaving brush, makeup brush, or soft paintbrush to work into the crevices. Never use scourers of any kind, because these may scratch surfaces. Rinse well—have a similar bowl, also lined with a towel, full of clean, warm water standing by. To finish, dry and polish with a soft cloth.

★ Adding a little white vinegar to the rinse water will give your glasses an extra gleam.

★ Use warm water rather than hot to wash fine or delicate glass or china.

CLEANING A STAINED DECANTER

Cleaning the inside of a decanter can be awkward. If soaking in warm, soapy water is not enough, this technique should do the trick. Cut up half a raw potato into cubes, as if you were about to make potato salad. Half fill the decanter with warm, soapy water.

Drop in the potato pieces and swirl around, allowing the potato to rotate around the bottom and sides to rub off any stains. Rinse and dry, either by twisting a fine, clean dishcloth as far into the decanter as you can, or leaving to drain.

Alternatively, if you don't have a potato handy, you can use uncooked rice with lukewarm water instead.

WATER, WATER

Always rinse china and glass in warm rather than cold water, because changes in temperature can make delicate items crack.

BLOW DRY

To dry china pieces that have intricate detailing, such as ornaments, use a blow-dryer on a warm or cool setting.

BOOKS AND PHOTOS

Protect your books with regular dusting and by storing them upright, rather than at a jaunty angle. Shelves of books are much loved by dust, so keep them clean by dusting regularly with a cloth, a feather duster, or the brush tool of your vacuum cleaner.

VACUUM WITH BRUSH TOOL

BLOT WITH TISSUE PAPER

CARING FOR YOUR BOOKS

☆ *When dusting, hold books closed to prevent loose pages snagging or ripping. Brush from the inside to the outer edge using a soft brush, cloth, or the brush attachment of your vacuum cleaner.*

☆ *If you find that your books are damp or show signs of mildew, dry them gently by placing blotting paper or tissue paper in between the pages and leaving them in a cool, dry place. Sunlight will help to dry out damp books and kill mold spores, but it may also discolor the paper.*

MILDEW
Never attempt to get rid of mildew or mold until the book is completely dry. Even then, it is advisable to approach a specialist.

SIMPLE MAINTENANCE

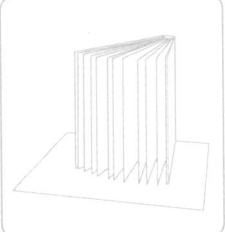

FLOOD DAMAGE

If a book gets seriously water damaged by flood, rain, or simply by accidentally dropping it in the bath, either stand it upright on an absorbent surface, like a towel or some blotting paper, fanning the book open and leaving to dry near, but not directly in the path of, a fan. Replace the absorbent paper the moment it gets wet. In a real emergency, put the book into a plastic bag and into the freezer. This will prevent further damage until a specialist can deal with it for you.

PHOTOGRAPHS

The best way to protect and keep photographs clean and flat is to store them correctly. Arrange them in a paper album using corner mounts. Albums that stick photographs into place or gluing them directly into an album yourself can cause damage.

PROTECTIVE FRAMES

Framing your photographs behind plastic or glass will not only keep them clean but also help protect them from drying or cracking. Be careful when cleaning the frames, though. If using glass or window cleaner, be sure to spray the cloth, not directly onto the glass. Drips can run behind the glass, staining the photograph below.

PAINTINGS AND PICTURES

Cleaning original paintings is a specialist job; even prints can be ruined by overenthusiastic amateurs. Restrict your cleaning work to a quick swipe with a feather duster or an ultra-soft cloth, remembering to refold to a clean patch with every sweep to prevent scratching the surface. Resist any temptation to vacuum your paintings.

PICTURE HANGING

☆ *To prevent your paintings and pictures from becoming soiled or damaged, consider carefully where to hang them. Don't position them above sources of direct heat, in damp, steamy atmospheres (such as the bathroom or kitchen) or near open windows (where direct sunlight, wind, or rain may damage them). Pictures and paintings may look lovely by candlelight, but burning candles can cause soot marks or even scorches if positioned too close.*

DUSTING

☆ *To keep frames free of dust, wipe regularly with a damp cloth, unless they are gilded. Water will damage the gilt paint. To remove dirt or marks from gilded frames, pour a little lighter fluid onto a cloth and wipe carefully.*

HAIRSPRAY FIX

You can't frame every masterpiece your child comes home with, but a quick burst of hairspray will preserve it for posterity and keep it from getting ruined by the first blast of steam that comes its way.

CARING FOR YOUR PAINTINGS

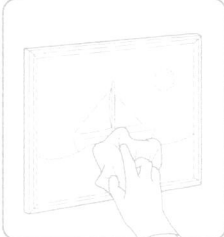

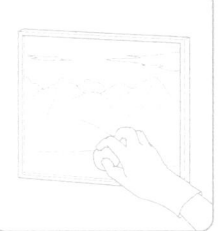

A WORD OF ADVICE

When you clean a framed picture, spritz the cleaner onto the cloth, not directly onto the glass or frame. That way there's no risk of spraying the surface of the painting or liquid seeping behind the frame onto the original.

CLEAN AND POLISH

Polish with a separate cloth. If the glass is very dirty, apply more cleaner then polish and buff the glass to a shine. Use a clean cloth to dust the frame. If the picture is at all unstable, or hung in an awkward position, remove from the wall and place on a flat surface to clean. If necessary, pad with an old towel or some rags to protect the surface underneath.

WATERCOLORS

If one of your watercolors gets grubby, roll up the inside of a baguette or a piece of sliced white bread and use it as an eraser to clean the surface gently. You can also use this method on other original paintwork, but save it for the cheap stuff. It's not recommended for old masters.

LAUNDRY

" *After enlightenment, the laundry.* "
ZEN PROVERB

Once upon a time it took all Monday to get the laundry done, and the rest of the week to dry, iron, and put it away. By the time you'd finished it would be time to start again. No longer. With a little planning, you can keep right on top of things, and it only takes a few minutes a day.

The key is organization. Some people can fly through the laundry because their massive basements enable them to keep everything at hand: the drying racks are always up, the ironing board is out, and shelves of detergents and miracle stain removers are within reach at all times. The rest of us may not have the space to devote a whole floor to the art, but a few well-chosen laundry baskets and a shelf or two will drastically reduce the hassle.

If you have any outside space, use it. Drying laundry outdoors is quick, cheap, eco-friendly, and efficient. No need to dominate the garden with a rotary drier—invest in a double-length line on pulleys, which means you don't even have to carry your laundry baskets far outside your front door in cold weather. Make sure that you have twice as many clothespins as you think you'll need. They always disappear.

Make friends with your washing machine—find out where the filter is and defluff it religiously. Check which compartment takes powder and which takes fabric softener: you'd be amazed at the number of people that get this simple system wrong. Keep a supply of stain removers and sprays handy so that they are on hand as needed. Stains are far more likely to disappear if treated immediately.

Finally, even if you don't have enough space to leave the ironing board up on a permanent basis, try to store it somewhere handy so that the ironing can become an automatic part of the job, not a huge extra effort. Bribe yourself with some fancy ironing water and keep a radio nearby to keep you company. If your iron is ancient history, treat yourself to a new, more efficient model.

WHICH WASHER, WHICH PRODUCT?

The choice of laundry products is bewildering, and you can be forgiven for just reaching for the first economy box you see and diving for cover. Just when you've finally settled on one particular product, fashions change and you can't buy it anymore. As technology progresses, laundry products are continually revised and improved, so it's worth spending a few minutes cruising the aisles and comparing the different choices.

BIOLOGICALLY SPEAKING

☑ Some laundry detergents and presoaks contain enzymes to dissolve fat and grease, but will not perform at very high temperatures. Some people find that enzyme detergents irritate their skin. You can reduce this risk by running your wash through an extra rinse cycle.

WHICH WASHER'S WHICH?

First, establish what kind of washing machine you have. These days, for example, you can save money and the planet by investing in a state-of-the-art, energy-efficient model. If you have one of these, you can wash just as thoroughly at lower temperatures, provided you use the right detergent.

POWDER, LIQUID, OR TABLET?

☆ This is a matter of taste and budget. Powders are easy to measure and you don't have to spend hours hunting round to rescue that ball dispenser from the inside the comforter cover, but liquids may be more efficient at getting to the dirt. Individually wrapped tablets or gel capsules look cute but face it: it's laundry—save your money for something that matters.

✰ Detergents designed for machine washing are usually too harsh for using on delicates and can also irritate the skin of whoever has the lucky job of washing them. Choose a separate powder or liquid specifically for hand-washing.

POWDER AND LIQUID DETERGENT

✰ Psychologically, fabric softeners do wonders—and of course they make the laundry smell nice, too. Today's softeners even have added benefits such as activated odor eliminators. However, whether or not fabric softener is strictly necessary is a matter of debate. So, if you live for fresh, fluffy towels and the smell of spring blossoms in your whites makes you think of home, there's no harm in indulging.

WATER SOFTENER

✰ Many people swear by water softener, claiming that adding a little to each wash allows them to cut down on the amount of detergent and gets the laundry cleaner, too. There is no question that, particularly if you live in a hard-water area, regular use of water softener will prevent buildup of lime scale and lengthen the life of both your fabrics and your washing machine.

FABRIC SOFTENER

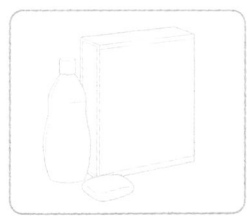

HAND-WASHING PRODUCTS

EFFICIENT SORTING

Getting yourself—and the rest of the household—into the habit of sorting laundry is half the battle. The first step is to dispel the myth of the laundry fairy. Contrary to popular belief, she does not simply appear in the middle of the night and whisk clothes off the bedroom carpet and into the dryer, nor does she magically pick them up off the bathroom floor.

BASKET CASES

☆ *Invest in two or three hampers and insist that they are used. Put them wherever is most useful, either near the washing machine or in the bathroom. If you have enough space: keep one for dark colors, one for whites and one for hand-washing.*

☆ *Try to treat the laundry like the dishes—as a quick, daily necessity rather than a huge weekly project. Once you get into the habit, you'll have a load on and another in the dryer before you've finished your early morning cup of coffee.*

☆ *Make any repairs before putting items in the machine, so that holes or tears are not made worse in the washing process.*

☆ *Brush off any mud, dirt or fluff and load items one by one, shaking them out to avoid them tangling in the machine.*

MATCHING PAIRS

Pin pairs of socks together—either buy specially designed sock clips, or use large safety pins to make sure that you don't end up with an odd sock.

ORGANIZING YOUR LAUNDRY

POCKET ALERT

Pockets cause more laundry disasters than anything else. Stray coins jam the works, cell phones and dollar bills end up going through the spin cycle; and pens and crayons can create complete havoc.

DOUBLE CHECK

Insist that everyone goes through their pockets before they put anything into the hamper, but make it a rule to go through every pocket yourself as you put clothes into the machine, just in case.

TAKING CARE

If you can't train everyone to sort their clothes into colors, do it as you load, but keep an eye on care labels. Keep woollens, delicates and dry-clean-only fabrics to one side, but have a strategy in place to deal with them, even if it's only once a week. Otherwise you'll be continually ferreting around for woollens and silk shirts. Mixed loads of laundry should be washed according to the label instructions on the most delicate item.

CARE LABELS AND WASHING CYCLES

Understanding the various different care labels will help you take better care of your clothes and avoid disasters. It's a hassle to learn them, but well worth it if it means that you don't have to throw ruined clothes away or attempt rescues with expensive color removers. Spend a few minutes deciphering the different labels on your clothes.

For more lightly soiled loads, wash at a lower temperature than the one suggested. This will save energy and also cause less wear and tear on your clothing.

HOW MUCH is enough? Don't be tempted to use extra powder to help things along. It's just a waste and will result in you spending hours with a spoon declogging the drawer, and you may damage your machine.

IT'S AS SIMPLE as ABC. Machines vary, so check the manual, but, as a rule, the first compartment is for pre-wash and bleach, the middle one for main-wash detergent and the last symbol is for fabric softener.

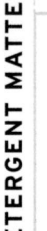

DETERGENT MATTERS

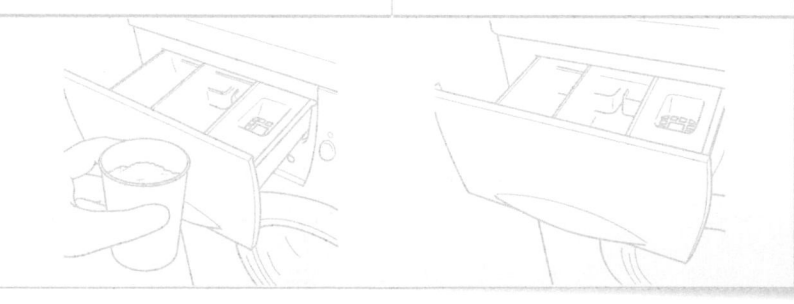

LAUNDRY SYMBOLS

MACHINE WASH, COLD
A single dot advises that the garment should be laundered at a cool temperature—a maximum of 30°C (85°F).

MACHINE WASH, WARM
Two dots indicate that the garment can be laundered at a warm temperature—a maximum of 40°C (105°F).

MACHINE WASH, HOT
Three dots indicate that the garment can be laundered at a hot temperature—a maximum of 50°C (120°F).

NORMAL CYCLE
No bar beneath the symbol means that the garment can tolerate a maximum-speed spin cycle.

PERMANENT PRESS CYCLE
A line beneath the tub indicates that the garment should be laundered on the permanent press cycle.

DELICATE WASHING CYCLE
Two lines beneath the tub indicate that the garment should be laundered on the delicate/gentle washing cycle.

HAND-WASH ONLY
Don't put the garment in a washing machine.

MAY USE BLEACH
A triangle indicates that it is safe to use any bleach on this garment.

ONLY NON-CHLORINE BLEACH
It's safe to use only a color-safe, non-chlorine bleach on this garment.

DO NOT BLEACH
It's not safe to use chlorine bleach on this garment.

DRY-CLEAN ONLY
Professional dry-clean only.

DO NOT DRY-CLEAN
Not suitable for dry-cleaning.

PRE-WASHING AND TREATING

Rushing stained clothes straight into a hot wash can do more harm than good. High temperatures will actually "set" protein-based stains (such as milk, blood and egg), making them even harder to eradicate. Using a pre-wash cycle on a washing machine with a low temperature is the equivalent of giving stained clothes a vigorous hand-wash, and it's a good way to deal with sports clothes before they get too horrible to handle.

TREAT WITH PRE-WASH SPRAY

SOAK IN HAND-HOT WATER

TACKLING STAINS

☆ *Individual stains can be treated prior to being loaded into the machine with a pre-wash spray, stick or foam. Some treatments only need to be left on for a few minutes before washing, while others can be safely left to work overnight.*

☆ *Soaking stained garments overnight in a weak mixture of detergent and water can take the sting out of a stain, but remember to keep the water cool if the stain is protein-based, and always make sure that any detergent has completely dissolved before adding the garments.*

BLEACH CARE

Remember, bleach can damage silk and wool and can cause some man-made fabrics to deteriorate, so always check the label before reaching for the bottle.

☆ Most items can be left to soak for several hours or overnight in detergent solution. Whites usually benefit from a longer, rather than a shorter, soaking. To achieve the best results, always allow sufficient time for the process; whatever garment is being left to soak, don't be impatient and take it out after only 30 minutes hoping that will do the trick.

SOAK FOR SEVERAL HOURS

☆ When preparing to soak in bleach, always run the water first and add the bleach to the water. Never run the water on top of the bleach. As a general rule, use one tablespoon of household bleach to one bucket of water, or, if you are using a milder type of bleach, such as hydrogen peroxide, one part peroxide to eight parts water.

ADD BLEACH TO WATER

☆ Remember, it is always much easier and effective to deal with stains, splashes, spots and spills as soon as they happen. Leaving any type of mark to be dealt with later is usually a recipe for disaster. If you are not able to properly clean a garment as soon as the accident happens, at least flush the stain through and try to keep the area wet until you are able to tackle it properly.

BRIGHT WHITES

If you are worried about over-bleaching, replace half the bleach with baking soda. To brighten up dingy whites, replace the bleach entirely with half cup of cream of tartar.

HAND-WASHING

Some delicate materials, such as silks, wools, and knitted cotton, need to be hand-washed, particularly if they are fragile or old. Gentle washing of these clothes by hand enables them to be thoroughly cleaned without danger of becoming misshapen or damaged.

SOAP SENSE

If you are using soap flakes or washing powder to hand-wash, make sure that it is thoroughly dissolved before adding the clothes, or difficult-to-remove flakes or lumps of soap will get stuck in your garments.

TOUGH LOVE

☆ Hand-washing is not only a method for cleaning fragile items. Sometimes you may need to hand-wash a sturdier item, either because you need a garment and don't have enough for a complete load, because a washing machine is not available, or simply because the item is so heavily soiled, it needs a good scrub to get it clean. In the latter case, if the item is colorfast, leave it to soak for an hour or two in hand-hot soapy water, then either scrub with a soft nail brush or rub the fabric together to loosen ingrained dirt.

SPIN DOCTOR

Some natural fabrics can be given a short spin after hand-washing to remove most of the water. Many modern washing machines have a special short rinse and spin cycle for hand-washed articles.

HOW TO HAND-WASH

SORTING COLORS

Separate colors into dark and light piles, and leave each set to soak for an hour or two in hand-hot soapy water. Keep woollens separate, because they can't handle hot water. Make sure the soap is completely dissolved before adding the clothes. Test dark clothes for colorfastness by wetting a corner, then squeezing in an (old) white towel.

HAND-WASHING

Try not to rub the garments, however tempting. Instead, squeeze the fabric gently through your fingers. You can double the life of underwear by washing it by hand, and stockings and panty hose should never see the inside of a washing machine. But be careful to squeeze out hosiery thoroughly after rinsing so that the weight of the water doesn't make your panty hose grow as they hang on the line.

COLLAR RING

Minimize "ring around the collar" by squirting dishwashing liquid along the cuffs and inside collar and scrubbing carefully with a soft brush. Leave a few minutes, then wash by hand. After washing, squeeze gently to get rid of as much soap as possible, then rinse in clean water two or three times—until the water runs completely clear. Soap can do as much damage as dirt, so be thorough.

DEALING WITH DELICATES

First you need to define your delicates. Anything made of silk, satin, or wool, or any item that is heavily embroidered, antique, fragile, or lacy comes under this category. You can also include most fancy underwear, especially bras, lacy lingerie, and panty hose and stockings. All of these items will benefit enormously from a little tender loving care in the laundry department. Never succumb to the temptation to throw fragile items into the washing machine to fill up a regular load—you will almost certainly regret it later.

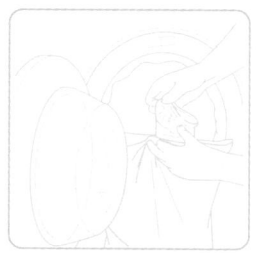

PUT DELICATES IN A PILLOWCASE

A DELICATE TOUCH

☆ If you are lucky enough to have a machine with a delicate cycle, you can almost dispense with hand-washing altogether, particularly if you tie the delicates inside a pillowcase or a specially designed net laundry bag, to prevent snagging. That said, purists would argue that if you want to care for your delicates properly, you should always hand-wash. Remember that with delicates, it is the agitation as much as the temperature of the water that you are protecting them from.

☆ Delicates need to be sorted and washed by color, too. Don't make the mistake of thinking that it is safe to throw them all in together.

✰ If you don't want to risk putting something into the machine, immerse it in cool water into which you have poured a capful of detergent suitable for hand-washing. Pat the foam gently into the garment to dislodge any dirt. Leave to soak if the dirt seems ingrained. Squeeze suds gently through the fabric—do not wring, because this can do real damage—and then rinse. Be prepared: you may need to rinse delicate items three or four times to get rid of the soap because you need to go easy on the squeezing.

PAT GARMENT GENTLY

✰ Instead of wringing dry, which can damage the fabric or pull it out of shape, roll the garments in a towel and squeeze gently to get rid of excess water. You may go through several towels, but it will be worth it.

ROLL GARMENT IN A TOWEL

SHAPING UP
Hang items on the line if they can take it, but if they are too delicate and risk stretching or sagging, dry them flat on an airing rack, making sure that you have eased them back into shape first if necessary.

FRESH AND DRY

Clothes dryers are a wonderful invention, although they can be heavy on electricity and therefore an expensive way to dry your clothes. It's also true that you can do more damage to some clothes in the dryer than in the washing machine—like when you turn cashmere to felt, and silk back into a sow's ear. So it's worth paying attention to the symbols.

ALL HUNG UP
Try to store clothespins indoors to prevent them from deteriorating or becoming dirty and staining your clean laundry. If you must leave them outside, at least keep wooden pins clean by boiling them in a solution of water and bleach occasionally.

Hang out your clothes to dry in the open air whenever possible, especially in the case of towels and bedding. You do not have to go for the full romantic Tuscan idyll and dry your sheets downwind of a lavender hedge for your laundry to smell "outdoor" fresh and clean, but don't ruin the effect by neglecting the simple task of taking care of your clothesline. It's horribly dispiriting to discover a black smudge along the length of your newly laundered sheets. Use a clean cloth wrung out in warm, soapy water to wipe down your line at least once a week.

☆ *Whites will benefit from being hung out in bright sunshine because the sunlight has a slight bleaching effect. For the same reason, protect colored clothes by hanging them in the shade, or turning them inside-out to prevent them from fading in the sun.*

DRYER SYMBOLS HERE'S WHAT THEY MEAN

EMPTY CIRCLE IN A BOX
Safe to dry on a normal cycle.
A line underneath indicates a
permanent press cycle; two
lines indicate a gentle cycle.

TWO DOTS IN A CIRCLE
Safe to dry on medium heat
setting. Three dots indicate
that it is safe to dry on a high
heat setting.

ONE DOT IN A CIRCLE
Safe to dry on low heat setting.

CROSS IN A CIRCLE
Do not put the garment in
the dryer.

☆ *Woollens, delicates and items that soak up too much water should be dried flat to prevent them from stretching. Lay them out on a large towel or an airing rack with a horizontal grid. If it's raining, use a blow-dryer on the lowest setting to dry these items rather than dangling them over the radiator, which can scorch and leave clothes crispy rather than fresh.*

☆ *To help them keep their shape, shirts and T-shirts can be put on a hanger and then hung on the line. To save space, pin socks to a hanger first, too. Pin hangers to the line, though, to keep them from blowing away.*

BLEACH WHITES IN THE SUN

LAY DELICATES FLAT TO DRY

IRONING

Take the headache out of ironing by doing your homework; spend a few minutes learning the various functions of your iron and the ironing symbols on your clothes labels. That way you'll save yourself a lot of heartache—and hours sweating over a not-quite-hot-enough iron.

CREASE-FREE SLEEVES

Stuff a rolled-up magazine inside the arm of a jacket so you don't iron an unwanted crease into the sleeve. The magazine will unfurl just enough to create a firm "ironing pad," enabling you to iron around the sleeve.

CARE SYMBOLS

Check the care labels of your fabric before ironing.

🔺	HIGH HEAT	🔺	MEDIUM HEAT
🔺	LOW HEAT	🔺	DO NOT IRON

IRONING TIPS

☆ *If you don't have a water softener, there is no need to distill water before you fill your steam iron. Instead, mix 1 tablespoon of ammonia to each cup of water. It will make ironing easier and will protect your iron from lime scale.*

☆ *Don't be too eager to get started on that pile of ironing. If you begin before your steam iron has reached the correct temperature, your iron will almost* certainly drip and leave water marks on your clean, pressed clothes.

☆ For persistent creases, if the spray function of your iron doesn't do the trick, rub the offending area with a damp sponge.

☆ If ironing a pleated skirt is driving you crazy, fix the pleats at the bottom of the skirt with a clothespin before continuing.

☆ If the base of your iron becomes stained or sticky, unplug it and rub it with a cloth dipped in vinegar. Wipe again with a clean cloth to remove any residue and continue ironing.

☆ If you don't already have a reflective ironing-board cover, speed up the ironing process by laying a piece of aluminum foil under your existing ironing-board cover. This will reflect the heat back up to the underside of the garment.

☆ Items with trim or edging that need ironing at a lower temperature should be ironed first, then the main body of the garment.

INSIDE-OUT

✓ Before you iron, turn heavy fabrics and acrylics, fluffy materials, or materials with a nap (raised fibers) inside-out and iron on the reverse side. This will prevent the nap from being flattened or damaged, or the fabric from becoming shiny.

LAUNDRY-DAY BLUES

It's all gone haywire. What can you do? If the colors have run or bled into one another, your first step is to minimize the problem by soaking the damaged garment in cool water. Do this the moment it comes out of the washer. If the patch is small enough, a spray-on stain remover may do the trick. Then wash (by hand, if necessary) and reassess.

SCORCH MARKS

Overdone the ironing? A clean white cloth dampened in hydrogen peroxide will remove a light scorch mark. Place over the scorch and press lightly with a warm iron. Repeat if necessary.

COLOR BLEACHING

Revive colored items that have dulled by treating them with an oxygen bleach that is suitable for use on all fabrics. You can even use a solution of chlorine bleach on some colored fabrics.

WHITE BUT NOT QUITE

To freshen white nylon socks that have lost their sparkle, add one or two tea bags to a pan of cold water and soak for several minutes.

LAST-MINUTE PANIC

If you don't have time to take a desperately needed item to the dry cleaner, put it in the dryer for a few minutes with a dryer sheet and a dampened cloth to freshen it up.

RESCUE REMEDIES

🔁 In-wash stain removers, which "oxidize" and get rid of stains and revive dulled fabrics, can be extremely effective, but be wary of using them on darker colors because they can cause fading.

🔁 Soak damaged items using a solution of specially formulated color-run powder for the classic pink shirt/red sock scenario. If that doesn't work, try a bleach solution (but read the care label on the garment first).

🔁 If your white shirts or sheets are starting to look dingy, a simple remedy is to try boiling them for a few minutes in a large pan of water into which you have added a couple of slices of lemon.

🔁 Revive linen or dress shirts with a quick squirt of spray-in starch. Tablecloths and napkins can be soaked in a solution of starch and water, but remember not to overdo it and make them too stiff.

FROM HATS TO HEELS

"You can't have everything.
Where would you put it?"

STEVEN WRIGHT

Caring for your clothes has never been easier, but it is a skill that is shamelessly neglected. In the days when women had just one coat and one good pair of shoes, they either had to take care of them or go cold. Now, if we scuff one pair of black boots we tend to stuff them under the bed and reach for our second-best pair. Maybe it's time to turn over a new leaf!

As with all things domestic, storage is the key. Stuff things in a drawer or at the bottom of the closet and you're inviting snags and scuffs. Start with your shoes and work up. The main thing is to find a storage method that works for your living environment, and one that you'll stick to. The idea of storing shoes in individual shoeboxes with a photograph of each pair on the outside for easy identification is appealing—but seriously, is it going to happen, or would you rather just reorganize your shoe rack? Whatever your approach, be ruthless. However much you loved them once, battered, ill-fitting, broken-heeled shoes should have no claim on your space. Fix them, clean them, or toss them.

The same goes for purses. Sort them, empty them, clean them, and then find them a home. Broken zips can be fixed, scuffs can be cleaned, and handles can be replaced, but don't give space to battered old shoulder bags that you wouldn't be caught dead wearing in public.

Hats, gloves, and scarves need a home of their own. If you insist on stuffing them in your underwear drawer, you'll never know what you've got or be able to find them easily when you need them, and what you do have will get ruined. If you don't have a spare drawer, put them in cardboard boxes, or invest in some decorative hatboxes or a vintage suitcase. The aim is to know exactly what you've got and where it is, so that you're more likely to use it. If something in the box needs cleaning or fixing, you won't be able to hide from it, so you'll be more likely to deal with it.

LEATHER SHOES

A CLEAN PAIR OF HEELS

✓ *Check over the heels for scuffs and scratches. If they are very badly damaged, you will need to take them to a cobbler to fix. Otherwise, use a marker in a matching color, which will disguise any scuff marks that have cut right through the leather.*

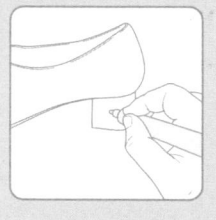

LEATHER CARE

Caring for leather shoes and boots used to be second nature. Whether you were in the brownies or the army, a weekly polish on a Sunday night and a daily buff to keep the shine was the absolute minimum level of maintenance. Nowadays, most of us have many more pairs of shoes than we could ever use regularly, and even the ones we do wear may be sadly neglected. Caring for your footwear will prolong the life of your shoes. It should also mean that you never again have to scrabble around the back of the closet or under the couch looking for a matching pair of shoes that aren't even fit to be worn in public.

LEATHER CARE
Regular polishing not only makes your shoes gleam, but it also keeps the leather supple and prevents it from cracking and leaking.

NEWSFLASH
To keep the polish off the inside of a shoe and to give it a little extra support, stuff the shoe with newspaper before you clean.

SOLE FOOD

Caring for your shoes begins with major organization. Gather all your shoes together and put them into matching pairs. Be honest with yourself and get rid of any that you no longer need or wear—don't be tempted to hang on to any "just in case." Where appropriate, remove and wash the laces and insoles of the ones you do decide to keep, or replace them if they are looking frayed or tattered. Finally, check the bottoms of your shoes and have any that are worn out or cracked resoled and reheeled.

YOU WILL NEED
- *Brushes*
- *Cloths*
- *Selection of shoe creams and/or polishes*
- *Markers to cover scratches*
- *Protective gloves*
- *Old newspaper to stuff inside your shoes and also to spread over your work surface or floor to keep it clean*

TAKE out any laces and go over the surface of the whole shoe with a soft, dry brush to get rid of any caked-in mud or dirt.

USING a soft, dry cloth, apply cream polish all over the shoe. Use a soft brush to apply wax polish if needed. Leave to soak in for a few minutes.

FINALLY, using a clean, medium-sized brush, polish the leather to a shine and buff the surface with a soft cloth or buffing pad.

BEST FOOT FORWARD

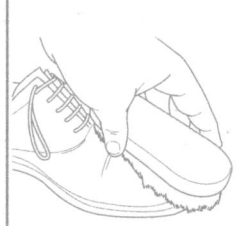
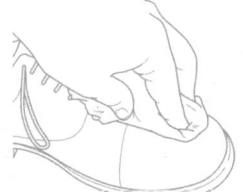

SUEDE SHOES

LOOKING AFTER SUEDE

Suede shoes can be very difficult to care for. One trip out in the rain can ruin them completely, so it's advisable to invest in a protective waterproof spray the moment you buy a pair. It's not a miracle cure, but it will help prevent them from unnecessary damage and protect them from water marks.

If your suede shoes or boots do get dirty, the main thing to keep in mind is that you need to go easy when cleaning suede items. Overly vigorous brushing can often do more harm than good, and you'll end up with a

YOU WILL NEED

- Cloths
- Velvet scraps
- Mild detergent
- Wire, rubber, or bristle brushes

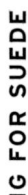

CARING FOR SUEDE

VELVET is excellent at picking up dust and fluff from suede. Wipe suede shoes and boots all over with a piece of velvet to get rid of dust and lint.

CAREFULLY, using a barely damp cloth wrung out in warm, soapy water, wipe the shoes to remove any stubborn marks.

LEAVE until completely dry, then, using a wire, rubber, or bristle suede brush, perk up the nap by brushing with gentle, circular strokes.

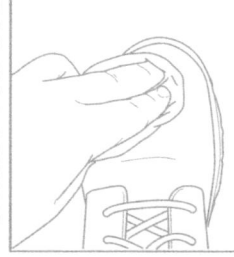

pair of shiny, bald-looking shoes. Always brush the surface with a special rubber, bristle, or wire brush, working gently in a circular motion. Never be tempted to scrub at suede to get it clean. Check the label or tag that came with your shoes for any cleaning recommendations—with both leather and suede, simply using strong detergents that you happen to have at home could damage the material permanently.

REVIVING

⭐ *To tackle persistent marks, brush the suede surface with a few drops of lemon juice on a cloth, then steam in front of a boiling kettle for a few seconds. (Wear oven mitts to protect your hands.) Then brush with a suede brush to revive the nap.*

⭐ *Worn suede shoes can be revived with a quick burst of steam. Hold each shoe in the path of a boiling kettle for a few seconds. Allow to dry, then go over it with a suede brush.*

⭐ *If your shoes are still looking dull or marked even after careful cleaning, applying a coat of suede dye in the original color can leave them looking almost new again*

SPEED DRYING
If you really don't have time to leave the shoes to dry naturally, use a blow-dryer on a low setting to speed up the process.

DRYING TIME
Do not leave shoes to dry near a direct source of heat, such as on top of the boiler or radiator, because this can stiffen and spoil the material.

CANVAS AND FABRIC SHOES

Canvas and fabric shoes look fabulous when they are new, but they get grubby and stained very quickly. Some time spent protecting your purchase before you wear them combined with day-to-day care will prolong the life of your shoes and keep them looking as good as possible.

SPIN CITY

✔ Canvas and fabric shoes can be washed in the washing machine (although some people are vehemently against this). Use a delicate or hand-wash setting if you have one, or otherwise use the most gentle cycle available. Select a cool or, at most, warm setting and do not spin. Hang your shoes up to dry or place them somewhere in the open air, away from direct sources of heat. If the shoes are white, put them outside to dry in the sun for that extra bleach effect.

HOT TIPS FOR COOL CANVAS

☆ Before spot cleaning to get rid of a stain, find a hidden area (such as inside the shoe) to test first, to make sure that the cleaning agent is compatible with your fabric and that it is not going to create a new stain or cause color to run or fade.

☆ If your Velcro fasteners (often used on children's shoes or canvas sneakers) have become dirty or have picked up fluff and lint, clean by running a separate piece of Velcro tape across it. The fluff and debris will transfer onto the tape, leaving your shoe fasteners clean.

☆ Be sensible with canvas or fabric shoes if you want to keep them looking good. They are not designed for tramping over fields or splashing through puddles, so, if it looks like rain, it's best to choose a more sturdy pair of shoes.

FABULOUS FABRIC

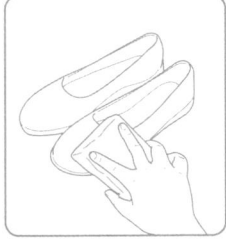

Heavily stained fabric or canvas shoes can be cleaned with carpet shampoo. Work into a lather, then scrub with an old toothbrush. Allow to dry.

Everyday marks can be cleaned off using a cloth dipped in warm, soapy water. Canvas and fabric should survive getting reasonably damp, but it's best not to soak the shoe, if possible.

Once you have cleaned off all the marks, rinse away the soapy water with a clean cloth that has been wrung out in warm water. Sponge the shoes dry.

To protect new or newly cleaned canvas or fabric shoes, spray with a specialized fabric protector or a starch spray before wearing them. This will provide a protective coating, making any splashes and stains easier to remove. It will also help the fabric keep its shape and stay looking new for longer.

SPORTS SHOES

Athletic shoes tend to absorb smells like no other and sometimes the house just isn't big enough for you and your gym shoes, so try to get into the habit of airing them outside for an hour or so every time you use them. Keeping them stuffed inside a dank sports bag all week is no way for them to stay fresh.

All footwear, regardless of the material it is made of, should be stored so that the air can circulate around it, in a dry environment and away from extremes of heat and cold. Sweaty sports shoes are particularly in need of a well-ventilated storage spot, so that they have a

YOU WILL NEED
- Foam fabric cleaner and a damp cloth to apply it with
- Specialist sneaker polish
- Baking soda
- Facial cleansing lotion and a cotton pad

SNEAKER SAVVY

TO GET rid of smells, try sprinkling a little baking soda inside to absorb odors. Leave overnight, then shake clean.	**SPECIALIST** polish is the best way to keep sneakers supple and clean, but foam fabric cleaner will remove most mud and scuff marks.	**TO KEEP** laces looking bright, wash them in the machine, but pop them in a white sock first to stop them getting lost or tangled.

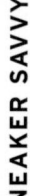

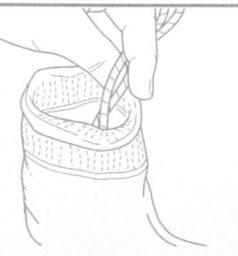

chance to dry out completely before being worn again. If you lead an active life and wear your sports shoes regularly, it's worth investing in a second (or even a third) pair, so that your shoes have plenty of time to air in between. This will not only make them more hygienic (as your feet will never again have to be encased in damp, potentially bacteria-infested shoes), it will also give the leather or fabric a chance to recover, and will therefore prolong the life of your sports shoes.

NO SWEAT
Wearing shoes that have not yet thoroughly recovered from their previous wearing and are still slightly damp is not only unpleasant but also unhygienic.

WHITE AND BRIGHT
• White leather sports shoes and bags (and regular belts, too) can be cleaned by wiping with a cotton pad dipped in facial cleansing lotion. Leave to dry for 10 minutes, then polish with a dry cloth.
• Non-gel toothpaste is fabulous for cleaning dirty white leather. Simply rub on with a cloth, rinse away, and then wipe the leather dry.

WORK BOOTS

Sturdy work boots and walking boots are, obviously, designed to take a great deal of wear and tear, but they still require careful maintenance. Although it may be unrealistic to try to keep them looking immaculate, making the effort to maintain them at a reasonable level of cleanliness will prolong their life and ensure that they are able to function efficiently and effectively for as long as possible, keeping your feet protected and dry.

USE PROTECTIVE SPRAY

☆ *Once your boots or shoes are dry, remove any laces and use a fairly stiff brush to get rid of any caked-on mud. Then wipe the surface with a cloth dipped in warm, soapy water and wrung out until almost dry. Leave until completely dry. Polish as you would any other leather shoes or boots. Finally, protect them from the elements with a waterproofing spray.*

☆ *If the boots are stained with salt water, wipe them thoroughly with warm water, apply a generous layer of olive oil with a soft cloth, leave to absorb for a few days, then polish as usual.*

☆ *Store boots somewhere dry, where air can circulate around them. You may only wear them every few months, but that is no excuse for stuffing them under the stairs or in the garage in a plastic bag.*

DRYING TIPS

⭐ *If your boots or shoes are completely soaked, simply stuffing them with newspaper and leaving them will not suffice. You will probably need to change the newspaper several times to help the leather dry.*

⭐ *Leave to dry either outdoors or in a well-ventilated room, but away from direct heat sources. If your shoes dry too quickly, the leather will stiffen and may even crack, which will ruin the surface of the leather and cause it to let in water in the future.*

⭐ *Once dry, polish footwear well before wearing it, to nourish and protect the leather.*

RAIN OR SHINE
To waterproof leather shoes and boots, coat them when they are new with boiled linseed oil. Repeat three times, allowing them to dry thoroughly after each application. If possible, leave them outdoors to dry.

GLORIOUS MUD

✅ *Water and mud are the greatest enemies of work boots and walking boots. Scrape off the worst of the mud with an old spatula or even a stick (before you even remove your boots, if possible). Then stuff them with newspaper and leave them to dry. The newspaper will help the boots retain their shape and will absorb the worst of the water. Don't even attempt to get the rest of the mud off until the boots have completely dried out.*

EVENING SHOES

Evening and party shoes need to be kept looking fresh in order for us to look our best. The effect of a gorgeous outfit is entirely lost if finished off with scuffed and scratched shoes. Unfortunately, evening shoes tend to be fragile and prone to damage. Here are a few tricks you can use to keep them looking good.

ALL WHITE ON THE NIGHT

Remove scuff marks from patent leather shoes by rubbing with a little egg white. Leave to dry, then polish with a soft cloth.

TWINKLE TOES

Gold- and silver-finish shoes can start looking tired and scruffy pretty quickly. Revive them by wiping with a cotton pad dampened with soapy water. Once the shoes are dry, wrap them in dark tissue paper before you store them to prevent them from tarnishing.

YOU SAY POTATO

If your dancing shoes have become so scuffed that they can no longer take any polish, first rub them all over with the inside of a raw potato. Leave to dry for a minute or two, and then try applying the polish.

FOOT NOTES

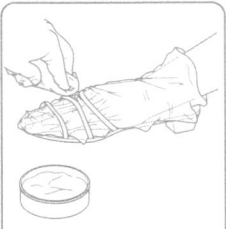

When cleaning strappy sandals, protect your hands and the insides of the shoes by putting a plastic bag over your hand and slipping it inside the sandal. If necessary, put a thick sock or two over your hand first, to provide a little extra padding and support for the sandal straps.

Polish patent leather with a little olive oil or milk to make it really shine. Rubbing the surface with petroleum jelly works just as well, but you need a little more elbow grease.

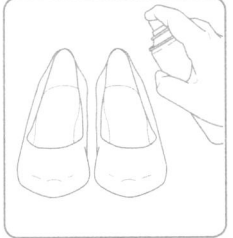

Once they're clean, protect your evening shoes from scuffing with a quick blast of hair spray. A coat of clear nail polish will protect the heels or any other vulnerable areas from getting scuffed too quickly. This is also a useful tip for shoes and sandals that have sequins or glitter decoration.

BELTS, BAGS, AND GLOVES

Even the smallest accessory benefits from a little attention to keep it looking its absolute best. Don't ignore scuffs, scratches, or drips on your bags or belts, but spend a few minutes every so often restoring them to their former glory.

BELTS AND BAGS

☆ *Never use color polish on leather belts because it will only transfer onto your clothes. If a quick wipe with a barely wet cloth doesn't do the trick, use a little saddle soap (very sparingly) and polish the belt well with a soft cloth before you wear it again.*

☆ *Keep polish away from leather purses, too, as, like belts, the risk of polish transferring onto your clothing is too great. A light rubdown with saddle soap will restore the shine and remove most water marks and stains. Suede bags can be steamed, then brushed. If stained, sponge gently with suede or fabric shampoo, or wipe with a little lemon juice. Steam once the bag is dry to revive the nap. (See also pages 178–179.)*

MATCHING SET

☆ *Clean matching items—such as gloves or shoes and bags—together, even if only one item actually needs cleaning. This will ensure the color and texture remain uniform for all pieces.*

Linings

✓ To clean bag linings, wipe gently with a barely damp cloth wrung out in warm, soapy water, turning the bag inside-out first, if possible. Be careful not to soak the lining or to allow any water to seep through into the leather. Leave to dry naturally. Alternatively, sprinkle the lining liberally with fuller's earth or bran. Leave it for a while to absorb any dirt, then brush or vacuum.

LOVELY GLOVELY

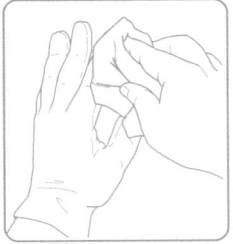

The best and easiest way to clean leather gloves is to put them on first. Leather gloves can be washed clean using gentle soap or soap flakes and water. Slip them onto your hands, run them under the faucet and then rub gently using cool water and a mild soap. Pale-colored gloves may need washing every time you wear them to prevent a buildup of dirt.

Rinse—it does not matter if a little soap remains in the leather. Then leave the gloves to dry in a well-ventilated room. You can buy specially designed wire or wooden "hands" to hold your gloves, or simply place them over a bottle to keep their shape and also to allow air to circulate around the leather. Do not dry in direct heat or place in direct sunlight. You can also use saddle soap to clean leather gloves and keep them supple.

Once the leather has been allowed to dry, gently work the leather through your fingers to soften it up again and ease the gloves back into shape. Put them back onto your hands to make sure they are the correct shape, remove and work the leather again if necessary. Finish by buffing gently with a soft cloth. To store gloves, always lay them flat, preferably wrapped in tissue paper first to protect them. Do not bunch them up in a ball with one cuff stuffed inside the other.

COATS, JACKETS, AND HATS

At the beginning and end of each season, spend a few minutes checking through and assessing all your outdoor wear. At the start of spring, when you think it's finally safe to pack away your heavy coats and jackets for the summer, make a careful check of all the pockets, inspect linings for rips and tears, and check for missing buttons. If any items require dry-cleaning, now is the time to get them cleaned and repaired—don't be tempted to pack them away while they are dirty.

CLEANING LEATHER COATS AND JACKETS

➦ Leather jackets can be dealt with at home. Mix up a strong solution of dishwashing liquid to water (1 part liquid to 5 parts water) and whip up into a foam.

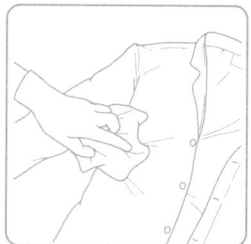

➦ Wipe the surface of the coat down with a damp cloth, being careful not to drench the leather. Leave to stand for a few minutes, then wipe down with a clean cloth wrung out in fresh water.

HEAD CASE

⭐ Hats can be a nightmare to clean. If your felt hat has been caught in a downpour, fold out the sweatband and let the hat stand on it to dry. Gently push out all the folds and creases so that the crown is as round as possible. Leave it to dry naturally and don't be tempted to put it near a radiator or use the blow-dryer. Once the hat is dry, gently fold the creases back in.

⭐ Straw hats should be given attention regularly with a clothes brush. This will prevent them from becoming damaged if they get rained on. To keep them clean, wipe with a cloth dipped in warm, soapy suds, then rinse with a cloth wrung out in clean water. Do not allow the straw to become soaked, otherwise it may shrink.

⭐ Stiffen limp straw hats by applying a thin coat of equal amounts clear shellac-and-alcohol solution to its surface. Leave to dry in a well-ventilated area and make sure the hat is thoroughly dry before wearing.

BRAN'S THE THING

✅ You can brush hats with a soft shaving brush or wipe with a stiff towel to remove dust and dirt. If the hat can't take water, use bran or fuller's earth to dry-clean it. Sprinkle bran or fuller's earth all over, leave for several minutes, and then brush off. This will absorb most greasy stains, but you may need to take the hat to a specialist cleaner if it has been stained with sweat.

THE GREAT OUTDOORS

"Gardening is the only unquestionably useful job."

GEORGE BERNARD SHAW

First impressions start at the garden gate, and if you haven't got curb appeal, you've already lost ground by the time your guests have reached the front door. Besides, coming home after a heavy day at work should give you a boost, rather than remind you of all the tasks that need doing. If your heart sinks before you even get inside, it's time to take action. We're all familiar with the concept of the garden as an extra room, but we have yet to get our heads around the idea of cleaning, maintaining, and decluttering it in the same way we do the house. If our gardens really are to function as spare kitchens and dining rooms, the surroundings—and that includes the gutters and drains as well as the flagstones—shouldn't ruin the alfresco experience for us. Sheds are not dumpsters, garden chairs do not automatically grow mildew, and rakes and trowels do not have to rust where they lie.

As with every other area of your home, the secret of a garden you can be proud of is to declutter, organize, and finally, once you know what you have, work out the best way to keep it clean and tidy (and by that we mean the simplest and quickest method). That way, using your garden becomes a pleasure, not a performance. If you don't have to trip over three deck chairs and a pogo stick to get to your lawn mower, cutting the grass becomes as straightforward as sweeping the kitchen floor. If you don't skin your shins dragging the barbecue out of the shed and work up a major sweat derusting it, you're likelier to use it more than once a year. If you can lay your hand on a trowel and a sack of soil without making a fruitless foray into the spidery recesses of your shed, then there's a chance that you'll actually wake up to a host of golden daffodils next spring, rather than have to throw away yet another bag of rotting bulbs. So, pick a sunny day, put on your oldest, scruffiest jeans and start blitzing the garden.

GARAGES, SHEDS, AND WORKSHOPS

Maintaining your garage, toolshed, or workshop in a clean and orderly state— free of dirt and cobwebs, where everything is put away in its own allocated place—is an ideal that, with a little dedication, is not too difficult to achieve.

☆ *Be brave. Giving your neglected garages, sheds, and workshops a good going over may take some time, and will almost inevitably involve grazed knuckles, bad language and probably a few tears, too, but it will be well worth it in the end. You will need your scruffiest jeans, some heavy boots, protective gloves, a hat and at least three uninterrupted hours (preferably when the sun's shining).*

☆ *Whatever type of outdoor storage space you have—a four-car garage, a wooden shed, or simply one of those lock-up tool boxes in the garden—unless you are naturally an extremely organized individual, it is almost bound to contain too much stuff. Most of it will be difficult to get at, and what you can* reach is likely to look suspiciously grungy and unpleasant.

☆ *Get into the habit of putting items away in their correct place as soon as you've finished with them. Do not simply leave them lying around the garden where they can quickly rust, corrode, or even go missing.*

Planning and organizing

☑ While your garage or shed is drying out from its washing down, take the opportunity to sort through the contents and organize some shelving or storage space so that you can not only see what you have, but can reach it easily when you need it.

AN EMPTY SPACE

Clear everything out, and that means everything. Apply the closet technique of dividing into three piles: one of items to keep, one of things that have seen better days and need to be chucked (or sent to recycling), and one of items that are to be cleaned and/or renovated or repaired.

Once you have entirely emptied your garage or shed, sweep all the surfaces thoroughly, not forgetting the walls and ceiling. Get rid of all the dirt and cobwebs, and don't overlook the corners. If your shed or garage is particularly dirty, or has not been cleaned for a while, you will probably need to sweep it twice to get rid of the buildup of dirt and dust.

Wash down all the surfaces with warm, soapy water and a rough cloth, scrubbing brush or old broom head. Hose the floor down. If your garage floor has any oil stains or ground-in dirt, scrub these areas first with undiluted detergent or neat dishwashing liquid. Allow to dry, leaving any doors and windows open so that the room can air completely.

Finally, hose down the outside of the building (including the roof, if you can get to it safely). If you do not have a hose, throw several buckets of water over the outside of the structure instead. Scrape away any buildup of moss. To get rid of patches of mildew or lichen, scrub the area with a solution of half cold water and half bleach, then rinse thoroughly.

TOOLS

Before you stash your tools away, make sure they are worth keeping, are clean and are still in good working order. Regular maintenance of your equipment will make caring for your garden easier, and will also extend the life of your tools.

SAND PIT

To help your tools stay clean, keep a bucket or small tub of sand in your toolshed or garage, and dig your tools into the sand after use, before you put them away.

LAWN MOWERS

☆ *The moment you've finished using your lawn mower, take a stiff brush and a hose and remove any residual grass and soil from the roller blades and grass boxes. Apply some grease to the height adjusters and turn them carefully to make sure they haven't seized up. Check that blades are still sharp. If necessary, get them sharpened professionally.*

☆ *If you have a gas-operated mower, always disconnect the spark plug and run the fuel down (or empty it out) before storing it away for the winter.*

HAND TOOLS

☆ *To prevent wooden handles cracking, splintering, or drying out, rub them with boiled linseed oil once a year, working the oil into the wood with a clean rag or some steel wool.*

☆ *Use a putty knife and a wire brush to scrape away dirt and debris.*

☆ Make sure that your tools are wiped dry before you store them, to prevent them from rusting or corroding.

☆ To prevent tools from rusting, they can be rubbed down with car wax before being put away; or put a lump of charcoal, chalk, or a few mothballs into your toolbox.

PRUNING TOOLS

Pruning tools should be cleaned between each plant or tree to reduce the risk of cross-infection. Using an antibacterial cleaner may not be enough; wipe the blades with wood alcohol or run them through a flame.

HAND-TOOL CLEANING MADE SIMPLE

 Begin by driving your garden tools into a bucket of sand a few times to get rid of dirt, grass, and mud.

To clean away rust, use a generous piece of steel wool or a soap-filled steel pad dipped in paraffin (kerosene), and scrub at any rusty patches.

Finish by buffing up the surface of your tool. Take a large piece of scrunched-up aluminum foil and polish the metal surface.

GARDEN FURNITURE

Most garden furniture—from wicker to cast iron—can be kept clean by regular wiping down with a damp cloth or sponge wrung out in mild detergent. Make sure the furniture is thoroughly dry before stacking or putting away.

☆ *Use an old nailbrush or toothbrush to scrub away dirt and lichen from awkward corners and intricate detailing on cast-iron or plastic furniture.*

STANDARD PLASTIC FURNITURE

White plastic furniture is one of the most frustrating things in the garden to keep clean, but it can be done. And don't fret if you're not successful—you can replace the chairs for a song if you know where to look.

➺ For general cleaning, use a scrubbing brush and a bowl of hot water with a squirt of dish soap. To clean a heavy buildup of dirt, add a couple of capfuls of bleach, then scrub, wipe, and rinse.

➺ Get rid of scratches using brass cleaner, graffiti wipes, or car cleaner. These will take away the top layer of plastic, thereby removing the scratches at the same time.

☆ To get rid of greasy spots on plastic or resin furniture, use a few drops of lighter fluid on a cotton pad or rag. Wash, then rinse well.

☆ If your aluminum tubular-framed furniture starts to corrode, give it a gentle polish with some fine-grade steel wool.

SHOWER POWER
If you can tell it's about to rain, dash outside and spray your garden furniture with a little cleaner, then let the rain do the rest!

TRADITIONAL WOODEN FURNITURE

Wooden furniture can be gently scrubbed with a softish brush soaked in warm water and detergent. Rub at persistent stains using a piece of fine steel wool. Work along the grain, not against it, to avoid marking the wood permanently.

Once the wood is clean and dry, you can seal it with a wax furniture seal or varnish. Dip your brush into the sealant or varnish, and apply it slowly and carefully in the direction of the grain. Take care not to overload the brush, or you may cause the sealant to pool.

PATIOS AND PATHS

U nquestionably, the easiest, quickest, most effective, and satisfying way to clean muck, moss, and mold from all the paved areas outside your home is with a high-pressure hose, so beg, borrow, or rent one if you possibly can. If not, you will need to resort to either a regular hose or a bucket of water and brush. Clean with a stiff broom designed for outdoor use.

SCRUB WITH A STIFF BROOM

AROUND AND AROUND THE GARDEN

⭐ *If your paving stones or paths still look soiled and stained, dissolve a cup or two of washing-soda crystals in a bucket of hot water, and scrub away with a stiff broom. Alternatively, use a specially formulated concrete or flagstone cleaner, which will lift away stubborn dirt and stains and kill any moss and lichen.*

OUT ON DECK

⭐ *Never place a barbecue directly onto a wooden deck, in case the coals, sparks, or hot ash fall out and burn the wood. Avoid the risk of such a calamity by resting your barbecue on some tiles or a piece of heatproof matting.*

⭐ *Move plant tubs regularly to prevent damp and stains or mildew rings, and ensure that they are either raised slightly from the ground on little feet or* protected with drainage saucers so that water can't linger underneath. Alternatively, place a tile between the bottom of the plant plot and the decking to act as a barrier.

⭐ Pay attention to the spaces in between the boards where dirt and dead leaves can collect. A pressure hose should get rid of them, but if not, use a putty knife to dig them out—but be careful not to scratch or gouge the wood.

⭐ Avoid leaving anything lying around on the patio (e.g., old pieces of board or bags of rotting soil) that can trap water and encourage mold.

CLEARING THE DECKS

✅ A high-pressure hose can be used to clean most plant-free areas of your garden efficiently and effectively, whether they are concrete, stone, or wood. On decking, it will lift away green algae and mold and blast away at debris which, left to its own devices, could form mold, encourage the wood itself to rot, and even cause blocked drains.

OIL STAINS

If tar or oil is a problem, try soaking up spills with cat litter, which will absorb a lot of it, then attack with a stiff brush, hot water, and laundry detergent.

PATIO SEALS

A specialist patio seal will help keep moss and lichen at bay and will ensure that oil stains are easier to get rid of in the future.

CARS AND BIKES

Never be tempted to wash down your car or motorcycle using dishwashing liquid—yes, it will clean the paintwork beautifully, but it will also strip it of its protective wax coating. Choose a detergent that is specially designed to clean car (or motorcycle) paintwork.

WASH WITH A SOFT BRUSH

POLISH WITH A CHAMOIS

CAR WASHING

☆ *Start with the roof, using a soft brush, a hose, and a bucket of warm water mixed with a solution of car-cleaning detergent. Rinse and dry as you go to prevent drips and water stains.*

☆ *Use a chamois leather to polish the windows and the light covers, but don't use a real chamois on the paintwork because it can strip off the wax. Use an old cotton towel to dry it off instead.*

☆ *Baking soda is the secret ingredient for stubborn stains on your car. Dissolve four tablespoons of baking soda in 1¾ pint (1 liter) of warm water and use it to clean the lights, windows, tires, tire trims, chrome fixtures, and interior vinyl seats and mats.*

☆ *Unless you have a particularly powerful vacuum cleaner, use the vacuum cleaner at your local gas station for the interior of your car.*

WASHING A BICYCLE

Begin by hosing down the bike with a regular garden hose. Don't use a high-pressure hose on a bicycle because it could force water into the gear system.

➡ Having hosed away most of the mud, sponge away the dirt and oil from the frame, wheels, and chain with warm water and some biodegradable detergent.

➡ Next, rinse with the hose and wipe dry using old towels. Relubricate the chain using a spray lubricant and a rag. Back pedal to ensure the chain is completely lubricated.

➡ Wax the frame, if necessary, and polish. Use a light engine oil on a clean rag to polish the chrome, but never use wax or oil on the inside of the wheel rims; otherwise your brakes will slip.

☆ You can, however, use the brush attachment of your vacuum to lift away dust and dirt from the dashboard and trims.

☆ An old dustpan brush is perfect for cleaning car wheels. Hose wheels down first to loosen the dirt and get rid of surface grime, then scrub with a strong detergent solution. You may need to rinse and repeat to get rid of the oil and gunk that collects here.

FINAL CHECK
To finish your maintenance session, check that your brakes and lights are working correctly, and that your lights are clean and not caked in oil or grime that has been thrown up from the road.

DRAINS AND GUTTERS

Unlike drain clearing, gutter clearing is not a job to try solo. Never climb a ladder if no one else is around. Always arm yourself with a pair of rubber gloves, an empty bucket, a sturdy ladder, and a friend before tackling the heights.

TWICE-YEARLY CHECK

Once you have cleared and cleaned the gutters, you don't need to repeat the process for another six months. As a rule of thumb, check and clear gutters twice a year—once in the spring and once in the fall.

SAFETY FIRST

If you feel at all unsafe climbing a ladder, call in a professional.

HOW TO CLEAN A DRAIN

☆ *Using a stiff brush, sweep any leaves and debris away from the external drain cover, then sprinkle with half a cup of baking soda.*

☆ *Pour a cup of white vinegar on top of the baking soda and leave for one minute.*

☆ *Flush the drain with a couple of kettles full of boiling water.*

☆ *Repeat the procedure about once a month to keep your drains flowing freely.*

The same method can be used to clear internal drains.

HOW TO CLEAN AND CLEAR A GUTTER

 Never rest your ladder on a gutter, because it won't be strong enough. Place it safely so that you can reach into the top of the gutter where it meets the downpipe. Avoid erecting your ladder in front of a door that is likely to be opened unexpectedly.

 Fix your bucket to the top of the ladder with a piece of sturdy rope or wire, so that you have one hand free to hold the ladder while you use the other to clear the gutter. Scoop out any debris and drop it into the bucket to save making a mess all over the walls of the house. Either use your free hand to scoop or a pair of tongs to lift out the residue.

 Once you have cleaned away as much debris as possible, get the hose and flush away any remaining muck down the downpipe. Ensure that it is flowing freely. You may be able to clear a blockage where the gutter meets the downpipe, but do not disconnect pipes unless you know exactly how to reconnect them.

EXTERNAL WINDOWS AND PAINTWORK

You can make your own window cleaner by mixing equal parts paraffin (kerosene), wood alcohol, and water. Store the solution in a plastic bottle, but label it carefully and keep out of reach of children. Spray onto external windows and polish with a pad of old newspapers for an excellent shine.

EXTERNAL WOODWORK

✔ External woodwork can be washed down or scrubbed with warm water and a mild detergent. Rinse and dry as you go to prevent watermarks forming.

✔ Keep an eye out for mold and rot on window frames. You can scrub with a solution of half bleach and half water to remove black mold and prevent it from forming.

GLEAMING WINDOWS

☆ *To prepare windows for cleaning, dust off both the windows and sills with a clean paintbrush.*

☆ *Heat a little vinegar and rub it on with a soft cloth to get rid of old paint and bird droppings.*

☆ *Use warm water mixed with a little vinegar to clean frosted glass. Then buff with a clean soft cloth.*

SPOTTING STREAKS

If you are cleaning both sides of your windows, work in one direction on each side—i.e., from top to bottom on the outside and side to side on the inside (or vice versa). This will allow you to locate any streaks quickly and easily, because it will be obvious which side they are on.

PATIO DOORS

Sliding patio doors should be given a thorough check every six months.

Scrub every month to six weeks with a wire brush to keep the tracks and bottom runners clear and rust free. For ease of cleaning, make sure the runners are thoroughly dry first. Use the crevice tool on your vacuum cleaner to clear away any loosened dirt particles.

Once you are satisfied that the runners are in good working order, sprinkle a little graphite powder onto the track to ensure they continue to run smoothly. Put a little powder onto the runners, then test the doors, then sprinkle a little more powder if needed.

☆ *Avoid cleaning windows and glass panels in doors while they are in direct sunlight because the sun will cause the cleaning solution to dry too quickly and streak badly. The best time to wash glass windows and doors is on a cloudy (but not damp or rainy) day. Do not clean external glass in frosty or freezing conditions.*

SHARING YOUR LIVING SPACE

"Cleaning your house while your kids are still growing is like shoveling the walk before it stops snowing."

PHYLLIS DILLER

Like it or not, sharing your home with others is never going to be a completely smooth ride. People have their own ideas about what a clean home means, and standards vary enormously. Some people think it's acceptable to dump clothes on the floor and leave dirty dishes in the sink for the dish fairy to do, while others leave their home so spotless that a forensic scientist would be hard-pressed to find anything out of place. Where does your household lie on the scale? Do you work as a team to help keep everything shipshape, or does everyone pile up the clutter and dirt and leave you to clear up the mess?

If you want a home that is orderly and uncluttered, where you can welcome unexpected guests at any time of day without embarrassment about the state of your surroundings, then you have to make sure that every member of your household is working with you and not against you. This applies to children as well as adults.

The key to a clean and well-run household lies in passing the dusting cloth to everyone who lives in the house. There is no reason why you should have to do everything by yourself. Share cleaning responsibilities with your partner, your children, your roommates, or anyone else who lives with you. Don't just go around picking up other people's clothes and cleaning up after them, expecting them to get the message. Encourage people to put away their own belongings and to leave the place as they find it. Make a list of tasks and let each household member pick his or her own. To keep things fair, rotate any undesirable chores each week, so that each person takes his or her turn. Encourage everyone to take responsibility for keeping the household space clean, and your home will be a pleasure to live in.

HOW TO HOUSE-TRAIN CHILDREN

Teaching children to help with cleaning isn't easy. Start them young if you can, and if necessary, use the old "carrot and stick" strategy, in other words, teach them that doing their cleaning task well and on time will result in a reward, whereas doing it badly or not at all will incur a penalty. Always praise a child for work well done, and give rewards where they are due. Agree with your family what the rewards and penalties will be in advance, so that no one can complain if you follow through with a penalty later. Make sure that parents also have penalties if they don't keep to their side of the bargain.

HOUSEHOLD TASKS FOR CHILDREN

AGE 2-5

- ☆ wash their hands after using the toilet, and before and after meals
- ☆ put away toys and books
- ☆ put their shoes away

AGE 6-9

- ☆ wipe up spilled food
- ☆ put their clothes away or in the hamper
- ☆ fold washed laundry

AGE 10-13

- ☆ make their bed
- ☆ set the table
- ☆ wash and dry dishes
- ☆ wash vegetables
- ☆ clean their room
- ☆ help to choose food items when shopping

AGE 14-18

- ☆ prepare simple meals
- ☆ clean the kitchen or bathroom
- ☆ clean the windows
- ☆ wash and iron clothes

COPING WITH LITTLE EMERGENCIES

What do you do when you are left with handprints of jam on your best wallpaper? Choosing washable furnishings and easy-to-clean flooring will make life easier. Here are some handy tips for those little emergencies:

☆ *To remove greasy fingerprints from wallpaper, place brown paper or blotting paper over the marks and press with a warm iron.*

☆ *To get rid of a dirt stain on wallpaper, roll a piece of white bread into a ball in your hands, then use it to rub out the mark.*

☆ *To clean jam from a carpet, scrape off the residue, then blot the stain with warm water. Clean with a little carpet shampoo. If the mark persists, remove with wood alcohol.*

☆ *To remove children's modeling clay from a carpet, scrape off the residue, then dab with lighter fuel.*

☆ *To remove felt-tip pen ink from upholstery, blot with paper towel, then dab with wood alcohol. If this fails, try using a specialist stain remover.*

CRAYON MARKS

✔ *To remove crayon marks from vinyl wallpaper, first spray the area with WD-40 (test on a hidden patch first) and leave it to work for 10–15 minutes. Then sponge it clean gently with hot, soapy water and rinse.*

DEALING WITH MESSY TEENAGERS

If you didn't manage to house-train your children when they were young, you will be tired of hearing yourself shout "Clean your room!" by the time they are teenagers. But all is not lost—there are ways and means of getting through to them, as long as you are prepared to be persistent.

MAKE IT FUN
Tasks are easier if we make them enjoyable. Be encouraging toward your teenagers; don't just nag them. Let them discover their own way of doing things; don't simply insist that they copy you.

TEENAGE HOUSE-TRAINING

If your teenager's room looks like the aftermath of a battle, the prospect of clearing it up may feel overwhelming. Help your teenager to start again with a clean slate by cleaning the room together. State clearly that this is the last time you will be helping, and what the consequences will be if the room is left a mess in the future.

Here are the consequences: When the room starts to look messy again, go in with a bag and take the items of clutter away. Insist that your teenager buys back items from you for a dollar each, or whatever sum you feel is appropriate. Assume that any items that are not bought back after three months are not needed and give them to charity. Your teenager may have a tantrum about this at first, but maintain a firm stance. Eventually, reason will break through and meek compliance should follow.

CLEANING TEENAGE SPILLS AND STAINS

☆ To clean nail polish from a carpet, remove the excess polish with paper towels, then dab a little non-oily nail-polish remover on the stain. (Don't let it soak through to the backing.) Then clean with carpet shampoo.

☆ To remove greasy fingerprints from books, place a piece of blotting paper over the marks and press with a warm (not hot) iron.

☆ To clean a grubby computer keyboard, use a dry cotton swab between the keys, then dampen it with a little wood alcohol and use to clean the dirty tops of the keys. Do not let any moisture penetrate the keyboard.

☆ To tackle chocolate dropped onto upholstery, first let it set hard, then use a blunt knife to scrape off the excess. Clean the stained area with a foamy carpet shampoo, and sponge off with a little water— but don't let the fabric get too wet or allow the water to soak into the padding inside. If this still doesn't do the trick, finish by applying a stain remover.

CHEWING GUM

✓ To remove chewing gum from a carpet, put some ice or an ice pack into a plastic bag, or wrap with plastic wrap. Place it over the gum until it hardens, then use a knife to crack the hardened gum and pick it off with tweezers.

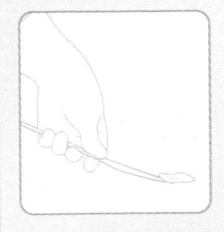

LIVING WITH HOUSEHOLD PETS

Household pets can be great company, but they need regular care and attention, particularly when it comes to cleanliness. Some pets need grooming—especially the furry ones—and some may have little accidents and leave odors on carpets and upholstery, and anywhere else within their reach.

CAUTION

Some people say you can vacuum your dog if you are gentle with the suction attachment, but it can still cause discomfort and is therefore not recommended. Don't ever attempt to vacuum a cat—you'll never pry its claws out of the ceiling.

FUR-FREE LIVING

The cleaner your pet, the cleaner your home. So regular grooming is vital. Brush your dog or cat daily; brushing is particularly good for your cat because it helps prevent hairballs. To keep your home as fur free as possible, choose a good vacuum cleaner that will pick up all the pet hair, and vacuum regularly. Use the nozzle attachment for vacuuming around the edges of the room between the carpet and the walls—this is a common place for fur to accumulate and, if left undisturbed, it will attract insects. You can also use the upholstery attachment to vacuum fur from upholstered furniture, or use a velour brush or tape wrapped around your hand. Better still, don't let your pet sit on the furniture in the first place. Vacuum all pet bedding regularly.

BATHING YOUR FURRY FRIEND

Bathe your dog regularly to minimize odors and keep it pest free. Bathe your pet every three months if you brush it regularly, more often if it starts to smell or if anyone in the house suffers from allergies. Use a good dog shampoo and rinse with warm water. Towel dry, then leave your pet to dry in a warm place, by a radiator or fireplace.

PERFUME YOUR POOCH

Steep some lavender and rosemary leaves in a pot of hot water. When the infusion has cooled, use it as a rinse for your dog. It will leave his coat shiny and healthy-looking, and help him smell nice, too.

FRESHEN UP YOUR FELINE

 If you can't persuade your cat to have a full bath once in a while, try a "dry-clean." Start by sprinkling baking soda down your cat's spine.

 Work it in with your fingers, then rub gently in a circular motion.

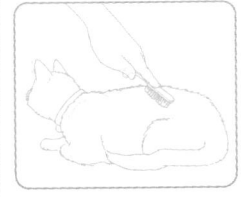

 Brush out any excess fur and baking soda, then rub down with a damp washcloth. Leave your cat to dry off in a warm place, by a radiator or a fireplace.

LIVING IN HARMONY WITH YOUR PETS

Dogs and cats have very different needs, as do fish, birds and other small creatures. Learn as much about them as you can so that you can live together harmoniously and hygienically.

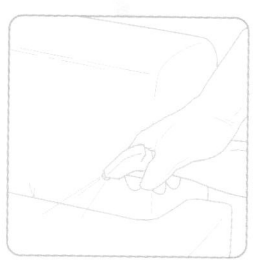

VINEGAR SOLUTION SPRAY

A WALK IN THE PARK

Dogs need to be taken out regularly for walks, not just for exercise, but also to relieve themselves. Take a scoop and a plastic bag with you so that you can pick up your pooch's little parcels. It's also a good idea to take a towel with you, so that if it rains, you can give your dog and his paws a quick rubdown before he gallops through your house leaving a trail of muddy paw prints and shaking dirty water all over your walls. Never leave it too long to take your dog outside, or you will be picking up little presents inside your home as well as outside.

TOILET TIPS FOR YOUR CAT

Cats are independent and clean animals by nature and will adapt very easily to using a litter box indoors. Position it in an accessible area for the cat, but out of the way of food preparation and marauding youngsters. Clean it daily and keep it fresh, or your cat will turn its nose up in disgust and relieve itself on a carpet or chair or some other inconvenient place to drive home its message of disapproval.

CARING FOR YOUR FISH

Always keep your fish in a tank—a goldfish bowl will not provide enough oxygen. Position it away from direct sunlight, and somewhere it cannot be knocked over. Clean it out well at least once a week, because stagnant water may make your fish ill.

BIRD TALK

Keep your bird's cage out of drafts and direct sunlight. Clean the cage regularly, but do not use carpet deodorizers or other strong chemicals, because they can be harmful to birds. Do not keep the cage in the kitchen: some fumes from non-stick pans can be toxic to birds.

RODENTS AND OTHER SMALL CREATURES

Keep these creatures out of the kitchen and bedrooms, and clean out their cages regularly. To avoid infection, encourage your children to wash their hands after handling these or any other pets.

SCRATCH STOPPER

✔️ To discourage your pet from scratching or chewing your furniture, rub it with a little clove oil or hot pepper sauce.

RODENTS

To help keep your rodent's cage clean, place an empty jelly jar on its side in the cage in the place where your rodent usually defecates. If necessary, put some of its deposits in the jar to reinforce the message.

TIPS FOR LITTLE EMERGENCIES

Even assuming the most thorough planning and organization, accidents can happen when the creatures that inhabit your home are four footed. First your dog regurgitates his dinner on the sofa, then the cat—not to be outdone—does a whoopsie on the carpet. No amount of planning can avoid these mishaps, but at least the following tips can help you clean up the mess with minimum fuss.

THE RING'S THE THING
Always tackle the ring around a stain first. After you have dealt with the ring, work from the outside in to prevent the stain from expanding.

If you don't have a commercial enzyme cleaner, treat the area with a solution of 2 pints (1.2 liters) water and 1 tablespoon white vinegar, or mix a little borax with water. Treat again with commercial enzyme cleaner as soon as possible. For fabrics, use a suitable enzyme cleaner and then apply a deodorizing fabric spray, which will neutralize the odor.

NATURE'S LITTLE PRESENTS

To clean fecal stains from upholstery, remove the excess with kitchen paper, then sponge the area with a solution of warm water mixed with a little ammonia. Apply a deodorizing fabric spray to neutralize the odor.

TUMMY TROUBLE

To clean up vomit and prevent it from damaging the dyes in a carpet, remove the excess with paper towels, then neutralize the affected area by treating it with a professional carpet detergent. Rinse with clean, hot water, then soak up the excess moisture with paper towels. To clean vomit from upholstery, remove the excess with paper towels, then treat with a deodorizing upholstery cleaner.

TROUBLESOME WET PATCHES

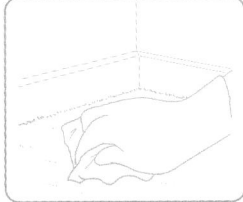

 Pet urine—especially a cat's—is notoriously difficult to eradicate once it has set in. Even if you can't smell it, your pet will, and he may return there at any time to update the odor. Whether it's on lino, carpet, or a wooden floor, act quickly if possible to prevent it from soaking through and into the floor.

 Sop up what you can with paper towels, then clean with a commercial enzyme cleaner, which you can buy from pet shops. The enzyme cleaner will clean the mess and neutralize the odor, whereas ordinary cleaners will simply clean the mess and leave the smell to linger.

SURVIVAL TIPS FOR SHARERS

You can learn more about people in a week of living together than you can through years of socializing. Sharing a house, apartment, or room with someone can be an economical and sociable way to live, but it requires a lot of organization, discipline, and tact. People have widely differing views on what constitutes a clean living space. Some people are very organized and tidy—they take responsibility for their surroundings and do their fair share to keep the home clean. Other people do basic things such as the dishes, but they never vacuum the floor or clean the windows. Some people are simply not interested in housework at all—they refuse to do anything, usually to the exasperation of their housemates.

A STITCH IN TIME SAVES NINE

In any shared household, it is vital to get into the habit of cleaning up as you go along. Five or ten minutes here and there will keep clutter at bay and things running smoothly.

NIPPING POTENTIAL PROBLEMS IN THE BUD

The best way to avoid potential problems is to try to assess other people's attitudes to household cleaning before you decide to move in together. Talk to them and consider their attitude to things such as friends, entertaining at home, smoking, and lifestyle. Are they sensible and considerate? Do they seem reliable? If you can, try to sneak a peek at their current living space to get an idea of how clean it is. This approach doesn't guarantee a problem-free home, but it could bring to light some potential problems before you get too involved.

PASS THE DUSTING CLOTH, PLEASE

Make a list of tasks and let each person choose his or
her own. Then create a schedule for unwanted chores,
so that each person takes a turn with these, too.

RESCUE REMEDIES

When sharing your
living space, it is vital to
clean areas where germs
can collect. Use a cloth to
wipe anti-bacterial
cleaner on light switches.

Door handles will
harbor germs, too.
Disinfect or spray with
anti-bacterial cleaner
once a week.

Use a cotton swab
dipped in disinfectant
to clean crevices
on telephones.

Keep a pack of anti-bacterial wipes in the bathroom
to encourage everyone to give a regular quick spruce to
the toilet and other fittings.

SHARING CHORES

Keep chaos and confusion to a minimum by making a list of all household tasks and ensuring that everyone is clear about their own cleaning duties. Here are some of the chores you will need to include in your list. Some of them need to be done daily, while others can be done less frequently.

WHEN PUSH COMES TO SHOVE

If your best efforts at resolving conflict fail, then it might be better for someone to make the break and move out.

HOUSEHOLD CHORES

☆ *Wash dishes* ☆ *Dry dishes and put them away* ☆ *Clean kitchen sink, stove (including oven), other appliances, and work surfaces* ☆ *Clean bathroom toilet, sink, bath/shower* ☆ *Dust and polish surfaces, ornaments, and mirrors* ☆ *Clean hallway*

NEGOTIATING A SOLUTION

1	2	3
If a person in your household is not pulling his or her weight, try to tackle the situation diplomatically by suggesting a mutually convenient time and place to talk about it. Allow plenty of time: what starts off as a "quick chat" may turn into a very long discussion.	Plan beforehand what you want to say. You need to state clearly exactly what the problem is and how you feel about it.	State the problem without sounding accusatory or overcritical. Be courteous and non-confrontational. Endeavor to show that you can also see things from his or her point of view.

✦ Clean bedroom/s (dust and polish surfaces, ornaments, and mirrors) ✦ Sweep and clean floors ✦ Vacuum carpets ✦ Shampoo carpets (every 6–12 months) ✦ Clean windows (once a month) ✦ Wash and iron curtains (or dry-clean them) ✦ Clean/defrost refrigerator/freezer ✦ Clean inside kitchen cupboards ✦ Tidy balcony or garden, including weeding and mowing grass ✦ Organize garage ✦ Feed/groom/walk any pets, and clean out cages or aquariums ✦ Wash/iron bedding, dish towels, and bathroom towels

RESOLVING CONFLICTS

✓ If a roommate is not doing their share of the chores, try to keep the atmosphere amicable. Leaving disgruntled notes or grumbling to other roommates will not encourage that person to cooperate—it is more likely to provoke a refusal to do any chores at all.

4

Explain the impact the situation is having on you and how you feel. For example, you could say, "When you don't wash your dishes, I get frustrated because I have to do yours as well as mine."

5

Give the other person a chance to explain his or her side of the story. There may be issues you have not noticed—for example, your housemate could be the only one who has been maintaining the garden and is sick of it.

6

Offer ideas for solving the problem, and invite ideas from the other person. Work out a solution between you that will keep everyone happy.

DEALING WITH HOUSEHOLD PESTS

Household pests are any insects or small creatures that come into your home uninvited. Central heating, wall-to-wall carpets, houseplants, or dropped food crumbs can all attract unwanted attention from pests. Scrupulous cleaning, regular vacuuming, efficient disposal of garbage, and careful attention to pets are key to pest prevention. However, if you still get invaded, here are some tips to help you evict unwanted guests.

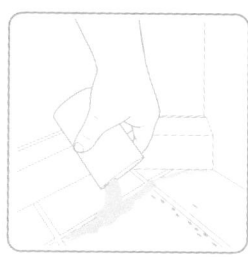

COMBAT ANTS WITH TALC

ANTS

If black ants become a nuisance, remove any food that might be attracting them and try pouring some peppermint oil into their nest and at points of entry to encourage them to move elsewhere. Ants don't like chili powder either, or dried bay leaves, dried basil, or lemon juice/lemon rind. You can also mix some sugar with talcum powder or borax and leave it near the nest. Keep children and pets away from it. The ants will take it back to their nest and eat the powder, eradicating themselves.

BEDBUGS

Bites from these oval-shaped, dark-brown little pests cause extremely uncomfortable itching and swelling and can spread diseases. Bedbugs can very easily hitch a ride into a clean home, so if you find your bedding has been colonized, throw out the mattress immediately. Put the bedding in a very hot wash with strong detergent to kill any remaining insects or eggs.

CARPET BEETLES

These little brown, ridged insects look like mobile coffee beans, but there the similarity ends. They adore carpets, fur, wool, and fluff—not because they make comfy bedding but because their larvae eat them. If you come across any of these little textile pests, the best way to rid your home of them is to vacuum regularly and thoroughly and spray the affected areas with an aerosol mothproofer. Pay particular attention to the edges of carpets because these bugs often head for the crevices between carpet and wall, where fluff and fur tend to accumulate.

HOT WATER
You can get rid of ants outdoors by pouring hot water over them, but beware of killing any plants that you wish to keep.

BEES AND WASPS

☑ If you need to move a bee or wasp outside, take a large jar or glass and place it over the insect, trapping it against a flat surface. Slide a piece of card or stiff paper under the glass, then go outside and release the insect into the open air. You can also use this method to evict spiders.

EVICTING OTHER HOUSEHOLD PESTS

MICE AND RATS

☑ These creatures can spread disease and are attracted to food, so keep all food well wrapped and out of reach. Instead of using cheese, which can spoil and smell, put a piece of chocolate in your mousetrap. You can also buy humane mousetraps, which catch the mouse but do not kill them. If you can find their hole, put a little dish of peppermint oil in front of it—this'll let them know they're not welcome.

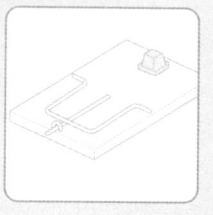

EARWIGS

These insects love houseplants, especially dahlias, so remove any infected plants and keep garden creepers away from entry points to your home. You can also ring-fence your home with a good barrier insecticide.

FLEAS

The most common way for fleas to come into your home is by hitching a ride on your pet. Consult your vet on the best way to treat animals; usually a flea spray will be recommended, and you can also get one for your home. Vacuum thoroughly, especially carpets, upholstery, and pet bedding, then throw away the vacuum cleaner bag or the fleas may continue to thrive in it. Spray your home according to the manufacturer's instructions. Repeat the process a day later to kill off any remaining eggs. A traditional way of keeping your pet free of fleas is to mash a clove of garlic into its food once a week.

FLIES

Flies have some unpleasant habits: they vomit on food before eating it to soften it up, they defecate

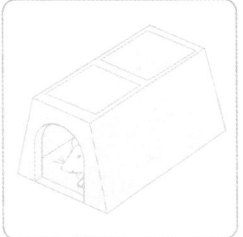

A HUMANE MOUSETRAP

every 4–5 minutes, and they spread disease. They are also attracted to food, so food preparation areas in the home are particularly vulnerable. Never leave leftovers lying around, and always seal garbage bags and take them out regularly. Make sure your trash can is clean and smells fresh. Citronella oil or citronella candles are a popular deterrent, and flypaper is an efficient way of catching flies without using aerosol sprays. If you do use a spray, choose one that is CFC-free.

ROACHES

These resilient creatures have an unpleasant smell and can spread dangerous diseases such as dysentery and typhoid through their excrement. If you find them in your home, you might be able to get rid of them by removing anything that may be attracting them, such as easily accessible food or old cardboard boxes, then clean everywhere thoroughly and zap their entry point with either a commercial product or some borax. If that doesn't work, you will have to call in specialist help.

SILVERFISH

 *These small, silvery insects are harmless to humans and adore damp environments. For some inexplicable reason, however, they like to eat wallpaper adhesive and book glue. To eradicate them, try to get rid of the source of the dampness. Mix some baking soda in a jar with a few drops of lavender water and leave for 24 hours. Sprinkle the mixture over your carpets, leave it for 30 minutes, then vacuum off. Alternatively, use half sugar and half borax if you keep children and pets out of the way.*

PLANTS AND FLOWERS IN THE HOME

Houseplants and flowers make wonderful decorations and bring the beauty of nature into our homes. However, they need care and regular cleaning to keep them at their best. Plants need to absorb sunlight and carbon dioxide to thrive, but if their leaves are covered with dust or grease, they won't be able to absorb as much sunlight through their pores, and this will make them look dull, unattractive and unhealthy. To a plant, it's like trying to eat your dinner through a colander.

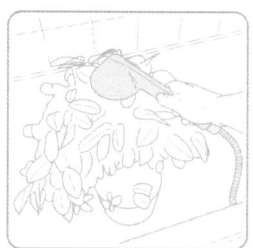

SHOWER LARGE PLANTS

WASH SMALL PLANTS IN SINK

BATHTIME FOR HOUSEHOLD PLANTS

Give your plants a bath every couple of months and they will love you for it. Wash small plants in the sink and larger ones under the shower or in the bath. You can also take them outside and hose them down gently. If your plant is too large or heavy to be moved, moisten a soft sponge with water and gently wipe the leaves clean. For really dirty plants, add a drop or two of mild liquid soap, not detergent. Rinse off afterward. Once the leaves are clean, some people shine them with all kinds of substances, such as milk, glycerine, egg whites, baby oil, and even mayonnaise. However, there have been claims that these block the pores and inhibit the plant's ability to absorb sunshine. The jury is out on that one.

LET PLANTS CLEAN YOUR INDOOR AIR

Recent research by NASA has shown that some plants help to purify and renew our stale indoor air by filtering out the toxins and carbon dioxide and replacing them with fresh oxygen.

Toxin/Source	Effects	Purifying plants
Benzene		
Inks, oils, paints, plastics, rubber, dyes	Irritates eyes and skin; causes headaches, drowsiness, loss of appetite, anemia	Gerbera Daisy Chrysanthemum
Formaldehyde		
Pressed wood products used to make household furniture, paper products, carpets, natural gas, cigarette smoke	Irritates membranes of nose, eyes, and throat; causes headaches and dermatitis; long exposure may also cause lung cancer	Spider Plant Golden Pothos Philodendron
Trichloroethylene		
Printing inks, paints, adhesives, varnishes	Can cause cancer of the liver	Peace Lily Chrysanthemum
Carbon monoxide		
Cigarette smoke, gas appliances	Low levels cause drowsiness and headaches; high levels can be fatal	All houseplants

CAUTION While houseplants will help to counteract low levels of household toxins in the air, they will not be effective against high concentrations. Always take added precautions—for example, in the case of carbon monoxide, check the safety of gas appliances and install carbon monoxide detectors where appropriate.

FRESHEN YOUR HOME WITH FLOWERS

Nothing makes a home look more beautiful than lovingly prepared arrangements of freshly cut or dried flowers, and the heady scent of fresh flowers can be intoxicating in any room. However, to get the most out of your flower arrangements, you need to keep them fresh and clean.

CHANGE WATER REGULARLY

KEEPING CUT FLOWERS CLEAN AND FRESH

The main thing to remember about freshly cut flowers is not to let the water in their vase stagnate or it will eventually smell very unpleasant. Change the water every other day, and remove any flowers and stems that are past their best. A pinch of salt will help keep the water fresh, and you can keep your flowers looking good for longer by dissolving an aspirin in the water.

REVIVING YOUR BLOOMS

When your cut flowers start to droop, snip off the end of each stem and stand the flowers in boiling water for a few seconds. Then plunge them up to their necks in cold water and leave them there for a few hours.

SPRUCE UP YOUR DRIED FLOWERS

Dried flowers are notoriously difficult to clean, so some people display them behind glass in order to protect them from dust and dirt. Dried flower arrangements can have thousands of tiny fragile parts, so it's little wonder that some people are unwilling to clean them. If your dried flowers are not behind glass, position them away from the kitchen, in a place that is as free from dust as possible. When you do need to clean them, try brushing gently with a feather duster. However, if the duster snags on lots of prickly parts, it might be better to start from scratch and replace the whole arrangement.

CLEANING SILK FLOWERS

Keep your silk flowers clean by dusting regularly with a feather duster. The occasional blast with a blow-dryer on a cool setting will also keep the dust at bay. If your silk flowers start to look really grimy, try washing them gently in a solution of cool water and gentle fabric wash that is suitable for silk. Rinse in cool water, shake off the excess and hang up by the stems to dry.

PROTECT YOUR FABRICS FROM POLLEN

Some flowers, such as stargazer lilies, have deeply colored pollen that stains if it comes into contact with fabrics. If pollen gets onto your upholstery or carpet, don't try wiping it up—that will cause it to stain. Simply lift it up with a strip of tape.

WASHING PLASTIC FLOWERS

✓ *A regular swish with a feather duster may be all that you need to do to keep plastic flowers clean and fresh. However, if they do become grimy or have grown a coating of dust that dusting simply cannot touch, wash them gently in a solution of warm water and dish soap, then rinse in clean water and dry with kitchen paper.*

TAPE LIFTS POLLEN

ALLERGENS

"After four years the dust doesn't get any worse."

QUENTIN CRISP

What exactly is an allergen? The answer is any substance that the body regards as foreign or potentially dangerous and that triggers a reaction in hypersensitive people. There are many different kinds of allergen. Pollens, dust, mold, fur, and feathers are allergens, and can trigger hayfever or coldlike symptoms in some people. House mites are believed to trigger some forms of asthma. Some drugs, dyes, cosmetics, and other chemicals can cause skin rashes and swelling. Sometimes allergens can trigger gastroenteritis or anaphylactic shock, and in extreme cases they can be fatal. So there are very good medical reasons for keeping your home as clear of allergens as possible.

People can develop allergies at any time of life—they are not necessarily born with them. Allergens can cause a wide range of symptoms, such as a runny nose, fatigue, red and irritated eyes, headache, problems with breathing or digestion, rashes, and insomnia. Symptoms can drag on for days, weeks, or even months. Some people have allergy symptoms for most of the year, while others have them during certain seasons. If you have an allergy sufferer in your home, or are likely to be visited by one, you need to be extra meticulous when it comes to cleaning. Although it is impossible to clear your home of allergens completely, you can reduce their effects substantially by taking extra precautions.

For seasonal sufferers, spring and summer—and sometimes fall—are usually the worst times of year. Tree and grass pollen counts are higher during these seasons, and fleas proliferate in the warmth. Cats and dogs are molting at this time, too, causing extra problems for hypersensitive people. The good news is that taking simple precautions, such as having a good cleaning regime, can substantially reduce the amount of allergens in your home during these periods and help allergy sufferers to feel far more comfortable.

COPING WITH DUST ALLERGIES

Some people are extra sensitive to dust, but what they are really reacting to is not the dust but the feces produced by dust mites. These tiny insects feed on the flakes of skin we shed in the home, and it is estimated that up to 2,000 dust mites can live in around 1 oz (25 g) of dust in an average mattress alone. Sneezing, coughing, streaming eyes and nose, rashes, and breathing problems are just some of the symptoms caused by sensitivity to dust mites.

DUST ANYONE?

✔ The recipe for your average household dust includes some unpleasant ingredients. First take a generous quantity of skin flakes, add some dust-mite corpses, droppings, and eggs, sprinkle in some volcanic ash, then throw in a dash of mold spores, bacteria, and viruses. Mix together well. This concoction is usually breathed in or consumed along with food and drinks.

☆ Taking a laid-back approach to dust in the house carries significant health risks. Dust attracts pests, and asthma sufferers in particular are at risk if exposed to high levels of house dust. People who suffer from hay fever or sinusitis are usually hyper-sensitive to it too, so it is important to keep your home as dust free as possible. The trouble is, dust doesn't simply settle on any accessible surface and stay there. It also becomes airborne easily and is quickly distributed throughout your living environment, so that the dust that was under the couch ends up in your nostrils or in your food. You may be breathing in a veritable soup of bugs and pests every time you disturb your household dust, just by flopping onto a couch or fluffing up a pillow.

DUST IN THE WORKS

⭐ *Electrical appliances are not keen on dust either, although you never hear them sneezing. Dust can clog up their components and cause operating faults in a range of appliances—if it gets into the RAM (Random Access Memory) of your home computer, for example, it can cause it to fail. Dust on electrical components is also suspected of causing house fires, so it is vital to keep your TV, computer, and any other electrical appliances dust free and squeaky clean.*

FIRE, FIRE
Dust on electrical components is suspected of being one of the causes of house fires, so it is extremely important to keep your TV, computer, and any other electrical appliances as dust free as possible.

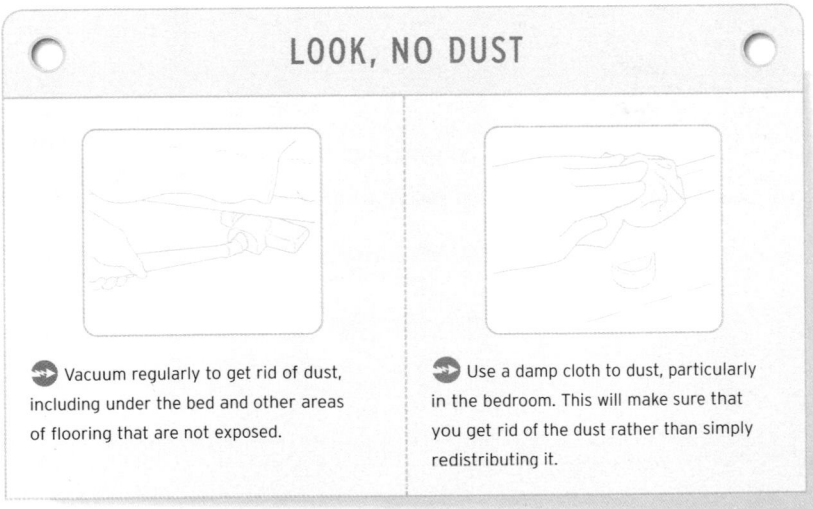

LOOK, NO DUST

Vacuum regularly to get rid of dust, including under the bed and other areas of flooring that are not exposed.

Use a damp cloth to dust, particularly in the bedroom. This will make sure that you get rid of the dust rather than simply redistributing it.

TACKLING DUST IN THE HOME

One of the worst things about dust is that it carries dust mites. Dust mites love a warm, dark, damp environment, and their favorite place is the bedroom. Humans regularly perspire and shed skin scales into their beds, and this is heaven for a dust mite. Not that they won't colonize every part of your home. Wherever there is a warm environment and flakes of skin—on pillows, bedding, mattresses, upholstery, carpets, floors, stuffed toys—dust mites will be having a field day.

HOW TO KEEP DUST AND MITES AT BAY

⭐ *The only way to keep dust and mites at bay is by frequent and thorough cleaning. Keep clutter in your home to a minimum, and dust and vacuum as often as*

SOFT toys can be a prime site for dust mites. Put the toy into a plastic bag and seal it.

LEAVE it in the freezer overnight. This will kill the mites, but you will also need to wash the toy to get rid of the dead mites or any allergen residue.

SOFT TOYS

you can. A daily clean is not excessive if you have an allergy sufferer in your household. Unfortunately, the very act of dusting and sweeping stirs up the allergens, so throw open windows and doors to air your house, and let the light in. Dust mites don't like sunny, airy places, so try to expose them to sunshine and ventilate your home as much as possible.

☆ Use allergen and mite-proof covers for pillows, mattresses and covers. You can buy these from large department stores, or by mail order from specialist suppliers. Throw back the covers each morning to air bedding and mattresses, and wash all bedding once a week on a hot setting (140°F/60°C or hotter). Recent studies show that feather pillows—when enclosed in allergen-proof covers—tend to accumulate fewer dust-mite allergens than polyester ones.

☆ If you can afford it, use a vacuum cleaner with an HEPA (High Efficiency Particulate Air) filter. Don't forget that clothes harbor dust mites, too. If you can, launder them at over 140°F (60°C). If the garment can't take that kind of temperature, wash or dry-clean often and air in a sunny place (preferably outside).

PRODUCTS FOR ALLERGY PROTECTION

You can go online to order products for your allergy-fighting arsenal, such as pillows, comforters, and dust-mite detector kits. Two websites to get you started are www.allergycontrol.com and www.natlallergy.com

ALLERGIES AND HOUSEHOLD PETS

People who are allergic to animals are not usually reacting to their fur, but to the animal's dander (skin flakes) and dried saliva. Animal hair is simply a carrier of these allergens, which is why most people think they are allergic to the fur. It therefore makes little difference whether your animal is short-haired or long-haired, except that long-haired creatures tend to have more fur with which to spread the allergens.

KEEP PETS OUTSIDE

Animal allergies among humans are on the increase. One of the main reasons for this is that we are spending more time indoors with our pets than ever before. More and more of us are working from home or spending long periods of time at home with our pets, and this change in lifestyle is a major contributor to the increase in allergy cases.

GROOMING YOUR PET

⭐ *If a member of your household is allergic to an animal, the most efficient way to keep your living space allergen free is to remove the pet from the house. If this course of action is unacceptable, you should at least shut your pets out of bedrooms and keep them off cushions and upholstered furniture. In any case, your pet needs to be groomed regularly* in order to keep allergens to a minimum. Ideally, this isn't a job for the allergy sufferer, but if you are an allergy sufferer who has to groom your own pet, then invest in a protective face mask and take a bath or shower once you've done grooming.

☆ Some experts recommend that in households with allergy sufferers, dogs and cats should be brushed daily and dogs bathed once a week (see pages 214–15). You can also buy special wipes containing anti-allergenic liquids to use between baths to keep the amount of allergens on your pet down.

PRECAUTIONARY MEASURES

☆ Reduce the amount of stray animal hair and allergens by vacuuming daily, if possible, including your pet's bedding. Some animals will even let you vacuum them, and even seem to enjoy it. If this is the case, use the small upholstery attachment, or even invest in a special animal vacuum.

☆ Keep litter boxes, pet bedding, and cages in a well-ventilated room.

CLEAN HANDS

 Always wash your hands after handling or playing with pets to avoid transferring allergens or bacteria.

KEEP YOUR PET WELL OILED

In order to keep your dog or cat in sleek condition and to prevent its skin from drying out from frequent bathing, add a few drops of olive oil to its food two or three times a week.

ELIMINATING PET ALLERGENS

Brushing and bathing your pet regularly is only part of the battle. Wherever your pet roams, allergens will be present. They can sometimes linger months after the pet is gone and you have cleaned the house. Pet allergens can stick to surfaces and fabrics, including walls, floors, carpets, drapes, clothes, and upholstery. They may also be present in an animal's urine, and when it dries, allergens become airborne and inhaled. Cat allergens are the worst because they are so small—they can float through the air to every part of your living space. A thorough cleaning regime is therefore essential to keep pet allergens out of your home.

GOOD HABITS
You will need to be vigilant and consistent when it comes to keeping pet allergens at bay. Don't let your pets in the bedrooms, and discourage them from climbing onto furniture. Making exceptions risks ruining the whole effect and also confusing your animal.

PROTECTING YOURSELF FROM ALLERGENS

Dusting, sweeping, and vacuuming your home will stir up the allergens so that they circulate in the air. If you are the allergy sufferer, it therefore makes sense to get someone else to do the cleaning for you. If this is not possible, then protect yourself by opening windows and doors, and wear a dust mask while you are cleaning and for at least half an hour afterward.

CHECKLIST FOR AN ALLERGEN-FREE HOME

Use the following checklist to keep pet allergens out of your home. If you can't manage to do some of these things daily, do them as frequently as you can.

☆ Keep any litter boxes in a well-ventilated space.

☆ Ventilate your home as much as possible by opening windows and doors, especially when you are dusting and vacuuming.

☆ If you have a garden or other outside space, let your pet go outside as much as possible to keep down the level of allergens in your home.

CLEAN CAGES OUTSIDE

☆ Keep your home clutter free and dust it daily.

☆ Vacuum your home daily, preferably with a vacuum cleaner that has a HEPA (High Efficiency Particulate Air) filter.

☆ Use the suction tool on your vacuum cleaner to vacuum drapes, upholstery, and the crevices between carpets and walls. Don't forget to vacuum your pet's bedding (or the places where pets sleep) daily, if possible, or at least every few days.

VACUUM YOUR PET'S BEDDING

☆ Wash down all hard surfaces and floors daily.

☆ Never wash animal bedding, cages, or tanks in the kitchen sink—clean them outside, if possible.

KEEPING MOLD UNDER CONTROL

Mold is a type of fungus similar to a mushroom or yeast. Its ability to decompose organic materials gives it a role as nature's declutterer. Without it, organic matter would continue to spread until virtually no room was left in the world. In order to establish itself, mold needs to suck nutrients from dead organic materials. Most people think that mold only exists when they can see it growing, but the truth is that mold spores may be present when you can't see anything at all.

WASH AWAY MOLD GROWTH

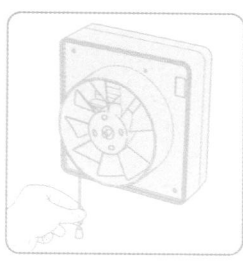

USE EXTRACTOR FANS

KEEP THAT MOLD AT BAY

Mold will proliferate in warm, damp environments, so look for it in places that gather moisture, such as window frames and the drip pan in your refrigerator. Bathrooms and kitchens are especially prone to mold. Here are some tips to keep your home mold free:

☆ *Make sure your home is well ventilated, and the air is dry. Open the window whenever the bathroom is in use, or install an extractor fan to help keep moisture levels at a minimum.*

☆ *Dry laundry immediately after washing—do not allow it to remain damp.*

☆ *To avoid condensation, fit sealed-unit double-glazed windows and do not leave damp clothes on warm radiators to dry.*

☆ Open a window or turn on your extractor fan whenever you are cooking.

☆ Use a HEPA filter. These devices can filter a substantial amount of particles from the air and reduce allergic symptoms significantly.

☆ Check any damp walls for mold, especially behind wallpaper. Strip off the wallpaper if necessary, then wash the wall with a solution of water and household bleach. Leave to dry thoroughly, then paint the wall with mold-resistant paint. If you want to hang more wallpaper, use fungicidal wallpaper paste.

☆ To remove patches of mildew in your bathroom or basement, clean the area with a solution of 9 fl oz (250 ml) household bleach to 1 gallon (4.5 liters) of water. Leave to dry and ensure that the area is well ventilated. For more serious problems, use a dehumidifier if necessary, or consult a specialist.

MOLD AS AN ALLERGEN

✓ Although mold has a beneficial role as a declutterer, and is a valuable source of medical drugs such as the antibiotic penicillin, it can also trigger allergic reactions in sensitive people. What is simply an unsightly fungus to one person can be a source of unpleasant symptoms to another. A mold allergy can be difficult to distinguish from a cold; it is often characterized by a streaming, itchy nose and sometimes difficulty with breathing. Coughing, wheezing and a general feeling of being unwell are all symptoms of a mold allergy. Mold can also trigger asthma attacks.

HOUSEHOLD CHEMICALS

Our households are full of chemicals that can trigger allergic reactions in sensitive individuals. It is hard to eradicate such chemicals completely from the home, because some are present in house-building and furnishing materials. Formaldehyde, for example, is used to bond plywood, carpets, and fabrics, and it contributes to that "new car smell." It is a pungent, colorless gas that is found in tobacco smoke, vehicle exhausts, and fumes from fireplaces. Symptoms of over-exposure to formaldehyde include irritation to eyes, nose, and throat; persistent cough and breathing problems; skin irritation; nausea; headache; and dizziness. (*See also pages 228–29.*)

IRRITANTS

The amount of household products containing allergy-inducing chemicals includes:

☆ *Antifreeze*
☆ *Pesticides*
☆ *Cleaning products—disinfectant, bleach, detergent, soaps, window cleaners, oven cleaners*
☆ *Toiletries*
☆ *Household paints, thinners, and other solvents*
☆ *Wood preservatives*
☆ *Aerosol sprays*
☆ *Moth repellents and air fresheners*

SIDE EFFECTS OF HOUSEHOLD CHEMICALS

The side effects of household chemicals depend on their toxicity, your sensitivity, and the level and duration of exposure. Symptoms range from eye, nose, and throat irritation, breathing problems, coughing, headaches, rashes, loss of coordination, and nausea. Some chemicals may trigger asthma attacks or cause liver or kidney damage—they may even be carcinogenic.

HOW TO PROTECT YOURSELF

In order to protect yourself and your household from the harmful effects of household chemicals, try to use products that are made from safe, natural ingredients as much as possible. However, if you do have to use strong chemicals, here are some tips to help you:

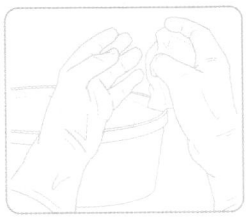

☆ Use protective gloves when using chemicals, and a face mask if necessary. If any chemical does come into contact with your skin, wash thoroughly in cool, clean water. If a reaction results, consult your doctor.

ALWAYS WEAR RUBBER GLOVES

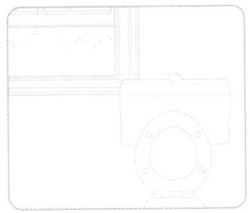

☆ Be sparing when using strong bleaches and disinfectants, or other hazardous products. When using cleaners, always make sure that there is plenty of ventilation to prevent you from inhaling toxic fumes. Never continue to use any products that make you short of breath or cause any other symptoms.

KEEP AREAS VENTILATED

☆ Read all labels carefully and follow the manufacturer's instructions. Never mix products unless the label says you can—some combinations, for example, can create fumes that damage your lungs. The chemicals used in some powdered laundry detergents can sometimes cause skin irritation or breathing difficulties. Switch to an enzyme-free, phosphate-free variety.

ENZYME-FREE PRODUCTS

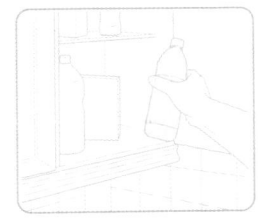

☆ Store products containing hazardous chemicals out of the reach of children, and label them well to avoid mistaking one product for another. Don't forget items such as mothballs, glue, and even some air fresheners.

KEEP CHEMICALS OUT OF REACH

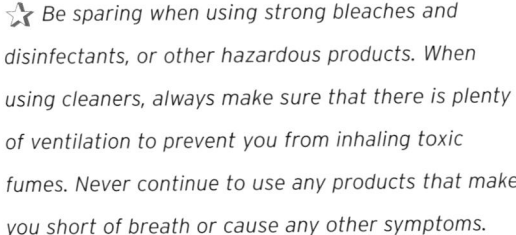

A–Z STAIN
REMOVAL
LIBRARY

THE SCIENCE OF STAIN REMOVAL

" Out, damned spot! Out, I say!"

LADY MACBETH, *MACBETH*

Nowadays you can buy a specialist remover for almost every kind of spill or stain. The focus is increasingly on producing substances that are both environmentally friendly and gentle on fabrics and surfaces.

Ideally, stains and spills should be dealt with immediately, or at least as quickly as possible—stains may not disappear entirely with the first treatment, but repeat applications will at least decrease their severity. Where possible, treat the stain from the back, and always work from the outside in toward the center to avoid spreading the stain further. If you can, pad the underside with paper towels or rags to soak up excess fluid and prevent the stain from transferring to the material underneath.

Commercially produced stain-removing products and solvents nearly all contain hazardous chemicals, so it is important to take time to read the manufacturer's instructions before you start using them. Always wear rubber gloves to protect your hands, and work in a well-ventilated space. Remember that the stronger the substance you are using, the more risk there is that some color may also be removed from the fabric or surface itself. Test all fabrics for colorfastness by applying stain remover to an inconspicuous patch first. Cheaper, greener alternatives to chemical cleaners—such as lemon juice, baking soda, and vinegar—can also be extremely efficient methods of getting rid of stains and marks. When taking items to be dry-cleaned, point out any stains that need to be treated.

Before settling down to a stain-removal session, make sure you have a supply of absorbent material such as paper towels, clean rags or cloths (preferably cotton), along with cotton pads, cotton swabs, soft brushes, and sponges. If you can't deal with the problem right away, a good way to remind yourself is to attach a clothespin to the offending garment before you throw it in your hamper.

A–Z OF STAINS

ACID

☆ Even weak acid solutions can damage fabric fibers (particularly cotton, linen, nylon, and viscose) and remove color, so any acid spills or splashes should be treated immediately. Flush with cold water and then dab on a little diluted ammonia (following the instructions on the bottle) or baking soda solution. Rinse well.

ADHESIVE

If possible, check the packaging for any recommendations or contact the manufacturer for advice. Many modern glues cannot be removed once they have dried, so they need to be treated as soon as the accident occurs.

Stickers and sticky labels

☆ Soak the item in warm, soapy water. If the glue is water-based, the sticker should come off easily. If you cannot immerse the item, place a wet cloth or paper towel over the sticker area.

☆ Rub with wood alcohol or mineral spirits.

☆ Fix a piece of sticky tape over the sticker or glue residue and peel away. Repeat until all the glue has been removed.

☆ For small items, such as glasses or containers, place the article in the freezer for an hour or two. Once the glue has frozen, lift or scrape it off, taking care not to damage your surface.

☆ On hard surfaces, pour a little oil (baby, vegetable, or eucalyptus) onto a paper towel or rag and rub into the area. Either peel the sticker away with your fingers, or use a blunt knife or spoon to lift it away. The oil will soften the adhesive, allowing it to come right off. Rinse and wash the area with warm, soapy water to remove any residue.

Animal and fish glues

☆ Soak in cold water. If this doesn't work, use an ammonia solution and rinse. Repeat if necessary, then wash with liquid detergent and rinse again.

Clear adhesives

☆ Dab the affected area with acetone or non-oily nail polish remover. (Do not use on acetate-based fabric.)

Contact adhesives

☆ Wash with cold water. If the glue has started to dry, dab with wood alcohol.

Latex adhesives (e.g., white school glue)

☆ Wash away with a wet cloth. Scrape or rub away if the glue has started to dry. If this doesn't work, try using paint thinner or paintbrush cleaner. On upholstery and carpets, wash the area with mild detergent, then treat the stain with a solution of 1 part ammonia solution to 6 parts water.

Model-making cement

☆ Remove as much residue as possible with a cloth, then dab with acetone or non-oily nail polish remover. (Do not use on acetate-based fabric.) On wooden surfaces, rub the area with a little sunflower oil.

☆ Contact the manufacturer for advice on solvents.

ALCOHOL

Washables

☆ Sponge with warm water, or soak with soda water, then wash as normal.

Non-washables

☆ Dab the area with a cloth dipped in warm, soapy water. Rinse and blot.

☆ On upholstery, treat with carpet or upholstery shampoo, if necessary.

See also Beer, Perfume, Wine

ALKALI

☆ Alkali substances can permanently damage fabrics, particularly polyester or polyester blends, so wash immediately, as for acid. Rinse in cold water and neutralize any last traces of alkali with vinegar. Rinse well.

AMMONIA

☆ Rinse with cold water and treat the area with a solution of equal parts white vinegar and water. Rinse and repeat if necessary. Wash as normal or sponge clean and blot dry.

ANIMAL STAINS

☆ Animal messes should be cleaned up as quickly as possible. To start, scrape or wipe away as much as you can and blot up liquids with paper towels.

Washables

☆ Soak in enzyme detergent for as long as possible and rinse thoroughly. For persistent stains, apply a solution of warm water and liquid detergent with a few drops of hydrogen peroxide. Rinse, then wash as normal.

Non-washables

☆ Scrape or blot as much as possible, then take to a dry cleaner.

ANTIPERSPIRANT *see* DEODORANT

BABY FOOD

Washables

☆ Wipe away any excess, then flush the stain with cold water. For dried-on stains, soak in mild detergent solution for 30 minutes or longer. Rinse well. If the stain remains, soak in enzyme solution. If necessary, apply pre-wash treatment and launder as normal. On white fabrics, treat persistent stains with lemon juice and hang out to dry in the sunshine.

Non-washables

☆ Remove excess and sponge with a mild detergent solution. Rinse and blot dry. Repeat if necessary. If the stain persists, take to a dry cleaner.

Upholstery, carpets

☆ Treat as for non-washables. For persistent stains, treat with dry-cleaning solution and follow with upholstery or carpet cleaner.

BABY FORMULA

Washables

☆ Soak in cold water, rubbing the stain occasionally. To tackle dried-on or persistent stains, soak in enzyme detergent for 30–60 minutes, or several hours if the stain is old. If necessary, apply a pre-wash treatment and wash as normal.

Non-washables

☆ Sponge with cold water, then wipe with liquid detergent solution. If the stain persists, treat with a solution of equal parts vinegar and water, or dry-cleaning solvent. Rinse and blot dry.

Upholstery, carpets

☆ Treat as for non-washables.

BAKED BEANS

Washables

☆ Flush the stain with cold water. Rub some enzyme detergent into the fabric and rinse. If the stain persists, sponge with dilute bleach, white vinegar, hydrogen peroxide solution, or lemon juice and rinse well. If necessary, soak in enzyme detergent or apply a pre-wash treatment, then wash.

Non-washables

☆ Remove any excess, then sponge the area with mild detergent solution. If the stain persists, treat with stain remover or dry-cleaning solvent.

Upholstery, carpets

☆ Treat as for non-washables. Finish with upholstery or carpet cleaner if necessary.

BALLPOINT PEN see INK

BARBECUE SAUCE see KETCHUP AND CHUTNEY

BEER

Washables

☆ Rinse with water. If the stain remains, wash with a solution of mild detergent and warm water. If needed, treat with a pre-wash stain remover and wash on as hot a setting as possible.

☆ For persistent stains, treat with a solution of 1 part white vinegar to 5 parts water and blot immediately. Rinse well.

Non-washables

☆ Treat with vinegar solution as above.

BEETS

Washables

☆ Soak in cold water for several hours, then rub the stained area with detergent. (For woollens, don't rub but gently squeeze the detergent solution through the wool.) If the stain persists, soak in enzyme detergent and sprinkle a little borax on the stain, flush with boiling water and then wash as normal.

Non-washables

☆ Sponge with cold water to dilute the stain, then have the item dry-cleaned.

Upholstered items and carpets

☆ Wet the stain with soda water or cold water and blot with paper towels, then treat with carpet or upholstery shampoo. Alternatively, soak a slice of white bread in water or soda water and place over the stain to absorb the color. Replace as necessary, then shampoo to finish.

BIRD DROPPINGS

Washables

☆ Soak washable articles in cold water, then rub the area with liquid detergent. (If the article is woollen, don't rub, but squeeze the solution through the wool.) If the stain persists, soak in a solution of enzyme detergent and warm water or apply a stain remover or pre-wash treatment, then wash as normal.

Non-washables

☆ Sponge or wipe with cold water, then treat with a solution of 4 tablespoons ammonia to half a bucket of water. Next, dab on a little vinegar and rinse. On canvas (such as umbrellas or awnings), brush with a stiff brush that has been run across a bar of laundry soap and sprinkled with washing soda crystals. Hose well and rinse.

BLEACH AND HYDROGEN PEROXIDE

☆ Rinse with cold water to remove as much of the acid as possible, then sponge with ammonia. (For silk or wool, use a solution of equal parts water and ammonia.) If possible, place paper towels or rags under the fabric to absorb any moisture. Alternatively, rub a paste of baking soda and water into the area, leave to dry, then brush or vacuum.

BLOOD

☆ Soak in cold water, then treat with a pre-wash stain remover, or rub some laundry detergent into the stain and wash as normal. For woollen items, don't rub—squeeze the solution through the wool. If the stain has dried, soak in enzyme detergent first or apply a pre-wash treatment. Or add 3 tablespoons of ammonia to a bowl of cold water and soak for 15–20 minutes.

☆ Coat fresh blood stains with a paste of water and cornstarch, or talcum powder. Leave to dry, then brush off.

Leather
☆ For fresh bloodstains, dab on a little hydrogen peroxide. Once it bubbles, wipe off.

Upholstery or mattresses
☆ Sponge fresh stains with cold water. Treat stubborn stains with hydrogen peroxide solution (1 part 20-strength peroxide to 4 parts water) plus a few drops of ammonia.

BRASS and BRONZE *see* COPPER

BURNT-ON FOOD

☆ Save old credit cards for scraping away burnt-on food from pots and pans.

BUTTER, MARGARINE, FAT, AND OIL

Washables
☆ Scrape off any excess, then, if appropriate, wash on as hot a cycle as possible.

Non-washables
☆ Blot, then treat with a grease solvent or enzyme detergent. On wallpaper, use a warm iron and paper towels. Treat remaining marks with a paste of cornstarch and dry-cleaning solvent. Allow to dry, then brush off. On carpets, after treating the stain, use a carpet-cleaning powder.

Upholstery and carpets
☆ Scrape off the excess, then dab with a little dry-cleaning solvent. Wash away with a mild detergent solution and blot dry. Alternatively, sprinkle with baking soda, talcum powder, or carpet-cleaning powder, and then vacuum. **See *also* Fat, Hot**

CANDLE WAX

☆ For spilled wax on fabric, carpets, and upholstery, scrape away excess, then place brown paper or paper towels over the dried wax and pass a warm iron over the area. (If possible, pad the underneath of the stain, too.) The paper will absorb the hot wax.

☆ On wood floors and hard surfaces, use a blow-dryer to soften the wax, then blot with paper towels. To finish, wash the area with a solution of vinegar and water. Alternatively, lift as much wax away as possible with a plastic knife or spatula, then clean and polish as normal.

☆ For small items, place in the freezer until the wax has frozen, then pick the pieces off. For larger items, rub the area with an ice cube (placed inside a plastic bag if you don't want the item to get wet). To finish, treat with a warm to hot iron and paper, if necessary, then wash as normal. On carpets, rub the area with wood alcohol, then sponge with diluted carpet shampoo.

CAR POLISH AND WAX

☆ Treat the stain first with some dry-cleaning solvent, then some liquid detergent. Rinse well.

CARAMEL

☆ Flush with cold water, treat with liquid detergent and rinse. If necessary, treat with a solution of equal parts hydrogen peroxide and water and rinse well. To finish, wash on as hot a setting as possible or sponge with detergent solution. Treat persistent stains with stain remover or dry-cleaning solvent.

CDs, MARKS AND SCRATCHES ON

☆ To get rid of marks or scratches on CDs or repair damaged disks, use a soft cloth and gently rub a little white toothpaste into the mark or scratch. Rinse with warm water and dry thoroughly. Furniture polish or peanut butter can be used instead of toothpaste.

CHALK

☆ Shake or vacuum to get rid of any loose chalk. If a stain remains, place the item stain down on some paper towels or rags and blot the back of the stain with rubbing alcohol. Replace padding as necessary. Wash or sponge with soapy water.

CHARCOAL see SOOT AND CHARCOAL

CHEESE see MILK, CREAM, CHEESE, AND YOGURT

CHEWING GUM

☆ Put small items into the freezer until the gum has set, then lift or chip off the gum with a knife or spoon. For larger items, rub the gum with an ice cube (inside a plastic bag if you don't want the material to get wet) until the gum hardens, then lift or chip it away. Any remaining pieces or marks can be removed with wood alcohol or a solution of white vinegar.

☆ Soften gum on clothes with egg white before washing, or sponge with a dry-cleaning solvent.

To remove chewing gum from hair
☆ Rub facial cleansing cream into the affected area, then pull the strands of hair through a piece of old towel—the gum will transfer onto the towel.

CHOCOLATE

Washables
☆ Soak or flush with cold water or soda water. Treat the area with liquid detergent, then rinse well. Treat any remaining stains with a solution of 1 part ammonia to 5 parts water and blot. Wash on a hot cycle if possible, or wash the area with warm, soapy water, rinse and blot dry.

Non-washables
☆ Scrape off the excess, then get the item dry-cleaned.

Upholstery and carpets
☆ Treat with mild detergent, a weak solution of upholstery or carpet cleaner, or a weak ammonia solution. Sponge with clean water and blot.

COD LIVER OIL

These stains need to be treated immediately, as they are otherwise almost impossible to remove.

☆ Scoop up or wipe away any excess, then treat the back of the stain with a specially formulated grease-removing solution and wash using a strong detergent.

On carpets

☆ Remove any excess and clean with a dry-foam carpet cleaner.

On baby clothes

☆ Sponge with a strong solution of mild detergent and wash as normal.

COFFEE AND TEA

Washables

☆ Wipe away excess, then soak or flush with cold water or soda water. Treat the area with mild detergent, then rinse well. Treat any remaining stains with a solution of 1 part white vinegar to 2 parts water, equal parts hydrogen peroxide and water, or a solution of 1 tablespoon borax to 2 cups warm water, and blot. If necessary, soak again in enzyme detergent solution. Wash on a hot cycle, if possible, or wash the area with warm, soapy water, then rinse and blot dry.

☆ For dried-on stains, work a little glycerine into the stain, then soak in a bowl of hot water, or treat with dry-cleaning solvent or wood alcohol.

Non-washables

☆ Sponge stains with dry-cleaning solvent or stain remover, or treat the affected area with borax solution (as for washables). If necessary, take to a dry cleaner.

Countertops and walls

☆ Coat the stain or mark with a paste of baking soda and water. Leave for 10–15 minutes, then wipe away. Rinse if necessary.

☆ Soak milky coffee stains in enzyme detergent and wash as normal.

Carpets and upholstery

☆ Spray with soda water, then wash the area with mild detergent solution, clean with carpet shampoo, or treat the area with borax solution (as for washables). For old stains, try treating with a solution of equal parts glycerine and water. Leave for 30 minutes, then rinse well and blot.

Mugs and cups

☆ Clean mugs and cups with tea and coffee stains by wiping with a damp cloth sprinkled with baking soda, or soak in a solution of enzyme detergent or a weak bleach solution. Rinse thoroughly.

COLA

Washables

☆ *Flush immediately with cold water, or leave to soak for 15–30 minutes. Treat from the back of the stain with a liquid detergent, then rinse well. For stubborn stains, treat with mineral spirits or a solution of wood alcohol mixed with a few drops of vinegar, then rinse.*

Non-washables

☆ *Dab with cold water or spray with soda water, but avoid drenching the area. Treat with wood alcohol, rinse well, and blot dry.*

Upholstery and carpets

☆ *Treat with a mild detergent solution, then treat with a solution of 2 parts white vinegar to 3 parts water. Blot dry.*

COLLAR AND CUFF GRIME

Washables

☆ *Scrub the affected area with shampoo or pre-wash treatment, leave for a few minutes, then wash as normal. Alternatively, soak in a weak chlorine bleach solution (3 tablespoons of bleach to one bucket of water) for 5–15 minutes, then wash as normal.*

Non-washables

☆ *Take to a dry cleaner.*

COPIER TONER

Washables

☆ *Rub the stain with some undiluted liquid detergent and rinse. If the stain remains, add a few drops of ammonia to the detergent and repeat. Alternatively, treat as for non-washables, below.*

Non-washables

☆ *Dab with wood alcohol or mineral spirits (unless rayon or acetate, in which case use a specially formulated stain remover).*

COPPER, BRASS, AND BRONZE

☆ To get rid of stains, spread the surface with tomato ketchup. Leave for 10–15 minutes, then wipe off. Rinse, then buff dry to finish.

CORRECTION FLUID

☆ Dab with amyl acetate and leave to dry. Repeat if necessary. Once the stain has completely disappeared, wash as normal or sponge the area with mild detergent solution.

COSMETICS

Washables

☆ Wipe away any excess, then rub glycerine or petroleum jelly into the stain to loosen it. On nylon fabrics, use wood alcohol. If the stain persists, use a stain remover or grease solvent.

☆ Alternatively, treat with some dry-cleaning solvent, then apply a weak detergent solution that includes a few drops of ammonia. Wash as normal.

Non-washables

☆ Apply a dry-cleaning solvent. If the stain remains, take to a dry cleaner.

Upholstery and carpets

☆ Remove excess. Treat with a dry-cleaning solvent. To finish, apply an upholstery or carpet shampoo.

See also Lipstick, Mascara

COUGH SYRUP

Washables

☆ Flush the area with cold water, then wash in a solution of mild detergent and warm water. Treat remaining marks with diluted ammonia, then mineral spirits. Rinse well and wash as normal.

Non-washables

☆ Sponge with cold water, then dab with mild detergent and warm water. Treat remaining marks with diluted ammonia, then mineral spirits or a little dry-cleaning solution. Rinse well and blot dry.

Upholstery and carpets

☆ Treat as for non-washables. To finish, clean the area with carpet or upholstery cleaner.

CRAYON

Washables

☆ For persistent stains, wipe with a cloth dipped in wood alcohol or mineral spirits, but be quick, or the fabric colors may run. Alternatively, treat with dry-cleaning solvent.

☆ Alternatively, dab away grease with mineral spirits, then soak in a solution of 1 part glycerine to 2 parts water for around an hour. Wash as normal.

☆ If a crayon has accidentally gone through the wash cycle, place the item face down on a wad of paper towels and spray with household lubricant such as WD-40. Turn over and treat the other side. Work some dishwashing liquid into the stain, then wash on as hot a cycle as possible.

Non-washables

☆ Remove excess and take to a dry cleaner.

Upholstery and carpets

☆ Brush or vacuum away any excess, then treat any remaining stains with wood alcohol or dry-cleaning solvent. Rinse well and blot dry.

Walls and ceilings

☆ Melt the crayon using a blow-dryer on a warm setting and wipe away with paper towels.

☆ Remove crayon marks from painted walls by scrubbing with toothpaste or a cloth soaked in ammonia. Rinse and blot dry.

CREAM see MILK, CREAM, CHEESE, AND YOGURT

CURRY

Washables

☆ Rinse in warm water, then rub in a solution of equal parts glycerine and water. Leave for a few minutes, then rinse. Soak in enzyme detergent, then wash. If the stain persists, soak in diluted ammonia or mineral spirits or, if the fabric can take it, 1 part hydrogen peroxide to 6 parts cold water. Then rinse well. Alternatively, try spraying the stain with hair spray, then wash as normal.

Non-washables

☆ Sponge with a solution of borax, then rinse and blot dry. For carpets, if the stain persists, treat with a solution of equal parts glycerine and water.

DEODORANT AND ANTIPERSPIRANT

Washables

☆ Coat the stain with a paste of baking soda, salt, and water, and leave for 15 minutes. Soak in enzyme detergent, then wash on as hot a setting as possible.

☆ Alternatively, treat with dry-cleaning solvent, then ammonia. Rinse thoroughly.

Non-washables

☆ Treat as above and then get dry-cleaned.

DYE

Washables

☆ Treat any splashes or spills immediately. Blot up as much as possible with paper towels, then rinse with cold water. (Hot water is likely to set the dye.) Treat with liquid detergent and rinse. Next, treat with ammonia solution and rinse again. Finally, treat with mineral spirits.

Non-washables

☆ Take non-washables to a professional dry cleaner.

Upholstery and carpets

☆ Treat small splashes with wood alcohol. Larger areas will require professional treatment.

EGG

Washables

☆ Soak in enzyme detergent. If the egg has started to set, soak in cold water first. Rinse and allow to dry. If the stain persists, treat with dry-cleaning solvent or stain remover, then wash as normal. Stubborn stains on white fabric can be soaked in a solution of 1 part hydrogen peroxide to 6 parts water plus a few drops of ammonia. Rinse well.

Non-washables

☆ Dab with dish soap, then treat with a specially formulated grease-removing solution.

Upholstery and carpets

☆ Scrape away any excess, wash with mild detergent solution, then treat with a specially formulated grease-removing solution or ammonia solution (1 part ammonia to 6 parts water). Shampoo with carpet or upholstery cleaner to finish.

FABRIC SOFTENER

☆ Moisten the stain and rub with a little soap to loosen it. Rinse or sponge with clean water. If the stain persists, dab with rubbing alcohol or dry-cleaning solvent. Wash as normal or sponge, then blot dry.

FAT, HOT

☆ Treat cottons, linens, and wool with undiluted liquid detergent, then rinse. Repeat if necessary. If any grease marks remain, dab with a little dry-cleaning solvent. Synthetic fabrics should be taken to a dry cleaner.

See also Butter, Margarine, Fat, and Oil

FECES

☆ Scrape away or blot as much as you can. Soak the area in a solution of 3 tablespoons of borax to half a bucket of warm water for 30 minutes and wash as normal, either in enzyme detergent or regular liquid detergent.   See also Animal Stains

FELT-TIP PEN see INK

FINGERPRINTS, SMUDGES, AND MARKS

☆ Dab fingerprints and smudges gently with a chunk of white bread or rub with an art eraser. Alternatively, rub gently with mild abrasive cream cleanser and a soft cloth.

☆ To get rid of heel marks, rub with a soft cloth or try using a pencil eraser.

FOOD COLORING see DYE

FRUIT AND FRUIT JUICES

Washables

☆ Rinse or soak immediately in cold water, then rub mild detergent into the stain, wash in warm water, and rinse. Treat stubborn stains (on colorfast fabric) with diluted ammonia (1 part ammonia to 8 parts water) followed by hydrogen peroxide solution (1 part to 6 parts water), then rinse well. Alternatively, leave to soak in enzyme detergent. Wash on as hot a cycle as possible.

☆ Dried-on stains can be treated with equal parts glycerine and warm water to loosen them before washing as normal. Wool should be treated with white vinegar after the glycerine treatment.

Non-washables

☆ Sponge with cold water followed by a specially formulated stain remover, or take to a dry cleaner.

Upholstery and carpets

☆ Mop up liquid with paper towels, then sponge with cold water and wash with mild detergent or carpet or upholstery cleaner. Rinse with white vinegar solution and blot dry. Treat persistent stains with wood alcohol.

To remove fruit stains from your fingers

☆ Wipe with a cotton pad soaked in nail-polish remover.

FURNITURE POLISH

Washables

☆ Blot any excess, then sponge with liquid detergent or treat with dry-cleaning solvent. Wash as normal.

Non-washables

☆ Sponge clean with liquid detergent solution. For persistent stains, apply dry-cleaning solvent, or take to a dry cleaner.

Upholstery and carpets

☆ Treat as for non-washables, then shampoo with mild detergent solution or upholstery or carpet cleaner to finish.

GASOLINE

Washables

☆ Blot the area, then sprinkle with talcum powder, baking soda, or cornstarch, leave to stand for 15 minutes, and brush. Treat the area with undiluted dish soap and leave to stand for a few minutes. Soak in hot, soapy water for 30 minutes and rinse thoroughly in hot water. Repeat if necessary. If the stain persists, apply a paste of water and baking soda, leave to dry, then brush off. Finally, apply a pre-wash treatment and wash on as hot a setting as possible.

Non-washables

☆ Blot the area. Then sprinkle with talcum powder, baking soda or cornstarch and leave to stand for 15 minutes to absorb as much moisture as possible. Then brush. Sponge the area with liquid detergent solution and blot dry. If the stain won't budge, take to a dry cleaner.

Upholstery and carpets

☆ Blot the area. Sprinkle with talcum powder, baking soda, or cornstarch and leave to stand for several hours. Then vacuum. Spray on some shaving cream or use foam upholstery or carpet cleaner and work it well into the fibers. Wipe with a damp cloth wrung out in cold water.

GLUE see ADHESIVE

GRASS AND LEAF

Washables

☆ Treat with wood alcohol or mineral spirits (unless the fabric is acetate-based, in which case treat with a specially formulated stain remover). Rinse, then wash as normal. If necessary, apply a pre-wash treatment before washing, or leave to soak in liquid detergent.

☆ Alternatively, rub a little toothpaste into the stain and rinse off.

Non-washables

☆ Coat the stain with a paste of equal parts salt and cream of tartar and a few drops of water. Leave to dry and brush off. If the stain persists, treat with a specially formulated stain remover.

GRAVY

Washables

☆ Wipe away any excess, then soak in cold water. Leave to soak in enzyme detergent for 30–60 minutes. If any stains remain, treat with dry-cleaning solvent or pre-wash treatment and wash as normal.

Non-washables

☆ Remove any excess and treat with dry-cleaning solvent.

Upholstery and carpets

☆ Wipe away any excess, then shampoo with a carpet or upholstery cleaner, or treat with dry-cleaning solvent. Rinse and blot dry.

GREASE

Washables

☆ Scrape away as much of the grease as possible, then apply some dishwashing liquid solution and leave for a minute or two to soak. Wash as normal.

☆ Alternatively, sprinkle with talcum powder, fuller's earth, cornstarch, or baking soda. Leave for a few minutes to absorb the grease, then brush off. Remove any remaining grease with dry-cleaning solvent, then wipe or wash as normal.

☆ For persistent stains, place paper towels on either side of the greasy patch (or on top only, if the underside is not accessible) and iron on a warm to hot setting.

Non-washables, upholstery and carpets

☆ Sprinkle with talcum powder, fuller's earth, cornstarch, or baking soda and treat as above.

On walls

☆ Apply a paste of fuller's earth to the stain. Leave to dry, then brush off. Repeat if necessary.

HAND LOTION see LOTION—HAND, BODY, AND SUNTAN

HONEY see JAM, MARMALADE, HONEY, AND MAPLE SYRUP

HUMMUS AND PEANUT BUTTER

Washables

☆ Scrape up any excess, then rub undiluted liquid detergent into the area and leave to stand for a few minutes. Wash on as hot a setting as possible. Apply a stain remover first.

Non-washables

☆ Scrape or wipe away as much as possible, then treat with stain remover or dry-cleaning solvent. Rinse and blot dry.

Upholstery and carpets

☆ Treat as for non-washables.

HYDROGEN PEROXIDE *see* BLEACH

ICE CREAM

Washables

☆ Scrape or wipe away any excess, then rinse in cold water or soda water to loosen the stain. Soak in enzyme detergent for 30 minutes. If the stain persists, use dry-cleaning solvent to get rid of the greasy marks. Dried-on stains can be treated with a solution of 1 tablespoon of borax to 1 pint (½ liter) of water.

Non-washables

☆ Use a specially formulated grease-removing solution to treat stains. If this doesn't work, take to the dry cleaner.

Upholstery and carpets

☆ Wipe with mild detergent solution, then treat any remaining stains with a grease solvent or a solution of 1 part ammonia to 4 parts water before cleaning with carpet or upholstery shampoo.

INK

☆ Rinse in cold water, then treat the stain with some liquid detergent and rinse. Any residual marks can be treated with a mixture of water, lemon juice, and ammonia in equal proportions.

☆ Alternatively, dab with or soak in a little rubbing alcohol, then rinse in warm water. Treat the area with liquid detergent, then wash. For persistent stains, relaunder, adding some bleach to the cycle. For non-washables, blot up as much of the ink as possible, then treat the stains with wood alcohol. If the stain persists, take the item to be dry-cleaned. Do not apply cold water to non-washables, as this may spread the stain. Carpets can be sprayed with soda water before treating with wood alcohol.

☆ To remove ink (and paint) stains from skin and nails, apply a blob of toothpaste and rub with a damp cloth.

Ballpoint pen

☆ Dab the stain with a cotton ball or a cloth dipped in wood alcohol or a solution of hydrogen peroxide. If appropriate, wash on a warm cycle or rinse, otherwise treat the area with a solution of mild detergent or dry-cleaning solution. Sponge with clean water and blot dry.

☆ On suede, rub gently with sandpaper, but be careful not to damage the surface.

Felt-tip and marker pens

☆ This ink cannot usually be removed but, on washables, try flushing with water to get rid of as much of the ink as possible. Then, when dry, treat with wood alcohol or stain remover, or soak for several hours in a bucket of warm water with 2–4 tablespoons of ammonia.

☆ Alternatively, loosen the stain by rubbing with glycerine, then wash as normal. Sponge persistent stains with mineral spirits.

JAM, MARMALADE, HONEY, AND MAPLE SYRUP

Washables

☆ Scrape away any excess, then soak in enzyme detergent and wash as normal. For persistent or dried-on stains, soak in a solution of 1 tablespoon borax to 1 pint (½ liter) warm water, then rinse and wash as normal. Alternatively, use a solution of 1 part hydrogen peroxide to 6 parts water or equal parts white vinegar and water.

Non-washables

☆ Scrape away any excess, then rinse in cold water and rub with liquid detergent. Treat persistent stains with vinegar solution, as for washables, or rub the area with a little borax, leave for a few minutes and then wipe clean. If the stain remains, get the item dry-cleaned.

Upholstery and carpets

☆ Remove any excess and sponge with warm, soapy water. Treat with dry-cleaning solvent to remove persistent stains, then clean the area with upholstery or carpet shampoo.

KETCHUP AND CHUTNEY

Washables

☆ Soak in cool water for 10–15 minutes, work liquid detergent into the area, and rinse. If necessary, apply a pre-wash treatment and then wash as normal. Soak persistent stains in a solution of 1 part hydrogen peroxide to 6 parts water, then rinse and dry. To remove residue, rub with some wood alcohol.

☆ Alternatively, stains can be treated with color-safe bleach or soaked for a few minutes in a weak chlorine bleach solution.

Non-washables

☆ Wipe away any excess, wipe with cold water, and apply a specially formulated stain remover. If necessary, take to a dry cleaner.

Upholstery and carpets

☆ Scrape away excess, sponge with cold water, blot, and apply carpet or upholstery cleaner. If the stain persists, rub a little glycerine into the area. Then shampoo, rinse, and blot dry.

☆ Remove ketchup stains from plastic food containers by filling with hot water and adding two denture tablets. Leave to soak for 20–60 minutes, then rinse well.

LEAF see GRASS

LIME DEPOSITS

☆ Boil potatoes or carrot peelings in water and use this water to clean away lime scale deposits from kettles and toilet bowls.

LIPSTICK

Washables

☆ Scrape away any excess, then soak in milk for 30 minutes. Rinse in hot, soapy water, then wash as normal.

☆ Alternatively, rub some vegetable oil into the stain and allow to stand for 10–15 minutes. Blot away excess oil with a paper towel, then sponge with a solution of equal parts ammonia and water (but not on silk or wool fabrics). Rinse with cool water and wring out. Sponge any remaining marks with rubbing alcohol. If necessary, apply pre-wash treatment and wash on the hottest setting possible. If necessary, take to a dry cleaner.

Non-washables

☆ Use a stain remover or dry-cleaning solvent, or take to a dry cleaner. Upholstery and carpets can be treated with upholstery or carpet shampoo to finish.

LIQUID PAPER *see* CORRECTION FLUID

LOTION—HAND, BODY, AND SUNTAN

Washables

☆ Blot, then sprinkle with talcum powder, baking soda, or cornstarch. Leave for a few minutes, then brush. Wash in hot, soapy water, then rinse. If necessary, apply a pre-wash treatment, then wash.

Non-washables

☆ Blot, then sprinkle with talcum powder, baking soda, or cornstarch and leave to stand for a few minutes. Then brush. Sponge the area with liquid detergent solution and blot dry.

Upholstery and carpets

☆ Blot, then sprinkle with talcum powder, baking soda, or cornstarch. Leave for a few minutes, then vacuum. Work some shaving cream or upholstery or carpet cleaner into the fibers. Rinse and blot dry. If the stain persists, sponge with dry-cleaning solvent.

MAKEUP *see* COSMETICS

MAPLE SYRUP *see* JAM, MARMALADE, HONEY, AND MAPLE SYRUP

MARGARINE *see* BUTTER, MARGARINE, FAT, AND OIL

MARMALADE *see* JAM, MARMALADE, HONEY, AND MAPLE SYRUP

MASCARA

Washables

☆ Rub the stain with undiluted dish soap and wash as normal. If the stain persists, treat with dry-cleaning solvent.

Non-washables

☆ Treat colorfast items with wood alcohol. Dab stubborn stains with a solution of 1 part ammonia to 3 parts cold water. Non-colorfast items should be treated with stain remover.

Upholstery and carpets

☆ Treat as for non-washables.

MAYONNAISE

Washables

☆ Treat with a grease-removing solution and soak in enzyme detergent. If necessary, apply a pre-wash treatment, then wash in lukewarm water. If the mark remains, treat again with the grease-removing solution .

Non-washables

☆ Remove excess with a warm, damp cloth, then treat with grease-removing solution. If the mark persists, take to a dry cleaner.

Upholstery and carpets

☆ Treat with a stain remover and wash with upholstery or carpet shampoo.

MEDICINE

Washables

☆ Soak immediately in cold water, then wash as normal. Treat any remaining marks with liquid detergent, wood alcohol, or lemon juice. Dry in direct sunlight, if possible.

Non-washables

☆ Wipe away any excess and take to a dry cleaner.

Upholstery and carpets

☆ Mop up excess with paper towels and rinse well with cold water, blotting between treatments. Treat persistent stains with upholstery or carpet shampoo.

See also Cough Syrup

METAL POLISH

Washables

☆ Blot up as much liquid as possible and treat with mineral spirits. Wash as normal.

Non-washables

☆ Blot with a cloth dampened with dry-cleaning solution, then apply a stain remover.

Upholstery and carpets

☆ Blot excess liquid, then treat the area with mineral spirits. Allow to dry thoroughly, then vacuum. If required, treat with upholstery or carpet shampoo to finish.

MILDEW

Washables

☆ Washing with enzyme detergent as normal should remove most mildew marks. Add a cupful of white vinegar to the wash to discourage mildew from returning. Alternatively, soak affected areas in a solution of half hydrogen peroxide, half water, but beware of color running. Wash as normal and repeat if necessary. White cottons can be soaked in a solution of 1 tablespoon bleach to 2 pints (1 liter) water plus 1 teaspoon of white vinegar. Alternatively, make a paste of borax and vinegar and apply to the affected area. Dry in direct sunlight, if possible.

Non-washables

☆ Take to a dry cleaner.

Upholstery and carpets

☆ Sponge with a mild disinfectant or weak solution of vinegar.

Books and papers

☆ Wipe with a soft cloth dampened in a mild anti-bacterial solution.

MILK, CREAM, CHEESE, AND YOGURT

Washables
☆ Rinse well in cold water, then apply a pre-wash treatment or soak in enzyme detergent for 30 minutes. Wash with enzyme detergent and warm water. If any marks remain, treat with a dry-cleaning solvent.

Non-washables
☆ Sponge with warm water or soda water, then allow to dry. Treat any remaining stain with stain remover. If the stain persists, take to a dry cleaner.

Upholstery and carpets
☆ Mop up any excess, then sponge with diluted upholstery or carpet shampoo. Carpets can be sprayed with soda water first to prevent an unpleasant smell developing. Treat persistent stains with dry-cleaning solvent.

MUD

Washables
☆ Allow the mud to dry and then brush off, working the fabric with your fingers to remove as much as possible. Wash as normal. Treat any marks with stain remover or dry-cleaning solvent and wash once more.

Non-washables
☆ Leave to dry, then brush off. If necessary, wipe with a detergent solution followed by a dry-cleaning solvent.

Upholstery and carpets
☆ Leave to dry, brush to loosen the dried mud, then vacuum thoroughly. If necessary, treat with a mild detergent solution, ammonia solution (1 part ammonia to 6 parts water), or upholstery or carpet cleaner. Rinse and blot dry.

MUSTARD

Washables
☆ Wipe or sponge away as much as possible and then soak in a liquid detergent. If necessary, apply a pre-wash treatment, then wash as normal. For persistent stains, treat with a solution of 1 teaspoon ammonia to 1 pint (½ liter) water. Rinse well.

Non-washables
☆ Treat the affected area with mild detergent solution, followed by ammonia solution (see Washables, above). If the stain persists, take to a dry cleaner.

Upholstery and carpets
☆ Treat as for non-washables. Dried-on stains on furnishings can be loosened with a solution of equal parts glycerine and warm water.

NAIL POLISH

☆ Blot away the excess, then treat with acetone, non-oily nail polish remover or amyl acetate, followed by mineral spirits. Use wood alcohol to remove any traces of color (except on acetate-based fabrics). Non-washable items will need to be dry-cleaned.

NEWSPRINT

Washables
☆ Dab with wood alcohol, then wash as normal.

Non-washables
☆ Dab with wood alcohol, followed by cold water. If the stain persists, take to a dry cleaner.

Upholstery and carpets
☆ Treat as for non-washables.

ODORS

Washables
☆ To remove unpleasant, lingering smells from lunch boxes and food containers, soak a sponge in equal parts vinegar and water. Place in the container and leave for at least 24 hours. Rinse well.

OIL, ENGINE

☆ *Scoop or blot away as much oil as possible, then treat with liquid detergent. Flush with a dry-cleaning solvent. Repeat the process as many times as necessary.*

OIL, VEGETABLE, NUT or MINERAL *see* BUTTER, MARGARINE, FAT, AND OIL

PAINT, ACRYLIC

Washables
☆ *Blot immediately and wash with soap and cold water. If the paint has started to dry, scrape away excess and treat with a dry-cleaning solvent, wood alcohol, or paint remover.*

Non-washables
☆ *Keep the stain damp, scrape off as much of the paint as you can and take the item to a dry cleaner immediately.*

Upholstery and carpets
☆ *Scrape or blot to get rid of as much paint as possible, then treat with upholstery or carpet shampoo and warm water. For remaining marks, apply wood alcohol or paint remover.*

PAINT, CELLULOSE

Washables
☆ *Treat immediately with cellulose thinner, then wash as normal.*

Non-washables
☆ *Take to a dry-cleaner immediately. Rayon fabric should be treated as non-washable.*

Upholstery and carpets
☆ *Treat the affected area with cellulose thinner. Then apply upholstery or carpet shampoo to clean. If the area is large, call in a professional.*

PAINT, ENAMEL

Washables

☆ Working from the front to the back of the fabric, wipe with a clean cloth soaked in paint remover until the stain disappears. Once the stain is gone completely, wash as normal.

Non-washables

☆ Take to a dry cleaner immediately.

Upholstery and carpets

☆ Blot away excess paint and treat with paint remover or dry-cleaning fluid.

PAINT, GLOSS (OIL-BASED)

Washables

☆ Treat with a cloth dipped in turpentine, brush cleaner, or mineral spirits. (Do not use on acetate- or rayon-based fabrics.) Sponge or wipe with cold water, then wash as normal.

Non-washables

☆ Treat as above. If the stain remains, take to a dry cleaner.

Upholstery and carpets

☆ Treat the affected area with dry-cleaner solvent, brush cleaner, or mineral spirits. Blot, then clean with upholstery or carpet shampoo.

PAINT, LATEX (WATER-BASED)

Washables

☆ Scrape away any excess, then flush with cold water. Keep rinsing until the paint has completely disappeared. Wash in enzyme detergent. If any marks remain, treat with a specially formulated grease-removing solution.

Non-washables

☆ Keep damp, remove any excess, then take to a dry cleaner immediately.

Upholstery and carpets

☆ Flush immediately with cold water, then sponge with warm, soapy water and blot dry. If necessary, apply a specially formulated grease-removing solution to any residual marks.

PAINT, WATERCOLOR

Washables
☆ Rinse in plenty of cold water. If the stain persists, dab with a little undiluted ammonia. Rinse well.

Non-washables
☆ Sponge or wipe with cold water. If this doesn't work, take to a dry cleaner.

Upholstery and carpets
☆ Sponge or wipe with cold water, then use undiluted ammonia followed by upholstery or carpet cleaner.

PAPER, STUCK ON

☆ To remove paper that is stuck to a hard surface, place a few drops of vegetable oil onto the paper and leave to soak in. After a few minutes, the paper should rub away easily. Wipe away any excess oil and buff with a soft cloth.

PARAFFIN (KEROSENE)

Washables
☆ Scrape away any excess and then sprinkle liberally with talcum powder, fuller's earth, or cornstarch to absorb as much grease as possible. Leave for a few minutes, brush away powder, apply a dry-cleaning solvent and wash on as hot a setting as possible.

Non-washables
☆ Cover the affected area with talcum powder, fuller's earth, or cornstarch, then treat with dry-cleaning solvent, as above. Deal with larger areas by placing them between two layers of paper towels and pressing with a warm iron. To finish, treat with dry-cleaning solvent.

Upholstery and carpets
☆ Blot away any excess, then apply stain remover to the affected area. Treat large areas by ironing between two layers of paper towels or blotting paper, as for non-washables. To finish, treat with stain remover and upholstery or carpet shampoo.

PEANUT BUTTER *see* HUMMUS

PENCIL

☆ Rub pencil marks with a pencil eraser. If the mark remains, treat with a stain remover or a pre-wash treatment. Launder as appropriate.

PERFUME

Washables

☆ Rinse immediately in warm water. If the stain persists, treat with undiluted ammonia, then wash as normal. Dried-on perfume stains can be treated with a solution of equal parts glycerine and water. Wash as normal.

Non-washables

☆ Rub a solution of equal parts glycerine and water into the affected area, then sponge carefully with a cloth or sponge wrung out in warm water. Delicate fabrics should be dry cleaned.

Upholstery and carpets

☆ Rub a solution of equal parts glycerine and water into the stain, then dab gently with a cloth or sponge wrung out in warm water. Blot well and clean the area with carpet or upholstery shampoo, if necessary.

PERSPIRATION

Washables

☆ Perspiration stains can be very difficult to get rid of completely. Soak in enzyme detergent and then wash as normal. Fresh stains can be treated with a solution of 1 part ammonia to 3 parts water. Rinse clean, then wash as normal. Alternatively, dab with lemon or white vinegar solution—1 tablespoon of vinegar or lemon juice to ½ pint (¼ liter) water—and leave for a few minutes. Old stains can be sponged with vinegar solution as above and then soaked in enzyme detergent. Persistent stains can be treated with a solution of 1 part hydrogen peroxide to 10 parts water. To get rid of lingering smells, soak the garment in a solution of 1 teaspoon borax to 1 pint (½ liter) of water with a few drops of ammonia. Rinse, then hang outside to dry.

Non-washables

☆ Dab gently with vinegar solution to get rid of the stain and freshen the fabric. If this doesn't work, take to a dry cleaner.   See also Deodorant

PETROLEUM JELLY

Washables
☆ Scrape away any excess, then wash on as hot a setting as possible using plenty of detergent. If the stain persists, treat with a little dry-cleaning solvent.

Non-washables
☆ Scrape away excess, then use a dry-cleaning solvent. If the stain remains, dry clean.

Upholstery and carpets
☆ Scrape away as much as possible, then treat with a specially formulated grease-removing solution, followed with dilute upholstery or carpet shampoo. Rinse well and blot dry.

PLASTICINE AND MODELING CLAY

Washables
☆ Scrape away excess, then apply a specially formulated grease-removing solution or a few drops of lighter fluid on some cloth. For man-made fabric, test on a hidden area first. Wash on as hot a setting as possible.

Non-washables
☆ Scrape away any excess, then treat with specially formulated grease-removing solution. If the stain persists, take to a dry cleaner.

Upholstery and carpets
☆ Scrape away excess and treat the area with a specially formulated grease-removing solution, followed by carpet shampoo, if necessary. Rinse well and leave to dry. If any stains remain, treat with wood alcohol.

POLISH *see* FURNITURE POLISH, METAL POLISH, SHOE POLISH

POLLEN

Washables
☆ Shake to remove any loose pollen and use some tape to lift away as much of what remains as possible. Rinse with cold water. If the stain persists, treat with a pre-wash treatment and then wash on the hottest setting available, or treat with stain remover or dry-cleaning solvent.

Non-washables

☆ Shake to remove any loose pollen and scrape or use some tape to lift away as much remaining pollen as possible. Sponge with cold water. If the stain persists, treat with a stain remover or dry-cleaning solvent.

Upholstery and carpets

☆ Treat as for non-washables.

RELISH see KETCHUP AND CHUTNEY

RING AROUND THE COLLAR see COLLAR GRIME

RUST

☆ Use a specially formulated rust remover and follow the directions on the packaging. Or treat with mild bleach, such as lemon juice, sprinkle with salt and rub gently. Leave to stand, then rinse.

Stainless steel

☆ To remove rust stains on stainless steel, rub with mild cream cleanser or lighter fluid. Rinse well and wipe with your regular cleaner.

SALAD DRESSING

Washables

☆ Blot away the excess and rinse with cold water. To remove grease and oil, work liquid detergent into the stain or treat with grease-removing solution. Wash on the hottest setting possible.

Non-washables

☆ Blot away the excess, then treat with grease-removing solution. If the stain persists, take to a dry cleaner.

Upholstery and carpets

☆ Mop up any excess liquid, then treat the area with a dry-cleaning solvent. Finish with an upholstery or carpet cleaner, if necessary.

SALSA see KETCHUP AND CHUTNEY

SCORCH MARKS

Washables

✩ Run the item under a faucet, rubbing gently. Next, soak in a solution of 2 teaspoons borax to 2 pints (1 liter) warm water or 1 part hydrogen peroxide to 4 parts water. Wash as normal.

✩ An alternative technique is to cut an onion (white) in half, and rub the cut side onto the scorch.

Non-washables

✩ Sponge with borax solution as for washables. Rinse well and blot dry.

Upholstery and carpets

✩ Treat as for non-washables. Or treat carpet marks with 1 part hydrogen peroxide to 10 parts water. As a desperate measure, trim away scorched tufts, or rub them with fine steel wool.

SHOE POLISH

Washables

✩ Dab with mineral spirits, or rinse and rub with dishwashing liquid. Rinse well. For tough fabrics, wipe with paintbrush cleaner. Wash with soapy water and a few drops of ammonia.

Non-washables

✩ Wipe away excess polish and treat with dry-cleaning solvent. If the stain persists, treat with mineral spirits or paintbrush cleaner. If necessary, take to a dry cleaner.

Upholstery and carpets

✩ Scrape away any excess and treat the area with mineral spirits, wood alcohol, or dry-cleaning solvent. Shampoo with mild detergent solution, or upholstery or carpet cleaner.

SOFT DRINKS

Washables

✩ Blot up any excess, then sponge or soak the area with cold water. Leave to soak in enzyme detergent, or apply a pre-wash treatment and wash as normal.

Non-washables, upholstery and carpets

✩ Sponge with a solution of mild detergent and warm water. Rinse and blot well. If the stain persists, dab with a solution of equal parts white vinegar and water.

SOOT AND CHARCOAL

Washables

☆ Brush, shake, or vacuum to get rid of as much soot as possible. Sprinkle with talcum powder, baking soda, or salt and leave to stand. Brush or vacuum. Apply stain remover or pre-wash treatment and wash on as hot a setting as possible.

Non-washables

☆ Brush, shake, or vacuum to get rid of excess, then treat with dry-cleaning solvent.

Upholstery and carpets

☆ Shake or vacuum thoroughly, then apply a stain-removing solvent. On light-colored carpets, try sprinkling with fuller's earth, leaving for a few minutes, before vacuuming again.

SOY SAUCE

Washables

☆ Flush with cold water, then apply a pre-wash treatment and wash. Rub laundry detergent into dried-on or persistent stains and leave to stand for a few minutes, then rinse in cold water.

Non-washables

☆ Blot any excess, then dab with mild detergent solution and blot dry. If the stain persists, treat with a solution of 1 part ammonia to 3 parts water. Rinse and blot dry.

Upholstery and carpets

☆ Sponge with a solution of mild detergent and warm water. Rinse and blot well. If the stain persists, dab with a solution of 1 part ammonia to 3 parts water. Rinse and blot dry.

SWEAT *see* PERSPIRATION

TAR

Washables

☆ Scrape away as much tar as possible, soften the remainder with a little glycerine, then apply eucalyptus oil to the back of the stain. Small marks can be removed with dry-cleaning solvent.

Finally, wash on the hottest setting possible. Remove stubborn stains with paintbrush solvent. As an alternative, try rubbing the area with peanut butter and then washing.

Non-washables

☆ *Scrape away the excess, soften the remainder with a little glycerine, and apply dry-cleaning solvent. If the stain persists, take to a dry cleaner.*

Upholstery and carpets

☆ *Dab with eucalyptus oil or olive oil and then sponge away with warm, soapy water or wash as usual.*

TEA *see* COFFEE AND TEA

TOBACCO

Washables

☆ *Treat with wood alcohol or, for acetate-based fabrics, benzene. Alternatively, try a solution of equal parts hydrogen peroxide and water. Rinse well. If necessary, apply a pre-wash treatment. Wash as normal.*

Non-washables

☆ *Take to a dry cleaner.*

Upholstery and carpets

☆ *Sponge with wood alcohol. Rinse well and follow up with carpet or upholstery shampoo.*

To clean tobacco stains from fingers

☆ *Dab stains on fingers with sterilizing liquid (used for cleaning babies' bottles).*

TOMATO SAUCE *see* KETCHUP AND CHUTNEY

TOOTHPASTE

Washables

☆ *Scrape away the excess, then sponge with a solution of enzyme detergent and cold water. Wash as normal or sponge with cool water and blot dry.*

TURMERIC

Washables

☆ Soak in warm water with a few drops of ammonia, then dab on some mineral spirits and wash as normal. White cotton and linen may need to be soaked in a weak bleach solution.

Non-washables

☆ Sponge with undiluted ammonia, then mineral spirits. If the stain persists, take to a dry cleaner.

Upholstery and carpets

☆ Treat the affected area with undiluted ammonia, then mineral spirits. Clean with foam cleaner.

URINE

Washables

☆ Flush thoroughly with cold water, then soak in enzyme detergent and wash as normal. Old stains can be difficult to remove; soak items in a solution of 1 part hydrogen peroxide to 6 parts water with a few drops of ammonia.

Non-washables

☆ Sponge with cold water, then with a solution of 2 teaspoons white vinegar to 2 pints (1 liter) water. If the stain persists, take to a dry-cleaner.

Upholstery and carpets

☆ Blot up as much liquid as possible, then sponge with warm water and blot. Carpets can be sprayed with soda water, then treated with warm water and a few drops of ammonia. Mattresses should be sponged with a solution of dishwashing liquid and cold water plus a little disinfectant.

VARNISH (SHELLAC)

Washables

☆ Wipe immediately with wood alcohol. Wash acetate-based fabrics in detergent and rinse.

Non-washables, upholstery and carpets

☆ Treat immediately with wood alcohol (unless on acetate). If the stain persists, take to a dry cleaner.

VEGETABLES AND VEGETABLE JUICE

Washables

☆ Scrape away excess, then rub mild detergent into the stain, leave to stand for a few minutes and soak in cold water for 10–15 minutes, rubbing the fabric occasionally to loosen the stain. Rinse well and repeat if necessary. If staining persists, soak in enzyme detergent for 30 minutes or more. Apply a pre-wash treatment if necessary and wash on hot, if possible.

Non-washables

☆ Remove excess and sponge with a mild detergent solution. Rinse and blot dry. Repeat if necessary. If the stain persists, take to a dry cleaner.

Upholstery and carpets

☆ Treat as for non-washables. Treat persistent stains with dry-cleaning solution and follow with upholstery or carpet cleaner.

VINAIGRETTE *see* SALAD DRESSING

VOMIT

Washables

☆ Scrape away as much as possible, then rinse well with cold water and leave to soak in enzyme detergent. If necessary, add a little disinfectant to the solution. Wash as usual. If the stain persists, and the fabric can stand it, soak in a solution of 1 part hydrogen peroxide to 6 parts water.

Non-washables

☆ Scrape away as much as possible and sponge with a weak solution of ammonia and warm water. If necessary, take to a dry cleaner.

Upholstery and carpets

☆ Remove as much as possible and sponge with a mild concentration of warm, soapy water. Carpets can be sprayed with soda water first and then treated with carpet shampoo. Mattresses should be sponged thoroughly with warm, soapy water, then rinsed in cold water with a little disinfectant.

WATER MARKS AND SPOTS

☆ Gently scratch off as much of the stain as possible with your fingernail. To remove any residue, use a steaming kettle to dampen the spot. As it dries, rub the stain, working from its outer edges in toward the center.

☆ Remove hot-water stains from glasses and bottles by rubbing them gently with steel wool dipped in white vinegar. Rinse and dry.

☆ To clean away spots and stains on chrome, rub the surface with a squirt of toothpaste and polish with a soft cloth. Alternatively, wipe the area with some cola and rub with a wad of aluminum foil.

☆ To remove rain spots or water marks on suede, rub gently with an emery board or extra-fine sandpaper.

☆ For water spills on carpets, mop or blot as much of the liquid as possible and apply cloths or paper towels to the area (above and below, if possible). Place heavy objects, such as books, on top of the cloth to help force the moisture into the absorbent pads. Remove the books and dry the area gently with a blow-dryer or electric fan on a warm setting.

WAX POLISH

Washables
☆ Treat with dry-cleaning solvent and wash on the hottest setting possible, or wash through in hot, soapy water and rinse thoroughly.

Non-washables
☆ Treat the affected area with dry-cleaning solvent, then sponge or wipe with warm, soapy water and rinse well.

Upholstery and carpets
☆ Treat as for non-washables.

WAX see CANDLE WAX

WINE, RED

Washables
☆ Sponge the fresh stain with white wine to keep it from setting, then soak in cold water. Spot treat with liquid detergent before washing. If it's still there, launder again using bleach.

Non-washables
☆ Blot away the excess, then sprinkle with talcum powder and take to a dry cleaner.

Upholstery and carpets
☆ Spray with soda water, then blot and leave to dry. Alternatively, treat with a solution of liquid soap and hydrogen peroxide. If the stained fabric is white, soak in a weak solution of bleach.

WINE, WHITE

Washables
☆ Wash the affected area with a solution of mild detergent and warm water. If the stain persists, treat with a solution of equal parts of white vinegar and water. Blot dry. Wash as normal.

Non-washables
☆ Blot away the excess with a paper towel, then sprinkle with talcum powder. If the stain persists or a ring forms, take to a dry cleaner.

Upholstery and carpets
☆ Blot away the excess, then spray with soda water. Blot, then sponge with lukewarm water and a little detergent. Old stains can be treated with wood alcohol.

WORCESTERSHIRE SAUCE *see* ACID

YELLOWING

Washables
☆ To get rid of yellowing on fabric, add 2 denture-cleaning tablets to a bucket of warm water and leave the item to soak. Rinse and wash as normal.

YOGURT *see* MILK, CREAM, CHEESE, AND YOGURT

HOME CLEANING
THROUGH CHEMISTRY

USING CHEMICALS SAFELY

Although synthetic chemicals are composed of the same molecules that make up all matter on earth, they are unlike anything that exists in nature. Some synthetic chemicals are harmless, but there are reasons to be cautious about our exposure to others. It can often take a significant amount of time to determine the health impact of a chemical compound, so we do not always know all the side effects of their use in our environment. For this reason, taking simple precautions when you clean can reduce your long-term exposure to potentially harmful substances and ensure that your home is a safe place to be.

HOUSEHOLD CLEANERS

DID YOU KNOW?

The average household today contains more man-made chemicals than an average-sized chemical plant contained 100 years ago. Each household uses approximately 55 gallons (250 liters) of hazardous household products per year, and produces 25 percent of all toxic waste.

There is some evidence to suggest that regular use of household cleaners that contain such chemicals may be responsible for a number of respiratory problems, skin irritations and diseases, and even, in some cases, cancers. So when using these products, make sure the area is well ventilated, and wear protective gloves.

SAFETY TIPS FOR DOMESTIC CHEMICALS

Here are some handy tips for using and storing your chemicals safely:

Keep all chemicals out of sight and out of reach of children. Install childproof locks on cupboards and drawers containing medicines or poisonous substances such as bleach and detergents.

Keep bleaches, cleaning fluids, dishwasher tablets, and other cleaning chemicals in their original containers, or label their new containers clearly, to prevent a chemical being mistaken for something else.

Buy products that have childproof caps or lids.

When you have visitors, put your guests' belongings out of reach right away. Babies and toddlers can be injured by pills and other potentially lethal items that they pull from guests' bags.

Use protective gloves when using household chemicals.

Use a face mask to protect your respiratory system from toxic fumes.

When possible, use chemicals outdoors. When using them indoors, keep your home well ventilated by opening windows and doors.

Read all labels carefully and follow the manufacturer's instructions.

Do not mix one product with another unless the instructions on the label say you can—some combinations create hazardous gases and fumes.

Dispose of used or unwanted products safely. Seal them well and follow the manufacturer's instructions or local authority guidelines.

WORKING WITH ABRASIVES

Abrasive chemicals usually contain tiny particles of grit or hard minerals. These particles have a rough quality that helps the cleaning chemicals do their job by scrubbing the area to be cleaned. Abrasives can be found in a wide range of chemicals, from scouring powder to toothpaste, and the harshness of the abrasive varies with each product.

CAUTION

Avoid rubbing fragile items the wrong way. Harsh abrasives will damage non-stick pans and highly polished metals and glass. Never use a scourer on car paintwork, no matter how gentle you are or how stubborn the mark is. It will look fine while it is wet, but just wait until it dries. Your local body shop will love you, but your car and your accountant won't.

Abrasives can also be used by themselves—for example, as pumice stones, sandpaper, nylon scourers, steel wool, and even salt and sand. Once again, the harshness of the abrasive action varies. It's important to be absolutely sure that your chosen abrasive isn't too harsh for the job, otherwise you take the risk that whatever you are cleaning will look as though it's done ten rounds in a boxing ring with a very angry cat. If in doubt, always opt for the most gentle abrasive to start with and switch to a harsher one if necessary.

SOFTLY, SOFTLY DOES IT

☆ *The commercial cream cleansers that are on the market today are usually reasonably gentle, but one of the gentlest and most useful and effective abrasives is the ubiquitous baking soda. You can use* it to clean any fragile items that would be scratched by the use of harsher abrasives. This handy, multi-purpose white powder also doubles as a mild bleach. Simply mix a little water with the powder to make it into a paste, and use it to loosen grease and send all those stubborn stains on work surfaces packing. To increase its cleaning effect and help eradicate marks, stains, spots, and discoloration, once you have worked the paste into the area, leave to stand for 15–30 minutes before rinsing and wiping clean.

BAKING SODA AND WATER PASTE

☆ Baking soda deodorizes smells, too; pour some into an open dish (or simply cut open the box) and leave it in a kitchen cupboard or a refrigerator, for example, to absorb unpleasant odors and leave the air smelling fresh. Sprinkle a little into drains, trash cans, or cat litter boxes to help combat unpleasant odors.

HOUSEHOLD ABRASIVES

POLISH THOSE PEARLIES

Run out of toothpaste? Mix a little baking soda and water to a paste and use that instead, or simply use plain old fine salt. Create your own instant mouthwash by stirring a little baking soda into a glassful of water.

UNDERSTANDING ACIDS

Acid-based cleaners have a valuable role to play in the home. They remove stains that are alkaline-based, such as lime scale and soap scum. They can also be used to treat discoloration on certain metals, including brass, bronze, copper, and aluminum, and it will eat away rust.

CAUTION

Some acids are very strong and can be extremely harmful if ingested. Keep them away from eyes and skin, and follow the manufacturer's instructions carefully. If an accident occurs, call for emergency assistance immediately, or go to your nearest emergency room.

☆ *Acidity and alkalinity are measured according to a scale system known as pH, which is numbered from 0 to 14. Anything with a pH of less than 7 is considered to be "acid," while anything with a pH of 8 or more is described as "alkaline."*

☆ *Pure water, which is thought of as a neutral substance, falls right in the middle of the scale with a pH of 7. As the water we use is rarely pure, water is usually either acid or alkaline, depending on what else is present. "Hard" water (water that contains too much of the minerals magnesium or calcium) is alkaline. Water that is too alkaline can cause color change in fabrics. Adding a little acid (such as vinegar) to water can counteract this effect.*

☆ *Acids dissolve in water and are considered to be "sour" in quality. Those used for cleaning are usually mild in nature, such as acetic acid and citric acid.*

LEMON REMOVES LIME SCALE

ACID CLEANERS AND THEIR USES

Acid-based cleaning agents vary in their strength and possible uses. Here are the main types and what they can do:

Vinegar (acetic acid)

Clear distilled vinegar is a mild descaling agent and can be used for cutting through calcium deposits and lime scale in toilets, sinks, and bathtubs, as well as removing rust. It can also be used to clean brass and bronze, and pots and pans made of copper, stainless steel, and aluminum.

Phosphoric acid

You can use this mild acid to clean your sink, bathtub, and tiles, and in low concentrations it will clean your metal pots and pans, too.

Lemon juice (citric acid)

Lemon juice is useful for removing mineral deposits around sinks and bathtub faucets, and for brightening up pots and pans made from brass, bronze, aluminum, copper, and stainless steel. Do not leave it in contact with metals for too long, however, or it may tarnish them. It can also be used as a mild bleach.

Hydrochloric acid

This acid is poisonous and can damage skin and mucous membranes, so use it with care. It can also corrode metals. You can use hydrochloric acid to clean toilet bowls and bleach nylon. Believe it or not, this is also the acid your stomach uses to digest food, making up around 2 percent of your gastric juice. In such a low concentration, it is not harmful.

Lime juice (acetic acid)

Lime juice can be used in the same way as lemon juice. (See above.)

Sulfuric acid

This acid cleaner is powerful enough for your toilets and drains, but keep it away from your skin and eyes.

USING ALKALIS

Most household stains, such as fats and grease, are acid-based, and respond best to alkaline cleaners. That's why the majority of cleaning products, including soaps and detergents, are alkaline.

HOUSEHOLD ALKALIS

CREATE YOUR OWN ODOR EATER

⭐ *Baking soda is not just an alkaline cleaner, it's a good deodorizer, too. To remove unpleasant smells from fabrics, sprinkle on some baking soda and leave for 30 minutes to allow the powder time to work. Wash normally.*

AMMONIA COMBATS GREASE

BRIGHTEN UP YOUR BABY'S DIAPERS

⭐ *You can make a good diaper soak using borax, which is gentle yet effective. Simply mix 3½ oz (100 g) of borax in a bucketful or sinkful of warm water and use as required. You can also add a little chlorine bleach for more heavily soiled white cotton diapers.*

⭐ *Alkalis are soluble in water and "bitter" in quality. Those used for cleaning are ammonia and caustic soda (which are both very harsh in quality) and other soda compounds. Alkalis can neutralize acids, but can also destroy natural fibers, weakening or damaging fabrics such as wool, silk, or rayon if used regularly.*

DETERGENT IS ALKALINE

ALKALINE PRODUCTS AND THEIR USES

The main types of alkaline household cleaners and their uses:

Baking soda

This is a very mild alkali that has a great many uses in the home. In addition to making an excellent scourer (*see Abrasives on pages 292–93*), this versatile powder can be used to clean bathtubs and sinks, polish silver jewelry, deodorize unpleasant smells, and soften water.

Borax

Borax is a white, crystalline powder. It is a moderate alkaline salt, stronger than baking soda but not as strong as detergent. It can be added to a washload of laundry for a more powerful clean, and it can also be used to help neutralize the strong ammonia smell of urine.

Detergent

Detergent is a popular alkaline cleaner in the home, most commonly used in dishwashers and to clean laundry.

Soap

Soap is on par with detergent on the alkali strength scale and can cut through dirt and grease.

Ammonia

This alkali is a little stronger than detergent, and is used to remove grease and dirt and to strip wax.

Lye (caustic soda and potash)

Lye is a very strong alkali and is used to manufacture soap. It is also an active ingredient in oven and drain cleaners. It can burn the skin and eyes, and the fumes are toxic. It is also very poisonous if taken internally, so keep it locked away, well out of the reach of children. Do not mix it with any other chemicals.

CLEANING WITH BLEACH

Household bleaches contain reductive or oxidizing agents to help deodorize and sanitize fabrics. They are also wonderful whiteners, but don't use them to whiten your fabrics too often, or it will gradually weaken and destroy fibers, damaging fabric and causing it wear out very quickly.

 ## TYPES OF BLEACH AND THEIR USES

Bleaches come in a variety of types and strengths. Use the table to see what they can do to keep your home as pristine as possible.

Sunlight	White distilled vinegar
Sunlight is a natural bleaching agent. To bleach white cotton, wash it and spread it out to dry in the sun or hang it on a clothesline. Leave it outside for at least a day, or two or three days if you can.	White vinegar is another mild bleach and is very good for removing stains on silk and wool. But beware: it should never be used on linen, cotton, or acetate.
Lemon juice	Ammonia
Lemon juice has a very mild bleaching action and can be used to remove organic stains such as blood and grass. It is also effective for removing mildew and stains on marble. Do not leave it on for too long, however, because it can cause discoloration.	Ammonia is a moderate alkaline cleaner and can be added to your laundry to boost brightness and help your detergent clean better. You can also use it to remove fresh perspiration and urine stains. Never mix ammonia with chlorine bleach because it will give off hazardous fumes.

CAUTION

Always take care to use chlorine bleach at an appropriate strength for the fabric. It is very strong, so needs to be diluted with water, according to the manufacturer's instructions, before use. Test it on an inconspicuous area of fabric first, or your favorite shirt may end up looking as though it has been munched by a colony of moths.

Oxygen bleach

Oxygen bleach is also known as "all-fabric" bleach. It is milder than chlorine bleach and can be used for most whites and colorfast dyes, but not on wool and delicate fabrics such as silk. Oxygen bleach needs hot water in order to become active, and it should be mixed with the laundry water before the clothes are added.

Chlorine bleach

Chlorine bleach is a strong household bleach that will whiten white cottons and is usually safe on colorfast cottons and some synthetic fibers. However, it should never be used on nylon, spandex, silk, wool, leather, fiberglass, or mohair. Be careful not to breathe in the fumes, and avoid contact with eyes and skin.

Hydrogen peroxide

You can use diluted hydrogen peroxide to bleach delicate fabrics such as white silk and wool. Leave the fabric to soak in the solution for around half an hour—unless wool, in which case you should remove after five minutes.

Color remover

Color removers do not remove dyes; they break them down so that they can be dyed with another color. When a dye from a colored fabric runs into a white or light fabric in the wash, a color remover can be useful for stripping out the unwanted dye and restoring the fabric to its original color. Follow the instructions carefully.

HANDLING DETERGENTS

Detergents and soap are used for similar cleaning tasks. However, that is not to say that dishwashing, dishwasher, and laundry detergents can be used interchangeably. The detergents we use to wash dishes by hand are the mildest and also the gentlest on our skin. Detergents for automatic dishwashers are harsher and will leave your hands feeling like you've just scrubbed them with sandpaper, so don't let them come into contact with your skin.

ADD VINEGAR TO DETERGENT

Laundry detergents come in two forms: liquid and powder. Liquid detergents are more expensive and are good for tackling oily and greasy stains, whereas the

ALLERGY-FREE DETERGENTS

If someone in your household has sensitive skin and your household detergent makes them feel like they've been sprinkled with itching powder, try using a gentler detergent that is free from dyes and fragrances.

cheaper powdered detergents are better at removing mud. Detergents labeled "automatic" produce fewer suds and are therefore suitable for use in automatic washing machines. Soaps and detergents are surfactants, breaking down oily deposits and allowing them to be washed away easily. Detergent is less effective in hard-water areas—adding some vinegar will help to counteract this.

SOAP OR DETERGENT?

Both soaps and detergents are anti-bacterial and work best in warm water. There the similarity ends. Soap is made from fats and alkalis, whereas detergents are made from petroleum products. Before detergents were invented in the 1930s, people always used soap flakes to wash their laundry. Nowadays, most soaps have been replaced by detergents, with the exception of a few brands. This is because soap causes scum to form in hard water, whereas detergent doesn't. However, soap is more environmentally friendly because it is made from renewable sources, whereas detergent isn't.

MILD DETERGENTS

 *Household detergents often contain petroleum by-products. Milder detergents tend to be neutral (with a pH of nearly neutral), which means that they can clean without damaging either skin or surfaces.*

PEP UP THAT POLYESTER

To whiten clothes made from polyester, pour 9 fl oz (250 ml) dishwasher detergent into 1 gallon (3.8 liters) water, mix together, then add the polyester. Leave to soak overnight, then wash as usual the next day.

USING SOLVENTS IN THE HOME

A solvent is any liquid that has the ability to dissolve other liquids or solid matter. Solvents are very useful for cleaning oily or greasy stains that cannot be removed by water, detergents or soap. They can be used to remove a variety of household stains, such as:

☆ Grease ☆ Tar ☆ Wax ☆ Crayon ☆ Ink ☆ Some types of glue

☆ Nail polish and makeup, including lipstick

DID YOU KNOW?

✓ WD-40 has solvent abilities and can be used to remove many types of gummy adhesives, road tar, grease and oil stains. It is also anti-corrosive and works well on rust. However, it has a slight yellowish-brown color, so keep it away from fabrics or it may stain. WD-40 is also a lubricant, so do not use it on surfaces that you cannot wipe clean afterwards.

USING SOLVENTS SAFELY

Take care not to breathe in the fumes from lighter fluid or other solvents. Solvents can give a temporary high when they are sniffed but can cause side effects such as vomiting and dizziness—and can even be fatal in extreme cases. Store all solvents, glue, and stain-removal kits in a cupboard that you can keep locked at all times, safe from children.

Many petroleum-based solvents are also highly flammable, so keep them away from sparks and naked flames.

LIGHTER FLUID MAGIC

Have you ever peeled a label off a jar and been left with a mass of sticky glue that refuses to come off? Take a soft cloth, add a few drops of lighter fluid, and rub it over the glue. The lighter fluid will melt away the glue like magic, and the glass will be left shiny and clean.

SOLVENTS AND THEIR USES

There are many different solvents and solvent-based cleaning products. The average household owns around 30 solvent-based products at any one time. The table below lists the most popular solvents and their uses in the home:

Water

Water is a solvent in its own right, and can dissolve a wide range of stains. However, you need the addition of a chemical, such as soap or detergent, to clean stubborn stains.

Dry-cleaning fluid

This solvent cleans grease and oil stains from fabrics. The fumes are toxic, so hang dry-cleaned fabrics outside if you can, and ensure that your home is well ventilated.

Alcohol

This is distilled from fermented plants and mixed with water. You can use it to dissolve greasy marks, dyes, inks, and grassy stains.

Limonene

This essential oil is made from citrus peel and is used in many commercial "citrus" cleaners.

Turpentine (paint thinner)

This solvent is used to remove oil-based paints. It is less effective for cleaning greasy stains.

Glycerine

This solvent is made from natural fats and is useful for cleaning dried-on stains on fabrics.

Acetone

Acetone is alcohol-based and a powerful solvent. It is quick to dry and is useful for cleaning off nail polish and glue. Never use it on acetate or plastic—it will damage them.

Liquid fuel

Liquid fuel solvents, such as lighter fuel, should be used in well-ventilated places because they have a very strong smell. Use them to cut through sticky, oily stains.

Lacquer thinner

This is a strong petroleum-based solvent, used for thinning lacquer and metal finishes. You can also use it to remove grease and paint from metal and glass.

THE WONDERS OF WATER

Water is a natural solvent and the safest, purest cleaning fluid you can use. It is the one solvent that you can actually sniff and drink safely. It is neutral on the pH scale, which means it is neither acid nor alkaline. When it is mixed with an acid or alkaline cleaner, it will dilute the potency of that cleaning agent and make it safer for cleaning more fragile items.

WATER IS A NATURAL SOLVENT

DISSOLVE THOSE DIRTY MARKS

Water is very versatile and has many uses, but on its own it will not be effective against stubborn dirt, or old stains or greasy marks. In these cases if you can't deal with the problem right away, soap or detergent needs to be added in order to cut through the dirt and grease. Water will hold a soils in suspension so that they can be cleaned at some later point. Although hot water usually works best for household cleaning tasks, it is often better to treat stains on fabrics with cold water before washing in order to avoid "setting" the stain.

WASH YOUR WINDOWS WITH WATER

Many people buy expensive solvent-based cleaners to clean their windows, but these sometimes leave the glass streaky, especially if you use too much. It is a much better idea to alternate your cleaning fluids with water; use solvents on one occasion, and just warm water the next. Keep alternating your cleaning fluids in this way. On the occasions when you use water on its own, you'll be amazed at the amount of residue from other cleaning products you have used that comes off your windows. Dry your windows afterward with a lint-free cloth. When you do use other cleaning products, keep the amount you use to a minimum—this will keep your windows residue free and will also save you money.

MAKE THOSE WATER STAINS DISAPPEAR

Although water is a good cleaning fluid, it can sometimes leave a stain. To remove a water mark from a delicate fabric such as silk, bring a kettle or saucepan of water to a boil. Hold the fabric in the steam until the stain is gone. (Keep your hands away from the steam to prevent burns.) To remove a water stain from wood furniture, quickly blot any excess liquid with a paper towel and dry off. Briskly rub cream metal polish in the direction of the grain. If this doesn't work, try putting liquid wax polish on fine-grade steel wool and rubbing gently.

HARD WATER
Hard water can reduce the power of soaps and deter-gents and encourages scum to form. It can also give your white clothes a gray look. To combat graying, add 14 fl oz (25 ml) white vinegar to your rinse water.

DIRECTORY OF HOMEMADE CLEANERS

Have you run out of a particular cleaning product? Why not create your own? Use this A–Z directory to discover common household uses for homemade cleaners.

AIR FRESHENER

☆ *Place a few vanilla pods in an open jar, or a few drops of vanilla extract on cotton balls, and leave in strategic spots around your home. Alternatively, add 3 cloves and 1 cinnamon stick to 4 fl oz (125 ml) water in a small saucepan and bring to a simmer. Leave to cool, then strain the liquid into a plant mister or spray bottle. Label clearly and use as required.*

ALL-PURPOSE CLEANER FOR HARD SURFACES

☆ *Mix 9 fl oz (250 ml) water with 2 tablespoons lemon juice, ½ teaspoon dishwashing liquid, 1 tablespoon of baking soda, and 1 teaspoon borax. Pour into a bottle with a tight-fitting lid, label clearly and use as required.*

BATHROOM CLEANER

☆ *Mix some baking soda and water into a paste and use to clean your bath, sink, and toilet.*

BATH SCRATCHES

☆ *If your acrylic bath is scratched, gently rub a little liquid metal polish over the scratches to make them fade or disappear altogether.*

BLEACHLESS LAUNDRY

☆ *Add 2¾ oz (75 g) cream of tartar or 4 fl oz (125 ml) lemon juice to your wash instead of bleach to brighten your dingy whites. If it's sunny, hang them out in the sunshine while damp to boost the bleaching effect. The "sunshine" technique can also be used with regular laundry detergent to increase its effect and get rid of stains. Wash items by hand, rubbing soap well into stains, marks, and spots, then hang the soapy items out in the sunshine for an hour or two. Rinse thoroughly and leave to dry.*

BLOOD

☆ Soak bloodstained fabrics in a solution of cold water and salt, then launder normally.

BRASS POLISH

☆ Mix 1 teaspoon salt with 9 fl oz (250 ml) white vinegar, then stir in enough plain flour to make a paste. Smear over the brass and leave for 45 minutes, then polish with a clean, soft cloth.

CANDLE WAX

☆ To remove candle wax from a carpet or fabric, scrape off the excess, then place a piece of brown paper over the area and press with a warm iron. If any color stain remains, remove with a little wood alcohol. To remove candle wax from a candlestick, scrape off the excess, then use a blow-dryer on low heat to melt the rest of the wax so that you can wash it off in warm, soapy water.

CARAMEL

☆ To remove caramel or toffee stains from a saucepan, fill the pan with warm water and bring it to a boil. This will loosen the stain and make it easier to clean.

CARPET CLEANER

☆ Fill a bucket with warm, soapy water, mix in 2 tablespoons each of white vinegar and salt, and use as required.

CARPET FRESHENER

☆ Sprinkle some baking soda over the dry carpet, leave for 2–8 hours, then vacuum.

CAR WINDSHIELD CLEANER

☆ Keep a spray bottle filled with soda water to remove grease from windshields. Also works on chrome or stainless steel.

CHROME POLISH

☆ Use cider vinegar on a soft cloth.

COFFEE

☆ To remove a fresh coffee spill from a carpet, mop up the excess with paper towels, then treat with a solution of salt and water. To remove a dried coffee stain from a carpet, rub a little glycerine into the pile and leave it for a few hours. Sponge with warm water and pat dry with paper towels.

☆ Alternatively, blot up as much excess coffee as possible before it has any chance to soak in, then pour a little soda water or sparkling mineral water over the area and blot, working from the outside in toward the center.

COPPER POLISH

☆ Mix some lemon juice with salt and smear over the copper surface. Polish gently with a scouring pad.

CREAM

☆ To remove stains on fabrics caused by cream, or a creamy sauce or soup, treat the stain with a little eucalyptus oil, then hand wash or launder in the usual way.

DISHWASHING LIQUID

☆ To make an economic and effective alternative dishwashing liquid, buy the cheapest brand and add a few tablespoons of vinegar to the bottle. You can do the same for dishwasher liquid.

DRAIN CLEANER

☆ Mix together 2¾ oz (75 g) baking soda and 3½ fl oz (100 ml) white vinegar and pour down the drain. Cover and leave for 20 minutes, then flush with boiling water.

DUSTING CLOTHS

☆ Recycle your old shirts, T-shirts, drapes, towels (and washcloths) by cutting them up and using them as dusting cloths or rags.

FABRIC DEODORIZER

☆ Sprinkle some baking soda over the entire area and leave for 45 minutes or more. Launder in the normal way, if the item is washable, or simply vacuum clean. Baking soda can be used to clean and freshen clothing, the inside of shoes, upholstery, cushions, and mattresses.

FLY REPELLENT

☆ Put some basil leaves into a bowl of water and leave in a strategic place, such as the kitchen or near a door or window.

FURNITURE POLISH

☆ Pour 9 fl oz (250 ml) linseed oil into a saucepan and bring to a boil. Leave to cool, then combine with 4 fl oz (125 ml) turpentine, 4 fl oz (125 ml) wood alcohol, and 4 fl oz (125 ml) white vinegar. Pour into a clean glass bottle with a cork stopper, label clearly, and use as required.

GARLIC

☆ To get rid of the smell of garlic from a chopping board, mix some baking soda and water into a paste and spread all over the board. Leave for 15 minutes, then rinse in cold water. To remove the smell of garlic from your hands, take a stainless steel teaspoon and some dish soap, and use your fingers to wash the spoon under cold running water.

GOLD JEWELRY CLEANER

☆ Rub with a cut tomato, then rinse well and dry with a soft cloth.

HAIRSPRAY

☆ To clean hairspray from a mirror, moisten a soft cloth with some wood alcohol and wipe. For a sparkling finish, clean with a little white vinegar mixed with water.

INK

☆ To remove felt-tip pen ink from a carpet, blot with paper towels, then dab on some wood alcohol. For fountain-pen ink, first sponge with warm water and pat dry with paper towels. Then mix some soap flakes, or detergent suitable for hand washing, with warm water and use to treat the stain. Rinse with warm water (don't allow the item to get too wet) and pat dry with paper towels. To remove ballpoint pen ink from vinyl, rub with a piece of raw potato.

INSECT REPELLENT

☆ Fill a plant mister with water, add a few drops of tea tree oil, and spray around doors and windows.

LIME SCALE REMOVER

☆ Mix together 4 fl oz (125 ml) water, 5 tablespoons cider vinegar, and 3 tablespoons salt. Use as required.

LINOLEUM CLEANER

☆ Use a mixture of 4 fl oz (125 ml) white vinegar and 1 gallon (4.5 liters) water.

MARBLE CLEANER

☆ Use lemon juice to remove stains from marble, but don't leave it on for too long or it will eat into the marble and cause discoloration.

MIRROR CLEANER

☆ Throw out those expensive solvents and use a little white vinegar mixed with water instead. Pour the mixture into a spray bottle, label clearly, and use as required.

MOLD AND MILDEW

✫ To get rid of mold or mildew, mix equal parts vinegar and salt into a bowl and use to scrub off the stain. Ensure the room is well ventilated.

ODOR ABSORBER

✫ Place a bowl of charcoal or coffee on a shelf in the refrigerator or wherever the offending odor is, and the smell will gradually be absorbed.

OVEN CLEANER

✫ Clean your oven with a solution of warm water and baking soda. To remove grease spills, sprinkle on some salt, then wipe clean. Loosen burnt-on stains by leaving a small dish of ammonia in the oven for a few hours.

PAINTWORK

✫ Clean grubby paintwork with a solution of 1 part ammonia to 3 parts warm water. Rinse the surface afterward with clean water. Be careful not to breathe in the fumes or splash the mixture onto your skin.

PERSPIRATION

✫ Use a solution of white vinegar and water to remove perspiration stains from cotton fabrics. If the material is synthetic, soak the stain in ammonia first.

PEWTER

✫ To clean, rub with cabbage leaves or a piece of orange. Polish with a clean, soft cloth.

PIANO KEYS

✫ Use a dollop of regular white toothpaste to clean and polish piano keys. Apply and rub well, wipe, then buff with a soft cloth. Be careful not to get any paste down between the keys, though. Toothpaste can also be used to brighten refrigerators and freezers.

RED WINE

On carpet

☆ Pour a glass of white wine over the stain. Blot off the excess with paper towels, then sponge the area with warm water. Treat the area with carpet shampoo and rinse with warm water. If necessary, treat again with a solution of half glycerine and half warm water. Leave for an hour, then sponge with warm water. Blot dry with paper towels.

On fabric

☆ To remove red wine from cotton fabric, sprinkle on some salt, then rinse out in warm water. Sprinkle on some borax, then pour on a little hot water. Leave for a few minutes. Launder in the usual way. For silk or white wool, soak for a few minutes in a solution of one part hydrogen peroxide to six parts warm water. Rinse and launder in the usual way.

On upholstery

☆ Blot with paper towels, then sponge with warm water and blot again. Sprinkle some talcum powder on and leave for 15 minutes. Brush off the powder, then sponge again with warm water and blot dry with more paper towels.

REFRIGERATOR CLEANER AND FRESHENER

☆ Use some baking soda and water mixed to a paste. If you are out of baking soda, try toothpaste instead, but choose a gentle, non-abrasive kind.

SCOURING POWDER

☆ Mix together 5½ oz (150 g) each of borax, baking soda, and salt, and use the paste to remove stubborn stains.

SHAVING LOTION

☆ Run out? Try hair conditioner instead.

SHOE POLISH

☆ Baby wipes can be used to give your shoes a quick clean and polish. Wipe on and then leave to dry and, if necessary, buff with a soft cloth to make your shoes really shine.

SILVER JEWELRY AND CUTLERY CLEANER

☆ Use baking soda and water mixed to a paste.

SILVERWARE

☆ Keep some chalk in the cupboard with your silver to help prevent tarnishing. To clean silver, use a few pieces of raw rhubarb. Alternatively, save some water after cooking potatoes and soak your silver pieces in it.

STAINLESS STEEL

☆ To remove spots on steel, clean with white vinegar. To remove rust on steel, rub with a cloth dipped in lighter fluid or paraffin (for stubborn rust, you may need to leave it to soak for a while.) Then clean with all-purpose cleaner (see page 306).

TOOTHPASTE

☆ Mix some baking soda and water to a paste, then use in the normal way.

WINDOW CLEANER

☆ Mix a little white vinegar with water, pour the mixture into a clean spray bottle, label clearly, use as required. You can also add a little ammonia.

WOOD FURNITURE CLEANER

☆ Mix some vegetable oil with a little lemon juice for wonderfully clean results.

WOODEN FLOOR POLISH

☆ Mix 4 fl oz (125 ml) white vinegar and 14 fl oz (125 ml) paraffin oil in a clean screw-top jar and label clearly. Apply with a soft cloth.

FURTHER READING

Clean House, Clean Planet, Karen Logan, *Pocket Books* (1997)

Cleaning and Stain Removal for Dummies, Gill Chilton, *John Wiley & Sons Ltd.* (2004)

The Cleaning Encyclopedia, Don Aslett, *Dell Publishing* (1999)

Cleaning Yourself to Death: How Safe Is Your Home?, Pat Thomas, *Newleaf Paperback* (2001)

Confessions of an Organized Homemaker: The Secrets of Uncluttering Your Home and Taking Control of Your Life, Deniece Schofield, *Betterway Books* (1994)

The Family Manager's Everyday Survival Guide, Kathy Peel, *Ballantine Books* (1998)

Field Guide to Stains: How to Identify and Remove Virtually Every Stain Known to Man, Virginia M. Friedman, Melissa Wagner, Nancy Armstrong, *Quirk Books* (2002)

Good House Magic, Natalia Marshall, *Mq Publications* (2003)

Home Comforts: The Art and Science of Keeping House, Cheryl Mendelson, *Scribner* (1999)

How Clean is Your House?, Kim Woodburn, Aggie MacKenzie, *Dutton Books* (2004)

How to Avoid Housework: Tips, Hints and Secrets on How to Have a Spotless Home, Paula Jhung, *Fireside* (1995)

How to Clean Absolutely Everything: The Right Way, the Lazy Way and the Green Way, Barty Phillips, *Piatkus Books* (2004)

The Life Laundry: How to De-Junk Your Life, Dawna Walter, Mark Franks, *BBC Consumer Publishing,* (2002)

The Life Laundry 2: How to Stay De-Junked Forever, Dawna Walter, Mark Franks, *BBC Consumer Publishing,* (2003)

Mrs Beeton's Book of Household Management (Oxford World's Classics), Isabella Beeton, Nicola Humble (ed.), *Oxford University Press* (2000)

USEFUL WEBSITES

The Naturally Clean Home: 101 Safe and Easy Herbal Formulas for Non-Toxic Cleansers, Karyn Siegel-Maier, *Storey Books* (1999)

The New Messies Manual: The Procrastinator's Guide to Good Housekeeping, Sandra Felton, *Revell* (2000)

The Queen of Clean: The Royal Guide to Spot and Stain Removal, Linda Cobb, *Pocket Books* (2001)

Rita's Tips for Domestic Bliss, Rita Konig, *Ebury Press* (2003)

Sink Reflections, Marla Cilley, *Bantam Books* (2002)

Talking Dirty with the Queen of Clean, Linda Cobb, *Pocket Books* (2000)

Vim & Vinegar: Hundreds of Ingenious Household Uses, Melodie Moore, *Perennial Currents* (1997)

Vinegar: Over 400 Various, Versatile, and Very Good Uses You've Probably Never Thought Of, Vicki Lansky, Martha Campbell, *Book Peddlers* (2004)

www.allabouthome.com/directories/dir_cleaning.html
Miscellaneous home cleaning tips

www.chemistry.co.nz/stain_frame.htm
Stain removal guide

www.cleaning.com
News, articles, and tips on cleaning

www.essortment.com/in/Home.Cleaning/index.htm
Advice on cleaning all around the home

www.furniturestuff.com
Leather, wood, and upholstery care

www.greenhome.com
Green cleaning products

www.hints-n-tips.com/household.htm
Hints and tips on cleaning and stain removal

www.howtocleananything.com
Cleaning hints for in and around the house

www.ivillage.com/topics/home/0,,167081,00.html
Links to cleaning topics

www.pioneerthinking.com/cleaningsolutions.html
Homemade household cleaning products

www.thriftyfun.com
Includes money-saving cleaning ideas

www.tide.com
Fabric care advice

www.tipking.com
Includes cleaning tips and laundry advice

www.virtuowl.com/household1.htm
Household cleaning hints and tips

www.wackyuses.com/uses.html
Little-known uses for well-known products

INDEX